The Microtheory of Innovative Entrepreneurship

KAUFFMAN FOUNDATION SERIES ON
Innovation and Entrepreneurship

Boulevard of Broken Dreams: Why Public Efforts to Boost Entrepreneurship and Venture Capital Have Failed —and What to Do about It, by Josh Lerner

The Invention of Enterprise: Entrepreneurship from Ancient Mesopotamia to Modern Times, edited by David S. Landes, Joel Mokyr, and William J. Baumol

The Venturesome Economy: How Innovation Sustains Prosperity in a More Connected World, by Amar Bhidé

The Microtheory of
Innovative Entrepreneurship

WILLIAM J. BAUMOL

PRINCETON UNIVERSITY PRESS

Princeton and Oxford

Published by Princeton University Press, 41 William Street,
Princeton, New Jersey 08540

In the United Kingdom: Princeton University Press, 6 Oxford Street,
Woodstock, Oxfordshire OX20 1TW

Library of Congress Cataloging-in-Publication Data

Baumol, William J.
  The microtheory of innovative entrepreneurship / William J. Baumol.
      p.   cm.   — (The Kauffman Foundation series on innovation
and entrepreneurship)
  Includes bibliographical references and index.
  ISBN 978-0-691-14584-6 (hardcover : alk. paper) 1. Entrepreneurship. I. Title.
  HB615.B398 2009
  338'.0401—dc22

                              2009047823

British Library Cataloging-in-Publication Data is available

Published in collaboration with the Ewing Marion Kauffman Foundation
and the Berkley Center for Entrepreneurial Studies of New York University

This book has been composed in Stone Serif
Printed on acid-free paper. ∞
press.princeton.edu
Printed in the United States of America
10 9 8 7 6 5 4 3 2 1

To my colleagues at the Accademia Nazionale dei Lincei

CONTENTS

CONTENTS

FIGURES AND TABLES

FIGURES

TABLES

PREFACE

The Innovative Entrepreneur in
Dynamic Microtheory

In Italy, the Antonio Feltrinelli International Prize is the highest
award offered to a non-Italian scientist. The award is decided
and governed by the Accademia Nazionale dei Lincei, the oldest
academic honorary society in the world, an institution founded
in 1604 and of which Galileo Galilei was one of the founders.
In 2005, the Feltrinelli International Prize for Contributions to
Economic and Social Sciences was awarded to Professor William
J. Baumol, a member of the Accademia, at a ceremony in Rome.
At that meeting, Professor Baumol addressed the members of
Lincei, and that lecture, considerably expanded, became the
basis of this book.[1]

I was led to begin work on this book in 2005, when I prepared my talk
for the award of the Antonio Feltrinelli International Prize for Economic
and Social Sciences at the Accademia Nazionale dei Lincei, the oldest of
the world's learned societies, in Rome. In connection with this honor, I
will always be indebted to my friend Professor Luigi Pasinetti, to whose
efforts I must accredit the award, gratitude thereby added to my admiration of his work.

This book can be described as my third try—my once-more reiterated attempt to bring systematic growth theory into the domain of microeconomics,
from which it is now largely excluded. As I will argue in the introduction,
in terms of the comparative importance of static and dynamic analysis,
as evaluated in terms of the welfare implications of microeconomics, the
current literature has the matter standing on its head. The really important
part of the story of economic well-being is all but banished from the literature. In particular, the near total omission of innovative entrepreneurs
and their role is a major element in this curious state of affairs.

Thus, the main conviction underlying this book is that the absence of micro growth theory from available scholarship on welfare economics leaves us with a crucial gap. There is a second conviction here, as well—that growth analysis requires a combination of two indispensable approaches: macroeconomic and microeconomic. Happily, a very substantial macro analysis is already available. But many of the decisions that primarily affect growth are made by individuals and individual firms. For that reason, the choices of the individual inventor, the individual entrepreneur, and the management of a firm that may spend heavily on R&D are surely at the heart of the subject. We are beginning to accumulate an invaluable body of empirical evidence on these matters, but the formal theory is still virtually nonexistent. The objective of this book is to show a promising way to begin filling this enormous gap.

I have already written about some of the subject matter covered in this book, so it seems appropriate to reproduce some of these earlier materials, suitably editing rather than completely rewriting discussions of topics on which I have little new to say. For this repetition, I trust I will be forgiven. This time, however, I finally may have gotten the story right, or rather, may at last be able to provide an outline of the *entire* story. Before closing this preface, I follow custom with my expressions of gratitude. Those I have given in the past were, I am convinced, richly deserved, but never so much as the two that appear here. For I will single out one organization and one individual to whom my debt is unequalled.

The organization is the Ewing Marion Kauffman Foundation, which has, of course, provided financing. But more than that, it has brought me friends, colleagues, and even coauthors. The pleasure of working with them has been a unique experience, and I look forward to its continuation. Given the commendable objectives of the foundation and the efficacy with which it pursues them, I can only be proud of and delighted with our association.

There are others to whom I owe great debts for constructive comments and suggestions. They include Professors Magnus Henrekson, Albert Lee, Simon Parker, and Mirjam van Praag—good friends and colleagues. They have stimulated my ideas, caught my errors, and added to the substance of my discussion. It is a pleasure, albeit meager reimbursement, to recognize their valuable assistance. At Princeton University Press, I wish to thank our editorial team, Seth Ditchik, senior editor; Sara Lerner, production editor; Janie Chan, editorial associate; and Richard Isomaki, copyeditor, with whom it was always a pleasure to work. Similarly, I owe many thanks to Konrad Grabiszewski, who saved me from error in the book's figures and equations, and to Aurite Werman, who gave up a summer to help by providing data that were more current and illuminating. And, finally, there is the substantive contribution of Zoltan Acs, who permitted me to build on one of his as yet unpublished ideas—philanthropy by entrepreneurs that creates and sustains programs, such as scholarships, that provide vital assistance to future entrepreneurs.

Most of all, I am indebted to Janeece Lewis and Anne Noyes Saini, who are best described as my partners-in-crime and without whom completion of this volume would have been immeasurably more difficult. Anne, who has recently become a co-worker in my enterprises and therefore has not been mentioned previously in my writings, has accomplished much more than sanitization of my grammar—her insight and capability have rightly elicited my admiration and feelings of friendship. Together, we three have become a team that works together most effectively and imparts pleasure to our activities.

The circumstances, however, call me to a far less happy task—to say some words about my late and beloved colleague, Sue Anne Batey Blackman. I was her partner for well over two decades. Now I constantly miss the contributions stemming from her intelligence, her ingenuity, and her love and mastery of language. But much more than all of that, I miss her as a person—calm, rational, delightful, always wanted, and always there when needed. Only the Bard can provide suitable words to describe Sue Anne: "Her life was gentle, and the elements / So mix'd in her that Nature might stand up and say to all the world, 'this was a woman!'"

Permission to reprint is hereby gratefully acknowledged for previously published extracts of this text. Portions of chapter 2 appeared in the *Journal of Entrepreneurial Finance and Business Ventures*, the official publication of the Academy of Entrepreneurial Finance ("Entrepreneurship, Innovation and Growth: The David-Goliath Symbiosis," vol. 7, issue 2, pp. 1–10); portions of chapters 3 and 4 are taken from *Entrepreneurship and Invention: Toward Their Microeconomic Value Theory*, an AEI-Brookings Joint Center for Regulatory Studies report (Baumol 2005); and excerpts from an article published in the *Journal of Political Economy* ("Entrepreneurship: Productive, Unproductive, and Destructive," vol. 98, no. 5, part 1, pp. 893–921, © 1990 by The University of Chicago) have been incorporated in chapters 9 and 10. The Von Mises epigraph in chapter 1 is taken from *Human Action* (Von Mises 1940, p. 270); the Dana epigraph in chapter 3 appeared in the *Journal of Political Economy* (vol. 106, no. 2, p. 395, "Advance-Purchase Discounts and Price Discrimination in Competitive Markets," by J. D. Dana, © 1998 by The University of Chicago Press); the Okun epigraph in chapter 5 is taken from *Equality and Efficiency: The Big Tradeoff* (Okun 1975, pp. 46–47), courtesy of the Brookings Institution Press; the Marx and Engels epigraph in chapter 7 is taken from the *Manifesto of the Communist Party* (Marx and Engels 1976, vol. 6, p. 487); the Schumpeter epigraph also in chapter 7 appeared in *Capitalism, Socialism and Democracy* (Schumpeter 1947, p. 83); and the Jones epigraph in chapter 8 was previously published in *France* (Jones 1994, p. 130). Table 2.1 appeared in *The State of Small Business: A Report of the President, 1994* (1995, p. 114) and is reprinted here courtesy of The Office of Advocacy of the Small Business Administration; tables 11.1 and 11.2 are taken from the website of the Center for Responsive Politics (Opensecrets.org); and figure 4.1 was previously published in a 2009 working paper by Michael A. Williams and Kevin Kreitzman, "Estimating Market Power with Economic Profits," available at http://ssrn.com/abstract=1167823.

The Microtheory of Innovative Entrepreneurship

Bringing Entrepreneurship
and Innovation into the
Theory of Value

I am an invisible man. No, I am not a spook like those who
haunted Edgar Allan Poe; nor am I one of your Hollywood-
movie ectoplasms. I am a man of substance, of flesh and bone,
fiber and liquids—and I might even be said to possess a mind.
I am invisible, understand, simply because people refuse to see
me. . . . When they approach me they see only my surroundings,
themselves, or figments of their imagination—indeed, everything
and anything except me.

—Ralph Ellison, *Invisible Man* (1952, 3)

THE INVISIBLE ENTREPRENEUR

My belief, delusory or not, is that I provide here the first quasi-formal, theoretical analysis of the role and activities of the *innovative* entrepreneur—an entrée into the elementary theory of value.[1] Through this book, I hope to introduce innovative entrepreneurship into the accepted body of mainstream microtheory.

However, this effort should also not be taken to imply that there exists no valuable research on the subject, or even that nontheoretical work on this topic is lacking. On the contrary, there is a profuse and rapidly growing body of empirical research—much of it imaginative, highly competent, and illuminating.[2] This work has begun to show, for example, the type of person most likely to become an innovating entrepreneur, the sources of financing available for this entrepreneurial activity, the institutional arrangements that stimulate it, the economic value of entrepreneurship, and a good deal more.[3]

In addition, as the reader need hardly be reminded, there is an invaluable macroeconomic literature on economic growth, stemming from the work of Robert Solow and including the writings of Paul Romer and Robert Lucas and, more recently, the outstanding volume by Philippe Aghion and Peter Howitt (1998). In these macrotheoretic writings, entrepreneurs usually lurk in the background—largely concealed, but present under certain interpretations. Finally, there also is a considerable body of microtheoretic work in the arena of invention, including the pathbreaking analyses of Karl Shell.

It is clear, then, that work much more profound than mine has been provided by others in more sophisticated and advanced theories of innovation that have indirect implications for the theory of entrepreneurship. Even more extensive is the fine body of empirical work on the subject provided by economists and sociologists, among others. But despite the existing literature and near universal acknowledgment of the entrepreneur's crucial contribution to economic growth and the general welfare, theoretical material on entrepreneurship has not yet become a required component of all training in microtheory, nor has it become a mandatory portion of every elementary textbook. In fact, the word fails to appear in the indices of many such textbooks.

Thus, even the valuable empirical and theoretical work in the microeconomic arena, to which I have just alluded, does not meet the goals of this book, for it lies outside the mainstream of basic microtheory. The theory of entrepreneurship does not go totally unrecognized or unappreciated in discussions of growth, but it remains relegated to the suburbs of the microeconomic literature. As things stand, few of us who teach economics, in designing a one-semester course on the theory of the firm, would be expected to assign much time to the writings noted in the previous paragraphs. Although few deny the importance of the entrepreneurs and many acknowledge their critical role, they are almost entirely excluded from our standard theoretical models of the firm.

There are obvious reasons why this state of affairs should be considered curious. Entrepreneurs seem to be widely recognized as prime contributors to economic progress. However, it also should be obvious that the current state of economic welfare and standard of living in industrialized economies owes vastly more to the market mechanism's past growth performance than it does to any static efficiency contributions for which it is arguably responsible. Thus, there is little reason to expect the need for the work of entrepreneurs to diminish substantially in the foreseeable future. Despite this, our lectures on microtheory of the firm and its contribution to economic welfare focus almost exclusively on the static side of the latter. Surely, something here is out of order.

The nearly exclusive focus by welfare economics literature on those "market failures" that are static in character—monopoly, externalities of the type usually cited, inadequate output of public goods, and the like—

Table I.1
Rise in Real Per Capita GDP, 1900–2001

	% Rise	Multiple
U.S.	583	6.83
France	633	7.33
Japan	1,653	17.53
Sweden	703	8.03
U.K.	348	4.48
Italy	967	10.67
Germany	526	6.26

Source: Maddison 2003.

is entirely indefensible because it neglects the welfare implication of micro-activities related to economic growth. The result is, arguably, a serious misallocation of classroom time and textbook space, in which a markedly excessive share is allotted to the stationary analysis, as will be argued next.

GROWTH: THE SIGNIFICANT SOURCE OF ENHANCED GENERAL WELFARE

It seems not very difficult to indicate, albeit in imperfectly rigorous terms, something a bit more specific about the relative importance of the statics and dynamics of policy for the economic well-being of the general public. For this purpose, let us begin by taking note of some important data estimates: the evaluation of the magnitude of growth in per capita income. Perhaps the most conservative estimate of the rate of expansion of per capita real income in the past century is offered by Maddison (2003), who reports that this increased nearly sevenfold in the United States—surely an impressive number (see table I.1). Roughly speaking, this means that in 1900, average per capita income was a bit more than $5,000 per year (in 2000 dollars)—a standard of living that is virtually impossible to comprehend today. Several other estimates of twentieth-century growth are far higher. Alan Greenspan, for example—who is not noted for exaggeration in his data estimates, is reported by DeLong (2000) to have concluded that the true figure is something like a thirtyfold rise.

In order to analyze what this implies for our subject, I will employ a conservative approach, taking the lower (near sevenfold) multiplication

3

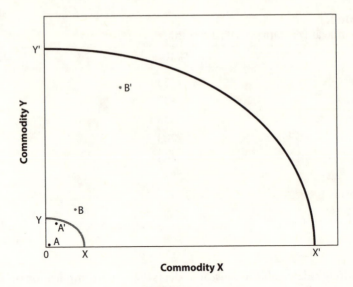

FIGURE I.1

Hypothetical Progress, 1900–2000: Elimination of Monopoly Power vs. Innovation

to be correct. Figure I.1 represents such an increase via two hypothetical production-possibility frontiers, XY and $X'Y'$ (in two commodities). The frontiers are drawn as replicas of one another, except that $X'Y'$ is magnified sevenfold and, therefore, placed seven times as far from the origin as XY. The frontier of 1900 is represented by XY, while $X'Y'$ signifies that of 2000.

Next, consider what a plausible increase in *static* efficiency could possibly have contributed to welfare, starting from the earlier date. We can, of course, take as the hypothetical initial position any point below the 1900 frontier, XY. However, in order to remain conservative, I select point A, which lies well below the 1900 frontier, as the initial position of the economy. This is a conservative assumption in that static inefficiency is taken to be implausibly enormous, leaving extensive room for improvement via static efficiency contributing measures. That is, under this premise, any move from A to anywhere on the XY frontier must be feasible.

In contrast, a sevenfold increase in every output from point A, permitted by the twentieth-century *growth* performance, brings us all the way from point A to point B—well beyond the 1900 frontier, XY. The disparity between the possible static change and the change made possible by growth is apt to be huge because the largest possible improvement in welfare at that date cannot take us any higher than some point on the (very low) 1900 boundary, which determines the maximal improvement technologically feasible at that time.

It is also illuminating to consider the implications of an alternative, initial 1900 position, point A', that already represents a state of relatively abundant welfare for that time, since A' lies very close to the 1900 frontier. Because point A' has far greater proximity to the 1900 frontier, as compared with point A, A' will have far greater static efficiency than A. With initial point A', the disparity between a move to the static frontier and the alternative contribution of growth to corresponding point B' of year 2000 is enormously larger than that permitted by point A. This is because point A' is already close to the frontier, so there is comparatively little room for contribution by *static*-efficiency increasing measures. Thus, my choice of A as the illustrative initial position can indeed be considered conservative.

In other words, if we take the position of those who believe that the performance of the unconstrained market is reasonably close to optimality, then there is necessarily an enormous excess of the welfare contribution offered by growth over anything a set of static programs can possibly provide.

The empirical evidence we do have appears to suggest that point A' in the graph is much closer to a true depiction of reality than point A. Although it has elicited a fair amount of criticism and reservations, the most noted evidence on the subject is that provided in Harberger's classic discussion (1954, 524), which concludes that "elimination of resource misallocation in American manufacturing in the late twenties would bring with it an improvement in consumer welfare of little more than a tenth of a percent [!] in present value. This welfare gain would amount to about $2.00 per capita." This astonishing estimate suggests that even point A' in the graph is far further from the frontier than it would be in reality.

More conservative studies raise the estimated figure for static efficiency gains from antitrust and regulatory activities, alone, to about 1 percent of GDP. This is easily shown to mean that, if we had completely eliminated all market failure attributable to imperfect competition, but the economy had failed to grow, the accumulated year-by-year gains from eliminating monopolistic distortions would have added up to about $5,000 per person over the entire twentieth century. The opportunity cost, in the form of the foregone accumulation of the benefits of growth (adding together the year-by-year gains), would have totaled about 300 times that amount—an incredible $1,500,000 per person (roughly) over the course of the century.

Other evidence also suggests that significant improvements in welfare have derived from the activities of entrepreneurs when they have devoted themselves to productive activities. Take, for instance, figure I.2, which

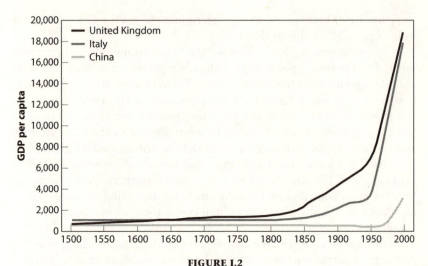

FIGURE I.2
GDP Per Capita, 1500–2006: China, Italy, and the United Kingdom (1990 international $). (Source: Maddison 2001, 264.)

shows the record of productivity growth over a 500-year period for China, Italy, and the United Kingdom.

Between 1500 and the middle of the eighteenth century, the curves representing the levels of per capita gross domestic product (GDP) in the three countries are virtually horizontal—a striking record of progress at a snail's pace.[4] But from then on, it is clear that the rate of improvement grows ever faster, until the curves jut sharply upward, and China's growth rate pulls ahead of both the U.K. and Italy in the second half of the twentieth century, as figure I.3 shows.[5]

What is striking here is the poor economic performance of China—until the late twentieth century, when its explosive productivity growth occurred.[6] That is, the recent explosion in output contrasts dramatically with China's earlier centuries of astonishing invention, which failed to produce anything like Western growth after the Industrial Revolution. One can argue that the extended medieval period in China was characterized by profusion of inventors, but with entrepreneurs seeking roles in the bureaucracy, rather than in industry. In contrast, in recent decades, entrepreneurship in China has directed itself to the business sector, while accompanied by no innovation comparable to its incredible earlier performance.

Add to this the more dramatic contributions of growing prosperity—for example, the striking increase in longevity that has doubled life expectancy at birth and the elimination of European famine that, until the end of the

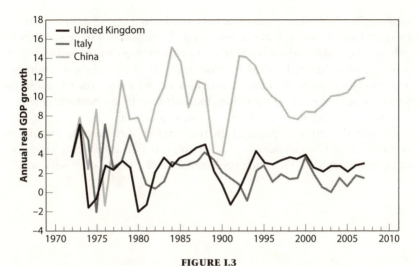

FIGURE I.3

Annual Real GDP Growth, 1972–2007: China, Italy, and the United Kingdom. (Source: Organization for Economic Cooperation and Development 2009.)

eighteenth century, occurred every decade, on average, and it becomes difficult not to acknowledge the enormously unmatched contribution to the general welfare of economic growth and, by implication, the critical role of the entrepreneur in this achievement.

THE OVERALL IMPLICATION

It appears evident that the really significant payoff to welfare economics lies in intertemporal, rather than stationary, analysis. One of the aims of this book is to suggest how a move in this direction can be carried out; another is to derive some pertinent results that fall within the domain of the welfare economics of growth.

Here there is one important exception: externalities. Static externalities can threaten enormous damage to the general welfare, as in the case of global warming. Still, where else are externalities more enormous than in the case of the huge spillovers from innovation? Consequently, we will pay attention to them in several of the chapters that follow.

However, the conclusions that emerge here will be far from the usual ones. Instead, I will argue that, unlike other externalities that invariably result in welfare-damaging market failure, the externalities of innovation have made an enormously beneficial distributive contribution to the general welfare. While the result may not pass any formal test of approximation to allocative efficiency, it nevertheless may be considered to be very desirable on the whole—most notably in its contribution to the reduction of poverty. In addition, I will show that in much of the affected economic activity, the market mechanism provides strong incentives for business firms to undertake *voluntary* actions that incidentally support and enhance this externality in a manner that is socially beneficial.

In sum, this book emphasizes the importance of redirecting microeconomic analysis from statics toward dynamics, as well as restoring attention to entrepreneurship, the much neglected, fourth "factor of production."

Entrepreneurship in Economic Theory: Reasons for Its Absence and Goals for Its Restoration

Man is not the only animal who labors; but he is the only one who improves his workmanship.

—Abraham Lincoln, "First Lecture on Discoveries and Inventions," 6 April 1858

The direction of all economic affairs is in the market society a task of the entrepreneurs. Theirs is the control of production. They are at the helm and steer the ship. A superficial observer would believe that they are supreme. But they are not. They are bound to obey unconditionally the captain's orders. The captain is the consumer.

—Ludwig Von Mises (1940, 270)

If we are interested in explaining what Trygve Haavelmo once described as the "really big dissimilarities in economic life," we must be prepared to concern ourselves with entrepreneurship. For the really big differences are usually those that correspond to historical developments over long periods of time, or to the comparative states of various economies—notably, those of the developed and the underdeveloped areas. It has long been recognized that the entrepreneurial function is a vital component in the process of economic growth. Thus, we are led to suspect that if we ignore the entrepreneur, we are prevented from explaining a very substantial proportion of historic growth in developed countries and its distinction from that of other lands. Those who concern themselves with development policy have apparently been driven to similar conclusions. If we seek to explain the degree of success of those economies that have managed to grow significantly in comparison to those that have remained relatively stagnant, we find it difficult to do so without taking into consideration differences in the availability of entrepreneurial talent and in the motivational mechanism that drives them on. Those who design plans to stimulate development devote a substantial proportion of their energies to providing the means for training and encouraging entrepreneurs. The entrepreneurs also are present in institutional and applied discussions of a number of economic arenas other than development. For example, their absence is sometimes cited as a significant source of the difficulties of a declining industry, and a balance-of-payments crisis is sometimes discussed in similar terms. Thus, those who study either macro or micro problems reserve a substantial place for innovative entrepreneurship within their analyses.

Whether or not they are assigned star roles in such discussions, entrepreneurs, in practice, play no minor role. In fact, the innovative entrepreneurs are among the most intriguing and elusive characters in the cast of characters that constitute economic analysis. They have long been recognized as occupants of the apex of the hierarchy that determines the behavior of the firm and, thereby, bears a heavy responsibility for the vitality of the free enterprise society. This is no recent phenomenon: in the writings of the classical economists, entrepreneurs appeared at least occasionally, though they remained a shadowy entity with no clearly distinguished form or function. Only Schumpeter, and to some degree, Say, succeeded in infusing entrepreneurs with life, assigning them the task of innovation as a specific area of activity that is commensurate with their acknowledged importance. In more recent years, the accumulating facts underscore the significance of their role,[1] but, at the same time, they have disappeared from the theoretical literature. In discussions of the doctrinal history of entrepreneurship theory, the consensus view now seems to be that there once was a theory of entrepreneurship found in the writings of the classical economists, but with the advent of neoclassicism, the entrepreneur was exorcised from that literature.[2]

However, a review of the literature should lead to some modification of these views, particularly those about the earlier period. First, the set of authors who constitute the "usual suspects" hardly includes all of the superstars of the classical arena. Neither Smith nor Ricardo typically is listed as a significant contributor on the subject. Instead, they frequently are replaced in this role by Cantillon and Say. Second, careful perusal of what these early authors have written on the subject should lead to the conclusion that, as far as theory—particularly of the neoclassical variety—is concerned, "There is no there, there." The writings offer us brief descriptions of the activities of the entrepreneur, such as organizing new firms and undertaking risky investments. But that surely is no more theoretical than a theory of labor that tells us carpenters are laborers and use saws to cut lumber. The material is brief—strikingly so—because, arguably, it contains nothing that can reasonably be taken to constitute operational theory.

This is not mere quibbling about the true definition, or connotation, of the word "theory." Rather, this highlights an important point about what we have a right to expect from work that qualifies as "theory." In the academic literature, the term is taken to mean two interrelated things. First, it can be interpreted to refer to a formalized and deliberately over-simplified version of some phenomenon, which, in its simplicity, reveals that phenomenon's basic working mechanism. Second, a theory is inter-pretable as a machine that can be used to generate operational theorems, which can assert that an increase in the magnitude of one variable—the relevant interest rate, for instance—will, other things remaining equal, lead to a new equilibrium in which the magnitude of another variable—say, investment by firms—decreases.

I will argue that Schumpeter and a few others who have been working since the appearance of his writings have created the beginnings of an op-erational theory of entrepreneurship. However, impediments created by the very nature of this topic, at least so far, have limited what we are able to provide by way of theory. Indeed, these handicaps have all but prevented a formal mathematical analysis, up to this point. Still, I aim to show that now we can provide a theory of innovative entrepreneurship that is at least as powerful as the theory of labor and wages, for example. If it is desirable for students of entrepreneurship to ground their learning in theory, there already exists substantial material with which to get them started.

First, however, we will look briefly, and rather superficially, into the doctrinal history and then consider whether the absence of the innovative entrepreneur from much of standard microtheory is, indeed, a needless failing of this body of analysis. After that, I will outline specifically what we can hope to obtain from a theory of entrepreneurship. Then we will examine the obstacles that impede it. Finally, we will turn to the most significant part of the discussion: what has already been accomplished in this arena, and what directions for future work appear to be most promis-ing. Later chapters will turn to the substance of my immodest claim that this book provides at least the beginnings of a theoretical structure that can fit entrepreneurship into the mainstream microtheory of value that has long been the focus of microeconomic analysis.

ENTREPRENEURSHIP: ORIGINS AND EARLY WRITINGS ON THE TOPIC

Until the twentieth century, writings in English referred to entrepreneurs as "adventurers" or "undertakers" (see, e.g., Marshall 1923, 172). The term "entrepreneur" was introduced by Richard Cantillon in the translation into French (suspected to have been carried out by Cantillon himself) of his great work (1755, 54). However, his original English text continues to use the appellation "Undertaker."[3]

These early writings were more descriptive than theoretical. Cantillon's discussion in chapter 13, for instance, is brief, focusing on entrepreneurs who create new firms that may not be innovative, such as "wholesalers in Wool and Corn, Bakers, Butchers, Manufacturers and Merchants of all kinds" (51). Like Knight, Cantillon's main point is the risk involved in the entrepreneur's task:

> These Undertakers can never know how great will be the demand in their City, nor how long their customers will buy of them since their rivals will try all sorts of means to attract customers from them. All this causes so much uncertainty among these Undertakers that every day one sees some of them become bankrupt. (51)

Writing nearly a century later, J. B. Say offers a similarly brief, but richer, discussion. In contrast to Cantillon, Say seems interested primarily in innovating entrepreneurs and, among them, he focuses on three types of "producers": scientists, entrepreneurs, and laborers. Using locks as an example, Say describes the scientist as the investigator of "the properties of iron, the method of extracting from the mine and refining the ore," while entrepreneurs deal with "application of this knowledge to an useful purpose," and the third group, the workers, actually make the product (1827, 20). According to Say, any successful economy needs all three: "Nor can [industry] approximate to perfection in any nation, till that nation excel in all three branches" (21). Thus, Say blames poverty in Africa, for instance, on that continent's lack of scientists and entrepreneurs. He is careful to note, however, that even with abundant scientific knowledge, a lack of entrepreneurs, alone, can undercut prosperity, for without the entrepreneur, "that knowledge might possibly have lain dormant in the memory of one or two persons, or in the pages of literature" (22).[4] Say also gives us a hint of Schumpeter's analysis, which I will summarize briefly later in this chapter. "In manufacture . . . if success [in innovation] ensue[s], the adventurer is rewarded by a longer period of exclusive advantage" (24). Finally, Say mentions the spillovers of innovation, which, he proposes, justify their governmental financing:

> The charges of experiment, when defrayed by the government . . . [are] hardly felt at all, because the burthen is divided among innumerable contributors; and the advantages resulting from success being a common benefit to all, it is by no means inequitable that the sacrifices, by which they are obtained, should fall on the community at large. (25–26)

Before Joseph Schumpeter's breakthrough, the theory of entrepreneurship was touched upon by economists like J. S. Mill, Alfred Marshall, and (a bit later) Frank Knight. Generally, their focus was not on innovative entrepreneurship;[5] they emphasized management's role in directing going concerns, rather than in establishing new firms. Today, however, these discussions would hardly be considered theory. Rather, they usually are narratives containing illuminating observations. For example, they assert that the entrepreneur's payment is a residual after other inputs are compensated and that compensation is determined by the entrepreneur's ability and the supply of entrepreneurship in the market. They also note that the occupation is risky and that entrepreneurs employ themselves, so that unlike other inputs, there is no demand function for their services. Beyond this, however, they offer little.

ABSENCE OF THE ENTREPRENEUR FROM STATIC THEORY OF THE FIRM AND PRODUCTION

Contrast even these limited observations with the entrepreneur's almost total lack of place in modern formal theory. Look for the innovative entrepreneur, or the entrepreneur of any sort, in the index of some of the most noted of recent writings on value theory, in neoclassical rent theory, or on activity analysis models of the firm.[6] The references are scanty—if not totally absent. Expunged from the discussion, the entrepreneur has become as invisible as Ralph Ellison's famous character.

It is not difficult to explain the entrepreneur's absence. Consider the nature of the model of the firm. In its simplest form (and in this respect, the more complex, sophisticated models are no better), the theoretical firm must choose among alternative values for a small number of rather well-defined variables: price, output, investment in plant and equipment, and perhaps advertising outlay. In making these choices, management is taken to consider the costs and revenues associated with each candidate set of quantities, as described by the relevant functional relationships, equations, and inequalities. Explicitly or implicitly, the firm then performs a mathematical calculation that yields optimal (i.e., profit maximizing) values for all of its decision variables. These values, which the theory assumes to be chosen, are taken to constitute the business decision. Matters rest there, at the values selected by the optimization process, and will remain so forever, or until exogenous forces lead to an autonomous change in the firm's environment. Until there is such a shift in one of the relationships that define the problem, the firm implicitly is taken to replicate its previous decisions, day after day, year after year.

The innovative entrepreneur is excluded from this model, which leaves no room for enterprise or initiative. As a result, the management group becomes a passive calculator that reacts mechanically to changes imposed on it by fortuitous external developments over which it does not attempt to exert any influence. One encounters no clever ruses, ingenious schemes, brilliant innovations, charisma, or any of the other stuff of which outstanding entrepreneurship is made. There simply is no way in which these elements can fit into this model.[7]

Nor can the practical pertinence of the decision variables make the difference in carving out a place for the entrepreneur. Already there are maximization models in which, instead of prices and outputs, the decision variables are the firm's real investment program, its financial mix (the proportion of equity and debt in its funding), or the attributes of a new product to be launched by the company. These decisions seem to smell more of the ingredients of entrepreneurship. But though such models may serve their objective well, they take us not a whit further in the analysis of innovative entrepreneurship, for their calculations remain mechanistic and automatic and call for no display of innovative initiative. Here it is important to emphasize that the timeless nature of these models has nothing to do with the invisibility of the entrepreneur. Professor Griffith Conrad Evans (1924) long ago constructed a model based on the calculus of variations in which the firm considered the consequence of its decisions for the time path of prices. In a number of more recent models, the firm chooses an optimal growth rate, rather than a stationary, once-and-for-all output level. But none of these alternatives helps matters. In all of these models, the businessmen are automaton maximizers, and automaton maximizers they remain.

This suggests why our body of theory, as it has developed, offers us no promise of being able to deal effectively with a description and analysis of the entrepreneurial function. Because maximization and minimization constitute the near ubiquitous foundation of the microtheory, the theory is deprived of the ability to provide an analysis of entrepreneurship.

There are at least two very good reasons why the entrepreneur virtually is never mentioned in modern theory of the firm and distribution. The first, and less significant, reason is summarized in what I call "Baumol's Third Tautology." According to this view, innovation is an entirely heterogeneous output—production of yesterday's invention is today's mere repetition. By such reasoning, there are no commeasurable items that can be added up, compared in magnitude, or otherwise quantitatively manipulated as, for example, we can add together the outputs of some commodity in different months of the year and analyze the effect of changes in prices on these totals. Simply put: in an analysis of entrepreneurial activities, there are none of the homogeneous elements that lend themselves to formal mathematical description, let alone the formal optimization analysis that is the foundation of the bulk of microeconomic theory.

The more critical explanation of the absence of the entrepreneur is that in mainstream economics, the microtheory generally is composed of equilibrium models in which, structurally, nothing is subject to change. By definition, however, this excludes innovative entrepreneurs. They are absent from such an innovationless model because they do not belong there—there is no task for them to carry out. This has been argued definitively by Schumpeter (1936) and Kirzner (1979), who demonstrated that sustained equilibrium is not tolerated by innovative entrepreneurs—any more than they tolerate sustained disequilibrium. Here Schumpeter's key insight is that the entrepreneur's occupation, in itself, is the search for profitable opportunities to upset any equilibrium—which is exactly what any innovation, in the broadest sense, entails. The rest of the story is told by Kirzner, who recounts that the entrepreneur, with her critical ability—her alertness—recognizes in any disequilibrium a profitable arbitrage opportunity. By taking advantage of that opportunity, entrepreneurs provide the pressures that move the economy back toward an equilibrium condition. So while Schumpeter's entrepreneur destroys all equilibria, Kirzner's works to restore them. This mechanism, which underlies continuous industrial evolution and revolution, surely is not the stuff of which stationary models are built. Thus, it is hardly surprising that a stationary, Walrasian model—even in a more sophisticated variant—has no room for the innovative entrepreneur.

This is evident particularly in the standard theory of the firm, which analyzes the repetitious decisions of an enterprise that already is present and fully grown. In such a scenario, entrepreneurs have completed their job and left for other places where their firm-creation activities can be used. Even if the creator of the firm has not departed, she will have transformed her role from entrepreneur to manager, so that although she, herself, remains in place, the entrepreneur has gone.

Here, I must emphasize that I do not mean to criticize—or even mildly reprove—the neoclassical model of the firm. That model does what it was designed to do, and does it well. Like any respectable analysis, one hopes that it will be modified, amended, and improved with time—but not because it is unable to handle an issue for which it is irrelevant. The model essentially is an instrument of optimality analysis of well-defined problems, and it is precisely such (very real and important) problems that need no entrepreneur for their solution. I conclude that the neoclassical theory is not wrong to exclude the entrepreneur, because it deals with subjects for which the entrepreneur is irrelevant. It would be as indefensible to require *all* microeconomic writing to give pride of place to entrepreneurship as it is to exclude it universally.

This does not mean, however, that a theory of entrepreneurship is not needed. In fact, its omission leaves us unable to deal adequately with a number of crucial matters. This omission, for instance, forces us to leave almost exclusively in the hands of economic historians what I regard as one of the greatest and most important mysteries in economics: why have free-enterprise economies in the past two centuries been able to outstrip—by substantially more than an order of magnitude—the performance, in terms of growth and innovation, of all other forms of economic organization?

MODELING PRODUCTION AND DISTRIBUTION

Economists are used to the idea that the entrepreneur is just another factor of production, albeit, one whose role is significant for growth of the economy and the general welfare but, at the same time, particularly difficult to analyze. For when the theoretical literature deals with individual factors of production (i.e., inputs), it tends to homogenize them. Granted, it still reluctantly preserves the distinctions among land, labor, and capital, but, more often, such inputs are described as an abstraction whose quantity is all-important and, consequently, easily can be represented as a variable—just another symbol in the production function. Where first and second derivatives are permitted by the assumptions about that function, this model also becomes the basis for the modern theory of distribution, which traces its primitive origins to the marginal productivity theory.

As already noted, even microeconomic theory does not concern itself with the details of the activities of any of the economy's inputs. It does not distinguish, for instance, the daily activities of a computer programmer from those of a plumber, and this is perfectly appropriate, given the objectives of theoretical analysis. In fact, as I will argue presently, this type of abstraction is especially appropriate and all but unavoidable for an illuminating theory of entrepreneurship.

Received theory of distribution and production focuses on a few key attributes of the broad classes of production factors. For these inputs, the theory seeks to provide results pertinent to five subjects:

1. The price that the input will command
2. The price of the output in whose production the input is used
3. The quantity of the input that will be supplied
4. The quantity of the input that will be demanded

5. The allocation of that input among its different possible uses and the distance of that allocation from the requirements of economic efficiency.

In addition, the theory deals with a number of ancillary matters, such as the optimal replacement dates of durable equipment, which will be ignored here.

The obvious question, then, is whether or not these same five issues also should be present in a theory of entrepreneurship. I will argue that they should be and, indeed, that considerable progress has already been made toward this goal. First, however, we must take a brief detour to discuss precisely what we mean by the term "entrepreneur." As we will see, this definition materially affects our conclusions.

DEFINING ENTREPRENEURSHIP: MANAGERS VERSUS ENTREPRENEURS, INNOVATORS VERSUS REPLICATORS

Clarity in the subsequent discussion requires us to pause for a few words about classification, emphasizing two distinctions—both somewhat artificial but, nevertheless, important—that already have appeared briefly in this discussion. First, it is necessary for us to differentiate between the entrepreneurial and the managerial functions. We may define the manager as the individual who oversees the ongoing efficiency of continuing business processes. Managers must see to it that available processes and techniques are combined in proportions appropriate for current and future output levels. They make sure that inputs are not wasted, that schedules and contracts are met, and they make routine pricing and advertising outlay decisions, among other tasks. In sum, they take charge of the more routine activities and decisions encompassed in traditional business models.

This description is not intended to denigrate the importance of managerial activity or to imply that it is without significant analytic difficulties. Carl Kaysen has remarked that, in practice, most firms find themselves in a position well inside their production possibility loci; one of the manager's most challenging tasks is to find ways of approaching those loci more closely, by, for example, increasing their firm's efficiency within the limits of known technology.[8] This is presumably part of the job of the manager, who is constantly on the lookout for means to save a little here and to squeeze a bit more there. For many purposes, the standard models provide an adequate description of the functions of the manager. Given that calculation, experience, or judgment can provide a reasonable approximation to the current optimum, it is the manager's task to see to it that such methods are instituted and retained wisely and accurately.

Next it will be helpful to proceed one step further and divide entrepreneurs into two subsets, which I call the "replicative" and the "innovative" entrepreneurs. Taken literally, the term "entrepreneur" refers to someone who undertakes. Accordingly, in the earlier literature, and even in much of current discussion, the word is taken to refer to anyone who organizes a new business firm of any variety, whether or not a number of similar firms exist already. This usage makes sense—even for the static analysis to which the bulk of micro theory has been dedicated—because, in reality, the vast majority of all entrepreneurs appear to be of the replicative variety.

Innovative entrepreneurs (whether or not they double as managers) have a different function. It is their job to locate new ideas and to put them into effect. They must lead, perhaps even inspire; for them, today's practice is never good enough for tomorrow. In short, they are the Schumpeterian innovator and even somewhat more, for they also must exercise what, in the business literature, is called "leadership." It is this type of entrepreneur who is virtually absent from the received theory of the firm.[9]

In the earlier literature, there are some hints—notably in Say's writings, as we have seen—that entrepreneurs sometimes produce innovative ideas in the process of their activities. However, it is only with Schumpeter that the term "entrepreneur" is redefined to connote an innovator. For analytic purposes the distinction is critical because presumably it is only the innovating entrepreneur who can be associated firmly with revolutionary growth of the economy. Thus the tasks and, consequently, the analysis of the two types of entrepreneur are very different. In what follows, the discussion will deal only with the innovating entrepreneur, except where the contrary is indicated explicitly.

THE SUPPLY OF INNOVATIVE ENTREPRENEURSHIP

In seeking to determine whether or not we can treat the innovative entrepreneur as the theoretical literature treats other factors of production, it may be noted that the distinctive supply conditions that characterize land, labor, and capital are often the primary attributes that distinguish each of these factors from another. The supply of land is fixed, but physical capital is made up of produced and often durable goods, so that variables, such as interest rates, determine its quantity. Meanwhile, the supply of labor largely is determined exogenously. In contrast, at least in marginal productivity theory, there is virtually no difference among these factors in the way that their demands are determined. But the services of the entrepreneur, as creator of a new enterprise—whether innovative or not—are not demanded primarily by others. Instead, it is the entrepreneurs themselves who, in normal circumstances, choose to demand their own services. Accordingly, it is difficult to distinguish the demand for entrepreneurship from its supply.

Still, looking at entrepreneurship from the supply side permits some interesting observations, which have not yet achieved general recognition, but which are based on clear historical evidence and offer insights for the design of policy.[10] The supply of entrepreneurship, for instance, provides yet another impediment to the subject's inclusion in standard theory and helps us to understand why a marriage between theory and policy is not arranged easily in this area. In its discussion of inputs, our formal analysis deals largely with the way in which these inputs are used, but tells us relatively little about where they come from. In our growth models, for example, the behavior of the labor supply exerts a critical influence on the economy's expansion path. The determination of the growth of the labor force itself, however, generally is taken to be an exogenous matter. Similarly, in a neoclassical or programming analysis of production, one investigates how the goal of efficiency requires inputs to be used in the production process. However, such discussions usually assume that the supply of inputs is determined outside the model. Thus, if we were to construct a model that advances the theory of innovative entrepreneurship to the level of sophistication of our treatment of other inputs, we are likely to succeed better in defining the role of the entrepreneur, but still would be able to add relatively little to our understanding of the determinants of the level of output of entrepreneurship.

From the point of view of policy, however, these priorities are reversed. The first order of business in an economy that exhibits very little business drive is to induce the appearance of increased supplies of entrepreneurial skills, which would then be let loose upon that economy's industries. Those concerned with policymaking are interested primarily in what determines the supply of entrepreneurship—particularly innovative entrepreneurship—and in the means that can be used to expand this. Effective allocation of entrepreneurship among *standard* production processes occupies a role of secondary importance.

Until recently, these matters—notably, the supply of entrepreneurial activity—were assumed to be governed, to a very considerable extent, by social psychology, social arrangements, cultural developments, and the like.[11] Focusing only on such matters, however, is tantamount to convening a counsel of despair for the planning of a policy to encourage entrepreneurship. After all, has anyone succeeded in designing reliable devices for modifying attitudes, cultural proclivities, and the institutional arrangements they entail? Who, indeed, knows how the "Protestant ethic" Weber identified can be disseminated and its wide adoption stimulated?

CONCLUDING COMMENT: TOWARD A MICROTHEORY
OF INNOVATIVE ENTREPRENEURSHIP

This book will undertake to show that we are on the verge of creating a rich body of microtheory on innovative entrepreneurs, their services to inventors, and their activities as suppliers of inventions—either directly to consumers, or to the large firms that develop and improve these discoveries into marketable commodities. As part of this broad theoretical development, I will provide models of pricing and of input supply. They are reasonably novel and will lend themselves to a considerable degree of formalization. Because these models also are intended to be operational, I hope that they will yield helpful conclusions—many of them not obvious to the intuition, at least not in advance. For instance, such models could yield insights into the pertinent welfare theory and its implications for entrepreneurial behavior.

In concluding this chapter, I will return to my argument that some of the things expected of a theory of entrepreneurship should not be demanded of it. I also will submit, in contrast, that there are other pertinent elements of such a theory that elude our grasp and may well continue to do so. Finally, I will discuss the special attributes of the innovative entrepreneur's inputs that impede and may prevent us from filling these gaps.

First, let me offer a few words on what should *not* be expected of such a theory. Particularly because those of us who write about entrepreneurship also are likely to be engaged in teaching prospective entrepreneurs, we are led in our teaching to focus on the details of replicative entrepreneurial activities. Much of what we teach future entrepreneurs relates to the legal prerequisites affecting the creation of the firm, bookkeeping and accounting, taxation, and marketing techniques, among other pragmatic concerns. In other words, prospective entrepreneurs who do not focus on innovation easily can be taught the details that make up their day-to-day activities. Surely, however, this is not the content we seek from the theory of the innovative portion of this input any more than it is the stuff of the theory of land, labor, or capital. Indeed, much of such subject matter arguably has less to do with innovative entrepreneurship than with management—not as it pertains to the creation of firms and the introduction of innovations, but, rather, to the ho-hum specifics of daily oversight of the ongoing enterprise. Of course, there still remain gaps in the theory of distribution and input use, in general, but further progress in that area of analysis does not face difficulties as severe as those that the theory of innovative entrepreneurship still must overcome.

Two key handicaps that do impede further development of a theory of innovative entrepreneurship and, particularly, its formalization have already been noted. First, there is the heterogeneity of the product—the fact that, by definition, an innovation is the ultimate unstandardized product. As we know, great product heterogeneity is a substantial source of difficulty for theory construction. Second, the activities of entrepreneurs are universally recognized as entailing relationships beset with uncertainty and discontinuity. Therefore, entrepreneurship cannot be described in neat, simple mathematical forms. As a result, the subject has offered little room for formal optimization analysis. Instead, this is surely an arena in which "satisficing," rather than maximizing, is apt to be attractive. But even here, as I will show, matters are more amenable to answers than might be expected.

In short, this book will describe ways in which such difficulties can be dealt with effectively. The book also will show how we can derive pertinent insight into each of the five subjects noted earlier in this chapter, which we can expect—or at least hope—that a microtheory of innovative entrepreneurship can resolve.

PART I

Pricing, Remuneration, and Allocation of the Agents of Innovation

Toward Characterization
of the Innovation Industry:
The David-Goliath Symbiosis

*In established businesses, innovation is mostly shaped through
small, incremental steps of additional features to augment basic
functionalities. With short product lifecycles, time to recoup
R&D investments is limited. . . . Success is relatively predictable
through the execution of well-defined innovation processes and
in-depth knowledge of their markets in the respective business
units.*

—Dr. Ad Huijser, executive vice president
and chief technology officer, Royal Phillips Electronics
(Tilburg, the Netherlands, September 2003)

This chapter lays out the attributes of the economy that create an environment in which the innovative activities we seek to analyze are apt to be
carried out. The main discussion of why and how to establish a theory of
entrepreneurship, on which this book focuses, is left for later. The magnitude and types of innovative activity vary among industries and different
types of firms, but this chapter describes a pattern that characterizes much
of this heterogeneity and helps us to understand the influence of the market mechanism on innovative activities. In particular, I will suggest that
there is a rough-and-ready division of labor between major corporations
and small, new enterprises in the high-tech sector. The smaller firms are
responsible for a disproportionate share of the breakthrough inventions.
Accordingly, they assume the risks and other special difficulties associated
with making new discoveries. The giant companies may account for the
major share of the economy's R&D financing, but these better-established
firms tend to minimize risk by specializing in incrementally improving the
most promising of the radical innovations they purchase, license, or adapt
from the smaller firms that created them. The implications of this pattern

of specialization, the David-Goliath partnership,[1] will be examined as we proceed.

PRELIMINARY DEFINITION AND DISTRIBUTION OF TASKS IN THE INNOVATION PROCESS

Before beginning the analysis, it is necessary to define some of the terms that will play a central role in our discussion. As already noted, we will classify entrepreneurs into two categories, *innovative* and *replicative*, focusing on the former, as Say and Schumpeter did, in contrast to Cantillon, Knight, and others. Replicative entrepreneurs are those who create companies that offer no significantly novel features, while innovative entrepreneurs focus at least a substantial portion of their efforts on new ideas. However, we will use Schumpeter's expanded definition of the term "innovation" so that it is not merely synonymous with the term "invention," but also entails all of the steps needed to adapt the invention to the desires of purchasers, organize its production, and put it to use—by selling or leasing the invention to others or by directly incorporating it into the production process of the final product to which it contributes. The steps between invention and final marketing are carried out by the innovative entrepreneur, who functions as a partner to the inventor. Such an entrepreneur is, in effect, a businessperson who recognizes the value of an invention, determines how to adapt it to the preferences of prospective users, and then brings the invention to market and promotes its utilization.

In our economy and others like it, innovation is characteristically pursued both by enormous firms and by individual inventors and their entrepreneur partners. Thus, there are two main classes of private suppliers to the innovation market: the large firms and the inventor-entrepreneurs. Despite his crucial role in the analysis of entrepreneurial activity, Schumpeter concluded that the day of the innovative entrepreneur was waning, as the expanding role of routinized innovation by big business threatened to make such entrepreneurs obsolete. I disagree and, in this chapter, will argue that the individual entrepreneur continues to play a critical role in economic growth.

Each side of large firm–small firm interaction is only part of the story of the evolving role of the entrepreneur, and, as a result, overlooks much of its essence. The entrepreneur, indeed, plays a critical part in the growth process, and there is no reason to expect that role to disappear.[2] But in the modern economy, entrepreneurs working alone in the marketplace cannot carry out their tasks most effectively. Fortunately, the market mechanism has provided the partners that entrepreneurs need for their purpose—for example, large firms like Boeing, which took on the task of improving the Wright brothers' invention.

In seeking to explain the unprecedented and miraculous growth performance of free-market economies, this chapter focuses on the difference in, but complementary relationship between, the characteristic innovative contributions of large and small entrepreneurial firms, emphasizing that these two groups have tended to specialize in different components of society's innovation process. The major breakthroughs have tended to come from small, new enterprises, while the invaluable incremental contributions that multiply capacity and speed and increase reliability and user-friendliness have been the domain of the larger firms. Together, the two have contributed far more than either would have alone.[3]

In addition, important innovations continue to flow from two groups outside the market sector: the government and the universities. Truly astonishing contributions have come from each of the four sectors, but the primary focus here will be on the activities and accomplishments of the private sector (it is not, however, my intention to denigrate the achievements of the others). In order to ensure that the pertinent arrangements and institutions really are effective in promoting economic growth, it is essential that each sector is provided with appropriate incentives to spur its role in the process. For any modern economy concerned with this issue, understanding the roles of the four key sectors and the requisites for their effective participation is essential for the creation of a road map for public sector growth policy.

MARKET PRESSURES FOR AN ENHANCED LARGE-FIRM ROLE IN TECHNICAL PROGRESS

Systematic R&D activity by large firms in the economy's high-tech sectors is reported to have originated in Germany in the mid-nineteenth century. Somewhat later, toward the end of the nineteenth century, this trend reached the United States. In 1911, when Schumpeter's pathbreaking work made its appearance, this method of organizing research activity still was a novelty. Until shortly before that point, the bulk of innovative activity had largely been in the hands of independent undertakers.

Free competition—that is, competition not handicapped by severe government regulations or tightly enforced customary rules, like those of the medieval guilds that prevented gloves-off combat among rival firms— arguably played a critical role in the move toward large-firm innovative activity. Of particular significance here are rivalries among oligopolistic firms—large companies in markets dominated by a small number of firms.

As will be discussed in chapter 4, these large firms constantly must be ready to respond to any major innovative steps taken by their very visible rivals and must possess the financial resources needed to support the R&D activities this readiness entails.[4]

In today's economy, many oligopolistic firms wield *innovation* as their main battle weapon, using it to wage both offensive and defensive campaigns against competitors. The result is precisely analogous to an arms race, in which two countries, each fearing attack from the other, feel it is necessary to match the other country's military spending. Similarly, two competing firms, each fearing the other will outspend it in developing and acquiring the battle weapons of their industry, are driven to conclude that not only maximization of profit (or minimization of loss), but their very existence depends on matching their rivals' efforts and spending on the innovation process. Because these giant warring firms do not dare to relax their innovation activities, a constant stream of innovations can be expected to appear in the economies in which they operate. The arms race character of innovation in these large firms drives each company to seek ways of minimizing the chance that its rivals will gain access to outside breakthroughs before it does. As a result, these firms are forced to undertake their own R&D by creating the necessary specialized internal organization. In their pursuit of risk reduction, the competing firms will be induced to proceed conservatively in the innovative projects they undertake.

The innovative entrepreneur naturally is associated with the small, start-up firm. Indeed, as noted in the previous chapter, widespread and long-employed usage simply *defines* such entrepreneurs as the creators of new enterprises. However, the apportionment of the task of supplying the resources invested in innovation has been changing materially. At least in the United States, funding for innovation increasingly is supplied by large, oligopolistic enterprises—hardly the sort of firms that one associates with entrepreneurs. Today some 70 percent of R&D expenditure in the United States is carried out by private business, most of it by larger firms. In 2000, 46 percent of all U.S. industrial R&D spending was attributed to just 167 companies, though more than 30,000 U.S. firms engaged in R&D activity (National Science Board 2000, 24).

In general, outlays on research and invention, like GDP per capita, have been exploding. Figure 2.1 shows real private business expenditures on R&D in the United States following World War II. The near-exponential growth path is observable immediately.

Note how little the recessions of the postwar period held back the growth in real expenditures on the invention process. The intervals of decline in R&D outlays are merely small deviations from what appears to be an inexorably rising path.

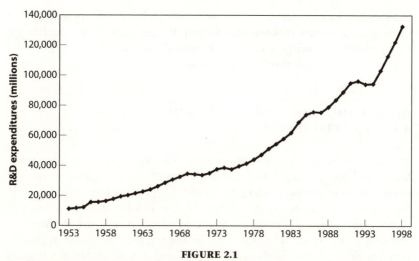

FIGURE 2.1

Real U.S. Private R&D Expenditures, 1953–1998 (millions of 1992 dollars). Note: expenditures are deflated using the GDP implicit price deflator. (Sources: National Science Board 2000; and *Economic Report of the President* 2001. Reprinted from Baumol 2002b, fig. 6.2, p. 77.)

As noted above, large enterprises account for the bulk of this private R&D spending. But because their innovative activities are designed to prevent unwelcome surprises and minimize risks, large firms' R&D incorporates little of the free-wheeling, imaginative, and risk-taking approach that characterizes the entrepreneur. Instead, management at large firms often maintains tight control of the activities of the company's laboratories, determining budgets, which, in turn, may dictate how many people at each level of specialization are employed in the firm's R&D endeavors. Indeed, it is not unusual for a large firm's top management, usually comprising people untrained or inexperienced in research, *to determine what new products and processes the laboratories should seek to discover.*[5] Sometimes, large firms try to loosen the leash that constrains their employees' innovative activity by organizing a subsidiary operation that is more inviting to the free exercise of creativity, imagination, and entrepreneurship, but it seems that these subgroups often fail to generate much success.[6]

A bureaucratically governed enterprise is likely to run research and development in accord with bureaucratic rules and procedures. This pattern leads to the conjecture, voiced by Schumpeter, that the work responsibilities the economy assigns to the entrepreneur are narrowing and are destined to shrink even further. One easily can surmise what prompted Schumpeter to predict a limited future for the entrepreneur, but I will argue next that his is a fundamental mischaracterization. Rather than being condemned to obsolescence, independent inventors and their partner entrepreneurs continue to play a vital role in innovation.

REVOLUTIONARY BREAKTHROUGHS:
A SMALL-FIRM SPECIALTY

It is convenient here to divide inventions into two, polar categories: revolutionary breakthroughs and cumulative incremental improvements. Of course, many new products and processes fall into neither extreme category, but are somewhere between the two. Still, it will become clear that this distinction is useful, as there are many examples that clearly fit into one category or the other. For instance, the electric light, alternating electric current, the internal combustion engine, and a host of other advances surely must be deemed revolutionary, while successive models of washing machines and refrigerators—each new model a bit longer-lasting, a bit less susceptible to breakdown, and a bit easier to use—constitute a sequence of incremental improvements.

The relevance of this distinction should be evident, given what has been said about the organization of R&D in large business organizations. The inherent conservatism of this process naturally leads to the expectation that these firms will tend to avoid the risks of the unknown that the revolutionary breakthrough entails, instead specializing in incremental improvements. The former is left most often to small or newly founded enterprises guided by innovative entrepreneurs. This was noted first by Acs and Audretsch (1988, 1990) and is suggested by much of the subsequent literature (albeit with some qualifications), as is shown systematically in van Praag and Versloot (2007, 15–19).[7]

The degree of asymmetry in the apportionment of R&D activity between large and small firms is illustrated dramatically in table 2.1, which identifies the breakthrough innovations of the twentieth century—from the airplane to the zipper—for which small firms are responsible.

This remarkable list includes a strikingly substantial share of the technical breakthroughs of the twentieth century. In addition to the airplane, the list features FM radio, the helicopter, the personal computer, the pacemaker, and a host of other inventions of enormous significance for our economy.

A very recent study sponsored by the U.S. Small Business Administration (2003) provides further evidence to similar effect.[8] The study, which examined technical change through patenting, found that "a small firm patent is more likely than a large firm patent to be among the top 1 percent

Table 2.1
Some Important Innovations by U.S. Small Firms in the Twentieth Century

Air conditioning	Heart valve	Portable computer
Air passenger service	Heat sensor	Prestressed concrete
Airplane	Helicopter	Prefabricated housing
Articulated tractor chassis	High-resolution CAT scanner	Pressure-sensitive cellophane tape
Artificial skin	High-resolution digital x-ray	Programmable computer
Assembly line	High-resolution x-ray microscope	Quick-frozen food
Audio tape recorder	Human growth hormone	Reading machine
Bakelite	Hydraulic brake	Rotary oil-drilling bit
Biomagnetic imaging	Integrated circuit	Safety razor
Biosynthetic insulin	Kidney stone laser	Six-axis robot arm
Catalytic petroleum cracking	Large computer	Soft contact lens
Computerized blood pressure controller	Link trainer	Solid fuel rocket engine
Continuous casting	Microprocessor	Stereoscopic map scanner
Cotton picker	Nuclear magnetic resonance scanner	Strain gauge
Defibrillator	Optical scanner	Strobe lights
DNA fingerprinting	Oral contraceptives	Supercomputer
Double-knit fabric	Outboard engine	Two-armed mobile robot
Electronic spreadsheet	Overnight national delivery	Vacuum tube
FM radio	Pacemaker	Variable output transformer
Freewing aircraft	Personal computer	Vascular lesion laser
Front-end loader	Photo typesetting	Xerography
Geodesic dome	Polaroid camera	X-ray telescope
Gyrocompass		Zipper

of most frequently cited patents."[9] The study also attributed the following innovation achievements to small firms.

> Small firms represent one-third of the most prolific patenting companies that have 15 or more U.S. patents.
>
> Small firm innovation is twice as closely linked to scientific research as large firm innovation on average, and so is substantially more high-tech or leading edge.
>
> Small firms are more effective in producing high-value innovations—the citation index for small firm patents averaged 1.53 compared to 1.19 for large firms.
>
> Small patenting firms are roughly 13 times more innovative per employee than large patenting firms.
>
> A small firm patent is at least twice as likely to be found among the top 1 percent of highest-impact patents as a patent from a large firm. (2)

Such results lead one to the plausible conjecture that a substantial proportion of the revolutionary new ideas of the past two centuries have been and likely will continue to be provided by independent, innovative entrepreneurs operating small business enterprises. Evidently, small entrepreneurial firms have come close to monopolizing the portion of R&D activity that is engaged in the search for revolutionary breakthroughs. Thus, we seem to have arrived at the opposite conclusion from Schumpeter's. Rather than the innovative role of the entrepreneur and the small firm disappearing as the R&D activities of the giant enterprises make the activities of individual inventors and entrepreneurs unnecessary, little appears to be left for large enterprise to do. This, as we will see next, also is a misleading conclusion. But such concerns may be exacerbated by statistics showing that the bulk of the country's R&D spending is contributed by large enterprises. Are the giant companies spending a great deal, but achieving very little? I will show next that this concern is also misplaced.

REVOLUTIONARY CONSEQUENCES OF AGGREGATED INCREMENTAL IMPROVEMENTS

As we have seen, the type of innovation in which giant enterprises tend to specialize primarily is devoted to improving products—by enhancing their reliability and user-friendliness—and finding new uses for these products. This approach tends to be conservative, as it seeks results that clearly are applicable within markets that are relatively unspeculative. Moreover, the bureaucratic control typical of innovative activity in large firms ensures that the resulting changes will be modest, predictable, and incremental.

These firms are not predisposed to welcome the romantic flights of the imagination, entrepreneurial leaps of faith, and plunges into the unknown that often lead only to disaster, but which also are part of the process of making breakthrough discoveries.

Having recognized the critical role of the smaller enterprises, one should not go to the other extreme and undervalue the incremental contribution of the routine activity that sometimes adds even more to growth than more revolutionary prototype innovations. Each small improvement may be relatively unspectacular, but when many are added together, they become very significant indeed. Consider, for instance, how little computing power the first clumsy and enormously expensive computers provided and, in comparison, what huge multiples of such power have been added by many subsequent incremental improvements.

Table 2.1 provided a set of the most notable examples of the contributions made by small, entrepreneurial firms. One also could obtain equally startling examples of the magnitude of the innovative contributions made by large companies, whose *incremental improvements* often add up to results of enormous magnitude.[10] Intel Corporation's progress in computer chip manufacturing dramatically illustrates this point. Intel, the leader in its industry, has brought to market successive generations of chips and transistors, on which the performance of computers depends heavily. According to a recent report, between 1971 and 2003, the "clock speed" of Intel's microprocessor chips—that is, the number of instructions each chip can carry out per second—increased by some *three million percent* to reach today's rate of 3 billion computations per second. From 1968 to 2003, the number of transistors embedded in a single chip grew by more than *10 million percent*, while the number of transistors that can be purchased for a dollar increased by *five billion percent* (Markoff 2003). These are hardly minor advances. Collectively, such improvements surely contribute far more computing capacity than was provided by the original revolutionary breakthrough—the invention of the electronic computer.[11] Of course, the initial invention is an indispensable necessity for all of the later improvements. For that reason, I argue that only the combined work of both blockbuster and incremental innovators made possible the powerful and inexpensive computers that serve us so effectively today.

DIGRESSION: ON THE ROLE OF GOVERNMENT AND THE UNIVERSITY IN INNOVATION

Our analysis of the forces driving technical change and economic growth must not overlook the public sector's role in promoting and expanding

33

economic output. In this book, I deliberately emphasize the importance of oligopolistic competition and independent entrepreneurship, giving less attention to the contribution of the public sector. There are, however, two key players in the innovation story that are not guided directly by market forces: universities and government agencies. Both have made direct contributions to technological progress—the electronic computer and the Internet are prominent examples of this participation. However, these institutions' contributions, which tend to be rooted in basic research, as distinguished from applied research, differ substantially from the private-sector accomplishments already discussed. This public-private division of labor can be attributed to the private firm's profit motive. From the point of view of the unthinking market mechanism, an outlay on basic research is apt to be a "wasteful" expenditure because it makes no substantial promises of adding to the firm's profits. By its very nature, it is nearly impossible to predict whether basic research will yield any financial benefit and, if it does, who will be the ultimate beneficiary. For these reasons, governments and universities have had to step in to ensure that basic research is accomplished. For, as we know, basic research is important for growth in the long run, and much applied innovation is made possible, or at least stimulated, by its results.

Government, in particular, plays two critical roles—one active and the other passive—in the innovation story. The passive contribution is provided primarily through the legal infrastructure and includes well-recognized provisions that guarantee property rights[12] and enforceability of contracts, as well as access to patented intellectual property, the lack of government interference in the exchange of technical information, and the absence of employment and rental rules that inhibit the formation of new firms. Such legal protections encourage entrepreneurship, the formation of new firms, and investment in the innovation process by larger competing enterprises. On the active side, the government's financial support of basic research has proven to be invaluable. Such research, with its uncertainties and unpredictable benefits, is not highly attractive to private enterprise, despite its critical role in long-term innovation and growth.

The importance for technological progress of this conjunction of academia, business, and the public sector was illustrated strikingly in an American Philosophical Society (2003) symposium on recent and projected biomedical advances.[13] There remarkable examples of the truly mind-boggling array of medical breakthroughs made by universities, government (notably the military), and small private firms were presented. One speaker, who quoted Hollywood's Steven Spielberg, aptly summed up the presentation, noting, "There is no more science *fiction*." Indeed, all signs indicate that there will be no break in the acceleration of innovation. For that reason, future innovations promise to be as difficult for us to anticipate as it would have been for our ancestors to imagine those inventions that are now thoroughly familiar to us. A sample of the innovations discussed at the symposium demonstrates this point:

- Surgery carried out by computer-guided robots, with immediate and automatic restocking of surgical equipment and medication, and remote surgery in which the operating surgeon, who guides the computer, may be thousands of miles from the patient during the procedure
- Growth of replacement bodily organs in specially maintained groups of animals (pigs are favored currently) for use in human transplantation
- Artificially induced hibernation and what can only be described as "reversible pseudo-death" of patients as a substitute for anesthesia, eliminating the latter's undesirable side effects and other perils
- Induced growth of new organs within patients as a substitute for transplants, eliminating the difficult and dangerous problem of transplant rejection and the need for postprocedure, antirejection medications, with their undesirable side effects
- Use of certain insects (notably butterflies, cockroaches, and sphinx moths, which have highly specialized, powerful senses) to transmit information about the presence of buried earthquake victims and dangers, such as buried land mines or anthrax spores.

This list, which stirs the imagination to overload, surely indicates that the end of innovation is nowhere in sight. Moreover, as the discussion in this chapter indicates, large corporations, working alone, apparently cannot be expected to produce the abundance of miraculous discoveries that our society has come to expect.

CONCLUDING COMMENT

This chapter describes the structure of what can be referred to as the "innovation industry" and the market forces that govern it. I contend here that market forces tend to divide private-sector suppliers into two primary sets: small and large firms. While individual inventors and entrepreneurs provide a disproportionate share of breakthrough discoveries, large, established firms take those breakthroughs and refine them by making incremental improvements. In order to grow, an economy requires both of these activities. Together, the activities of these two subsectors are superadditive—the whole is indeed greater than the sum of the parts, in terms of the benefits offered to society and the contribution made to economic growth.

Entrepreneurship, Invention, and Pricing: Toward Static Microtheory

Casual observation suggests that price discrimination is common in many industries that appear to be extremely competitive. . . . [F]irms in the airline, car rental, moving, hotel and restaurant businesses practice common types of price discrimination, and much evidence suggests that high-valuation consumers pay higher average prices than low-valuation consumers. Yet these markets are not characterized by unusually high entry costs, economies of scale, product differentiation, or market concentration.

—James D. Dana, Jr. (1998, 395)

There is almost no industry where this phenomenon [price discrimination] is not present.

—Jules Dupuit, 1853 (in Ekelund 1970, 270)

In this chapter, we take the first steps toward our main goal—bringing independent inventors and entrepreneurs to their proper place in production and distribution theory. The Schumpeterian model of his earlier volume (1936), of course, already brings us a good part of the way. But because it lacks formal structure—that is, it provides nothing like the *wage = marginal revenue* product formula for the remuneration of labor, which the undergraduate student can be asked to master and manipulate—this model largely has been excluded from standard textbooks. This chapter attempts to fill that gap, using the formal structure concealed in Schumpeter's informal discussion as a starting point.

The theory I will construct here contains conventional elements that are in keeping with the standard theory of pricing and input supply, an analysis not previously in the literature. The analysis also will have some unexpected features. Notably, it will demonstrate that it is the presence of *competitive* market forces that generally imposes discriminatory pricing as a normal state of affairs in the arena of innovative activity. This is implicitly true even in the classic Schumpeterian model. The theory of entrepreneurship presented here will depart from the widely held view that price discrimination requires monopoly power and constitutes an exercise of that power. Instead, I will argue that, in many cases, competitive market forces transform those who conduct innovative activities into de facto *discriminatory price takers.* Moreover, if competitive pressures are sufficiently strong, the vector of discriminatory prices that a supplier of innovation is forced to adopt will tend to be *Ramsey optimal.*[1] Here, Ramsey optimality means that the selected allocation yields the greatest possible contribution to the general welfare, among all of those allocations of the economy's inventive and entrepreneurial resources that yield profit sufficient to permit survival of the affected firms.

I will argue that this state of affairs fits right in with the Schumpeterian model, in which the discrimination entails prices that differ over time (I will call it "intertemporal price differentiation"), rather than among contemporaneous submarkets, as occurs in common models of differential pricing. The noteworthy observation that will emerge here is that there is no difference in the formal analysis of intratemporal and intertemporal price discrimination, in terms of the role of differences in elasticities of the firm's demand functions in its different submarkets—for example, the differences that result from inequality in the availability of competing products. I also will argue that since the pertinent discriminatory prices need not entail any element of monopoly power, a competitive equilibrium here will yield, as usual, no returns exceeding those of investment in fully competitive markets.

This chapter also will provide some theoretical discussion of a related matter: the empirical evidence that, as a class, innovative entrepreneurs should expect to earn *negative* economic profits. That is, on average, entrepreneurs' monetary rewards apparently are significantly lower than those of employed personnel with similar education and experience. In chapter 4, I will argue a related point, that the tendency for breakthrough inventions to come from the independent entrepreneurs and inventors represents a process of outsourcing by the large firms to low-wage independent inventors and innovative entrepreneurs.

The discriminatory pricing model on which my analysis focuses is not applicable only to entrepreneurs. Rather, it deals with a considerably broader arena in pricing and distribution theory. However, as a particular application, this body of theory deals with the pricing and remuneration of entrepreneurs, which brings us, perhaps for the first time, toward incorporating the fourth factor of production—entrepreneurship—into established value theory. I will argue in chapter 4 that this model also is applicable to the large firms that specialize in making incremental improvements to breakthrough innovations.[2]

Here I should emphasize again that the analysis in this book deals with innovative, rather than what I have called "replicative," entrepreneurs. That is, my discussion will focus on those entrepreneurs who launch firms with the aid of new products or other innovations, rather than those who open companies similar to a multitude of existing enterprises. It is important to note that the theory I offer here rests on the fact that much of today's innovative activity is carried out by the economy's giant corporations. Contrary to Schumpeter's prediction, however, this has not marginalized the role of the independent entrepreneur. Instead, as I argued in chapter 2, large and small firms have taken on complementary roles, with each undertaking a critical portion of the economy's innovative activity. In chapter 4, I will show that these two types of firms have analogous formal value theory analyses. That is, the appropriate pricing models applicable to the two types of innovative enterprises are very similar in formal structure.

To create a systematic microanalysis of entrepreneurship, it will be necessary to discuss the supply of innovative activities provided by both groups, as well as the equilibrium pricing structures to which they are driven by market forces. Of course, for independent inventors and entrepreneurs, who are self-employed and self-appointed to their occupations, the usual ways of analyzing demand for their services will not apply. Such demand nevertheless will pervade this analysis, via the general market's demand for innovative products and corporations' demand for the rights to use innovative inventors' and entrepreneurs' intellectual property.

ENTREPRENEURIAL PRICE DISCRIMINATION: SEVERAL SUBVARIANTS

I will begin my price discrimination argument with the case of innovative entrepreneurs and their inventor partners (who, of course, can be the same person). As already pointed out, the story pertinent to the independent entrepreneur will turn out to be essentially the same as that in Schumpeter's 1911 model. However, my recapitulation of that story entails an entirely new way of looking at it.

For this purpose, I will deal with different guises of the most common type of price discrimination in which different sales of a given commodity are carried out at different prices. However, my argument requires some extension of this concept of discriminatory pricing. Specifically, I will distinguish three types, which will be called "interpersonal discrimination," "interlocational discrimination," and "intertemporal discrimination." The first and most commonly discussed in the literature is illustrated by student discounts or senior citizen discounts, which divide customers into separable classes and sell a given commodity at different prices to the members of the different classes. Interlocational, or geographic, discrimination occurs when prices differ from one city to another—for instance, from one airline route to another—even though supply costs do not vary geographically. Finally, intertemporal discrimination is illustrated by the reduced prices in annual, post-Christmas sales, which provide the same commodities as were supplied during the pre-Christmas shopping season, but at very different prices.[3] Often, several of these pricing practices will be employed simultaneously, as in a food retail emporium that declares Tuesdays to be "senior citizen discount days."

For our purposes, it is important to recognize that a common analysis is applicable to all of these types of price discrimination. Profit maximization calls for equality of marginal revenues in all market segments in which prices differ, but supply costs are similar. Generally, prices will be highest in submarkets where demand for the firm's product is most inelastic. All other things being equal, the firm's elasticity of demand will be highest in submarkets where the number of competitors is greatest—whether the discrimination is interpersonal, interlocational, or intertemporal. As I will demonstrate next, Schumpeterian entrepreneur-inventor partners may engage in all of these types of price discrimination, but it is the intertemporal variant that lies at the heart of the story. I will return to Schumpeter presently, but first I will demonstrate how, contrary to widespread assertion, competition characteristically tends to enforce discriminatory price taking—particularly where firms are motivated repeatedly to incur sunk outlays, as in the Schumpeterian story.

MANDATORY PRICE DISCRIMINATION IN SEPARABLE MARKETS WITHOUT ENTRY BARRIERS

The discriminatory pricing scenario that applies to the independent entrepreneur also can be applied to the innovative, high-tech oligopoly industries. For, as I will argue in chapter 4, in both cases, price discrimination is the normal state of affairs. My analysis of the discriminatory pricing scenario, as applied in this chapter to the independent entrepreneur, rests on five fairly common assumptions:

1. Prospective inventors can enter and exit innovative activity at low cost and with little delay, doing so whenever there are profits to be earned—i.e., the markets are "contestable" with no Stiglerian

barriers to entry, so that expected equilibrium profits also must be zero.[4]

2. Customers are divisible into different submarkets with different, finite demand elasticities (with negatively sloped demand curves) for the firm.

3. If such a customer group is offered a lower price than another, it is not feasible—or, at least, is very difficult—for the former to resell purchases to the latter.[5]

4. The average cost curves of the firms are roughly U-shaped, at least in the relevant portion of the loci.

5. The firm repeatedly sinks R&D outlays—expenditures that do not enter marginal costs, since total R&D costs do not rise when users increase.

The second and third premises are the standard assumptions of any price discrimination model, while the first assumption—zero entry barriers and entry whenever profits are available in a market—is an extreme case. Indeed, interpreted strictly, the first assumption rules out sunk costs, as the need to incur such costs constitutes a barrier to entry and imposes risk costs on the entrant, from which the incumbent is immune.

The sunk costs that are important here are not once-and-for-all outlays. Rather, they are continuing expenses, as when competition forces the firm in a high-tech industry to sink money repeatedly in R&D. As we know, in these industries, a firm that introduces a superior product or production process cannot rest on its oars, for the firm and its rivals are engaged in a kind of arms race, in which expenditures on further innovation are the prime weapons. Success in this race ultimately is a matter of life and death for such firms.

The role of sunk costs in this discussion of price discrimination may require some explanation. For, according to traditional theory, sunk costs do not matter because a firm's current decisions cannot change any costs incurred in the past. The sunk outlays that are relevant here are very different, however, since they are still to be incurred and repeatedly will be sunk over and over again for the foreseeable future. They surely do affect pricing decisions, and it is these expectable and recurring sunk outlays that directly drive the firm to discriminatory pricing. These are not barriers to entry in Stigler's pertinent sense because they are equal burdens for the entrants and the incumbents. Accordingly, they offer no substantial competitive advantage and, hence, no monopoly power to incumbent firms. This brings us to the first proposition of my central result:

PROPOSITION 3.1: Entry enforces discrimination. In a market with no barriers to entry, the firm's equilibrium economic profits will be zero. If a seller can separate its customers into distinct submarkets with different demand elasticities of the firm's submarket demand curves and the firm can prevent its product from being transferred from one customer to another, then the normal assumptions of the theory of the firm require discriminatory prices to avoid losses. Consequently, equilibrium will entail such prices.

Note that the assumed differences in demand elasticities in the different submarkets preclude perfect competition, with its universally horizontal supplier demand curves. Accordingly, it should be clear, intuitively, that the first three of our five assumptions yield Proposition 3.1. For if freedom of entry forces the firm to charge profit-maximizing prices in order to break even—and if those prices permit it to get by—then those are the prices the firm will have to select in equilibrium. However, if there are discriminatory prices that yield profits higher than those that are possible under uniform pricing, then *tautologically*, in the (zero-profit) equilibrium, the profit-maximizing prices must be discriminatory. Moreover, if the profit maximum is unique, the firm will be a price taker with a unique vector of discriminatory prices that are dictated, element by element, by the market. Note that we have not yet used the U-shaped, average cost premise, which will be employed later, in discussing the existence and stability of the competitive, discriminatory equilibrium.[6]

From the premises discussed above, we can provide a formal model that yields the relevant prices and output quantities. For simplicity, I will deal with the case where the marginal costs of serving consumers in the different submarkets are all the same and equal to C', while the demands of the different submarkets are independent, so that all cross-elasticities of demand are zero. Thus, using obvious notation, equilibrium requires maximization of profit,

(3.1) $$Max \sum p_i y_i - C(y_1,...,y_n),$$

subject to the zero-profit requirement,

(3.2) $$\sum p_i y_i - C(y_1,...,y_n) \leq k \text{ (where we select } k = 0).$$

The Lagrangian is

(3.3) $$L = (1 - r)[\sum p_i y_i - C(y_1,...,y_n)] + rk,$$

where r is the Lagrange multiplier, and L is to be maximized by appropriate choice of the y variables.

But, letting E represent the price elasticity of demand, for any $y_i > 0$, the first-order (Kuhn-Tucker) conditions for maximization of (3.3) obviously include

(3.4) $$(1-r)\,p_i\left[1+\left(\frac{y_i}{p_i}\right)\frac{dp_i}{dy_i}\right]=(1-r)\,p_i\left[1-\frac{1}{E}\right]=(1-r)\,C_i'$$

or

(3.5) $$\frac{p_i-C_i'}{p_i}=\frac{1}{E}$$

This formula, which is familiar from the price discrimination literature, is clearly the formalization of the Schumpeterian story.

EXISTENCE AND STABILITY: MUST ENTRY UNDERCUT DISCRIMINATORY PRICES? CAN DISCRIMINATORS COEXIST?

The preceding arguments can be expected to raise at least two questions in the reader's mind. First, will not the assumed easy entry (a premise justified by my claim that competition is not inconsistent with discriminatory pricing) force prices toward uniformity? Second—the other side of the matter—will not the discriminating firm be able to take over the market and evolve into a monopolist? The general answer to both questions is that, in some circumstances, either can happen, but normally not in the situation described by our model. These questions also draw our attention to the existence and uniqueness of the discriminatory equilibrium, an issue that will not be examined formally here, but will be considered intuitively.

To deal with this issue most directly and heuristically, next I will go over the workings of the model with the aid of some simple diagrams. To avoid complications, I assume that there are two customer groups, each with downward-sloping, linear demand curves, $p_i = AR = a_i - b_i y_i$ ($i = 1, 2$). Hence, their marginal revenue also will be linear, with twice the slope of the demand curves, as shown in figures 3.1(a) and (b), for Submarkets (customer groups) 1 and 2, respectively. As usual, to find the profit-maximizing decisions for the firm as a function of its total output in the two submarkets, we add the marginal revenue curves horizontally to obtain the kinked marginal revenue curve for the firm as a whole, since, as we know, profit maximization at any given output level of the discriminating firm requires marginal revenue in the two markets to be equal. This produces the familiar, kinked marginal revenue curve of figure 3.1(c). At low levels of total output, $y = y_1 + y_2$, the firm serves only the more lucrative submarket, that is, Submarket 1, which, at low volumes, offers higher marginal revenue than the other submarket at any output level.

When the amount of output sold in Submarket 1 becomes sufficiently large, say at $y = y^*$, it will pay to supply some amount of product to Submarket 2. From the marginal revenue curve for the two submarkets

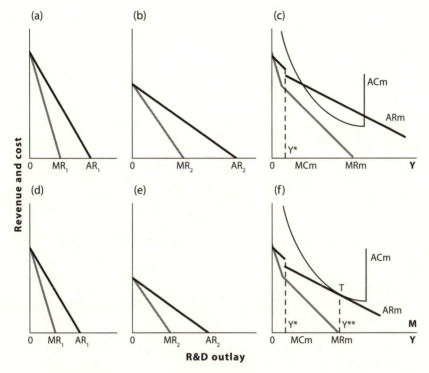

FIGURE 3.1
Price Discriminatory Equilibrium: R&D Expenditure in Two Markets

together, we can derive a curve of average revenue for the firm as a function of its total output, based on the assumption that the price in each submarket is set so as to maximize the total revenue derived from that level of y. To the left of y^*, the firm's average revenue curve will have the usual relationship to Submarket 1's MR curve—both start at the same point, and MR has twice the downward slope of AR. At y^*; however, the firm's average revenue curve has a downward discontinuity at y^*, as shown. This is because, at higher values of y, the firm obtains part of its revenue from a submarket with lower average returns than the submarket it initially served exclusively, thereby reducing the average of the returns from the two sources together. Thereafter, to the right of y^*, the average revenue curve will be linear, with a slope that is intermediate between those of the two submarkets' AR curves.

Now suppose that the average cost curve for the combined market lies partly below the market AR locus, as shown by AC_m in figure 3.1(c). Here it is clear that in the absence of barriers, as assumed in our model, we can expect entry to occur. As in the usual story, the result will be a downward

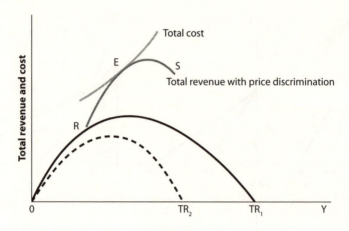

FIGURE 3.2
Total Cost and Revenue with and without Price Discrimination

(leftward) shift in one or both of the submarket demand curves. This shift will proceed to the point of tangency, T, between the AR and the AC curves, if such a point exists (see figure 3.1(f)).[7] If the curvatures of the average cost and revenue loci are appropriate, there will be only one such tangency point at a unique output level, y^{**}. At any other output level, the firm will incur losses.

Figure 3.2 shows *total* revenue and cost in the circumstance described in figure 3.1(f). With linear demand curves of the form $AR = a - by$, the total revenue curves will satisfy $TR = ay + by^2$. These will be parabolic, as shown by curves $0\,TR_1$ and $0\,TR_2$.

As before, when total output is small, it will pay the firm to serve only Submarket 1, so the total revenue curve for the firm will coincide with that for this submarket. Moving to the right, to larger values of y, we reach a point where the slope of $0\,TR_1$ equals that of $0\,TR_2$—meaning that marginal revenues in the two submarkets are equal at these points. Here, it will pay the firm to begin to supply some of its product to Submarket 2. From that point onward, the firm's TR locus will be above the $0\,TR_1$ parabola, shown as the locus labeled RS in figure 3.2.[8] The figure also shows an illustrative total cost curve and its tangency point, E, with this TR curve. Here E is the equilibrium point corresponding to T in figure 3.1(f).

These two figures demonstrate that, in the situation with which our model deals, at any output *other* than the equilibrium output at the tangency points in figure 3.1(f) or figure 3.2, the firm will lose money and be unable to survive. This is where our fourth assumption, the U-shaped average cost curve for the firm, comes into play. The linear demand curves in figures 3.1 and 3.2 show that the firm's linear submarkets are sufficient to produce the uniqueness result, though the linearity is evidently not necessary. Clearly, the curvature (convexity) of the *AC* curve must be greater than that of the *AR* curve. The former contains a downward-sloping segment whose slope, if continuous, decreases in absolute value, as *y* increases from a level initially higher than that of the corresponding point on the total market *AR* locus. Consequently, the slope of *AC* finally will exceed that of *AR*.

Now we are in a position to answer the two questions posed at the beginning of this section. First, we see that there is nothing in our equilibrium analysis that precludes the existence of a multiplicity of firms that compete in the markets in question. The nature of the cost and demand relationships prevents expansion of the firm's output level above the equilibrium amount. Consequently, total market demand for the product may well be many times as large as the equilibrium output of our firm. This means that a plurality of such firms with similar demands, costs, and equilibrium outputs can coexist, thereby establishing a stable industry equilibrium.

Similar reasoning suggests that, in such an equilibrium, it will not be possible for the discriminatory pricing to be undermined by a "cream-skimming" entry that attacks only the most lucrative segments of the overall market. For in the circumstances depicted in figures 3.1 and 3.2, any firm with the same revenue and cost possibilities will incur losses by serving only one submarket or fewer submarkets than are served in our firm's equilibrium. It follows that, even with the competitive pressures that characterize a market with absolute freedom of entry and exit, there need be no force that drives prices toward uniformity. The argument suggests that, while successful entry into our industry is possible, at least in the unique equilibrium case, only entrants fully grown to the equilibrium output will be able to survive. Of course, reality is somewhat different from this model. To that end, we conclude this part of the discussion with a few remarks on the implications of this model for the existence and uniqueness of the discriminatory prices equilibrium. What has been shown here indicates that, with little more added (such as continuity of the relevant portions of the derivatives of the *AC* and *AR* loci), we can expect this equilibrium to exist. Uniqueness is more complex, given the obvious possibility of a multiplicity of tangency points. However, the U-shaped *AC* curve assumption makes such multiplicity implausible. All of this calls for further exploration.

DISCRIMINATORY PRICE MAKERS OR PRICE TAKERS?

The discussion in this and the following section is expressed in terms of discriminatory pricing, in general—not only that which applies to the services of the entrepreneur, on which this book focuses. This is intended to show how the entrepreneur's pricing fits in with that in the more general models of competitive pricing.

Of course, firms with monopoly power do exit, and some of them do charge discriminatory prices that yield monopoly profits. However, as we have seen, where entry is sufficiently easy, discrimination brings no such profits. The reason for this should be easy to see—we need consider only the likelihood that, in practice, the profit-maximizing price vector for the firm will be unique. If that is so, where that price vector and no other yields zero profits, the firm will have no choice—any enduring deviation from that vector must be suicidal. Consequently, the firm will be a price taker, though not one that follows a posted price that emerges publicly on a market, such as that for, say, pork bellies.[9]

This is not mere theory. In practice, we see marginally surviving firms scrambling for every perceived source of potential revenue and, in doing so, adopting for every such source the price they believe necessary to capture that revenue. Neither the impecunious theater nor the marginal airline can tolerate empty seats. Each seeks desperately to fill them with whoever can help its finances—students, leisure travelers, and others who are unwilling to pay high prices, but who will pay a price that contributes *something* in addition to marginal cost. Similarly, that airline cannot forgo the higher price it imposes on business travelers who book at the last minute—without their contribution to total cost recovery, the firm's financial problems would be exacerbated. To the best of their ability, the airline's executives will select the prices that promise to maximize profits and minimize losses. Experience may well enable them to come close to selecting those most lucrative prices. If, however, they do not succeed in doing so, they will be replaced by others who can do so more effectively.

Thus, market forces impose the selection of approximations to the profit-maximizing discriminatory prices. The profit-seeking firm that charges a lower price to union members or to older customers does not do so out of charity, but because market conditions force it to do so in order to survive. Similarly, the supplier firm that charges higher prices for its product when it is sold in the United States than when it is sold in Africa is forced to do so. In particular, airlines that charge higher fares on routes served by few other carriers are not manifesting a monopolist's ability to select an exploitative price. One cannot doubt that any airline would want to adopt such lucrative prices if entry were difficult and those prices could bring in substantial economic profits. Even if that were not so, entry would still force the airline to adopt prices whose magnitude is dictated by the competitive rule that maximum profits are zero profits. Discriminatory pricing is not a sign of a breakdown of contestability, but rather a manifestation of its normal functioning. If the constraint on profit imposed by entry is potent, the only way for the firm with large, fixed, and continuing sunk costs to survive will be to engage in price discrimination of the most sophisticated variety that is workable. The firm that is more efficient in finding and carrying out better pricing strategies will survive against less creative firms.

The bottom line here is that *where entry is easy, price discrimination is not to be taken as a manifestation of monopoly power.*[10] It is true that a monopolist also may be able to engage in this practice. Indeed, if it is feasible, the monopolist generally will prefer to do so. However, in effectively competitive markets, the same type of prices can be expected to emerge as a mandate of the market throughout the industry. The firm that charges discriminatory prices in such an environment is, effectively, a price taker, not a price maker, because there is no substantial range of prices from which management can select. Rather, it is the need to survive that imposes those selections, which may well be unique.

Lest this conclusion seem to conform awkwardly to reality, two things must be said here. First, as we know, in markets of this sort, it is not unusual for prices to change frequently—indeed, sometimes with astonishing frequency. The fact that airlines change prices hundreds of thousands of times every day may elicit skepticism about the assertion that firms have little choice about the prices they adopt. However, in the most competitive of markets, the commodity and the securities exchanges, prices vary from moment to moment, yet no one is led by this phenomenon to suspect that a relatively small wheat farmer, for instance, really is a price maker. Indeed, it is mostly in industries where there is reason to suspect that firms possess market power that prices tend to persist unchanged, often for many months. Sticky prices are not a hallmark of industries in which pricing is controlled by the market.

Second, I must be careful not to exaggerate how closely management can approximate profit-maximizing pricing. Unlike a wheat farmer or a purchaser of stocks, the executives in charge of pricing for an airline, for instance, cannot communicate electronically with any organized market in order to determine what fares are imposed by current circumstances. Instead, an airline's executives must do their best to find the current, profit-maximizing prices for their firm, but at best, they do so very imperfectly. They do not have access to current demand functions for their products, nor even to a set of accurate demand functions for some time in the past. They do not know their marginal costs or even their average costs, as is confirmed dramatically by the records of any substantial antitrust trial in which predatory pricing is an issue. In these trials, when pertinent cost data are not available in the records of the firms, specialists on both sides are employed, at great expense, to determine their own greatly differing and imperfectly accurate cost estimates. Given the unavailability of the requisite information and the speed with which a firm must respond to changing market conditions, the prices selected at best will be imperfect approximations of the profit-maximizing prices determined by market pressures. That is still very different from the leisurely and considered pricing choices available to a firm that, as a genuine price maker, really is protected, by a lack of competition, from having to obey the dictates that emanate from a powerful market.

RAMSEY OPTIMALITY OF THE PRICE TAKER'S DISCRIMINATORY PRICES

I come next to my second central result:

> PROPOSITION 3.2: Ramsey optimality. If the profit-maximizing equilibrium that yields zero profit with discriminatory pricing is unique, then it is a Ramsey optimum.

That is, the equilibrium will entail the vector of prices that is Pareto optimal, subject to the constraint that the (expected) economic profits of the firm (and the industry) are zero. This argument is almost trivial: if there is only one set of prices that meet the zero-profit requirement, then no other prices can satisfy the Ramsey constraint. Hence, there are no other zero-profit prices that can add to consumers' and producers' surpluses or that can benefit some individuals without harming anyone.[11]

That is all there is to the argument, but we can do a little better than this formulation. Earlier in this chapter, our brief mathematical derivation of the requirements of the equilibrium in our model readily shows that these requirements lead to the usual Ramsey formulas. As is well known, in the simplest state of affairs, where cross-elasticities in the pertinent markets are all zero, the Ramsey analysis yields the usual inverse elasticity relationship: the Ramsey-optimal prices obtained in the various pertinent markets differ from the corresponding marginal costs in inverse proportion to the elasticities of demand for the product at issue in the markets in question. Equation (3.5) in the earlier discussion is precisely the formal statement of the inverse elasticity rule, the most elementary form of Ramsey equation:

$$\frac{p_i - C_i'}{p_i} = \frac{1}{E}.$$

The presence of nonzero cross-elasticities complicates the relationships entailed, but it is easy to show that this possibility will not change our qualitative conclusion, though this demonstration is left as an exercise for the interested reader.

The preceding discussion applies generally to all competitive markets that satisfy our five premises. For our current purposes, however, I have emphasized how the discussion applies, in particular, to independent inventors and their entrepreneur partners.[12] Obviously, there is no difference between the formal analysis of price discrimination among customer groups, in general, and the discrimination among time periods described by Schumpeter. For Schumpeter's story, figure 3.1 remains totally unchanged—except that, now, figure 3.1(a) must be interpreted to represent the firm's year t submarket, while figure 3.1(b) now pertains to the year $t+1$ submarket, rather than to a set of submarkets with different customers—all in year t. Therefore, Propositions 3.1 and 3.2 remain applicable to Schumpeter's model. Moreover, as we will see in chapter 4, in this respect, the analysis of the independent entrepreneur's pricing under market pressures is structurally similar to that of the innovative oligopoly firm. Yet, as we will see next, the data indicate that there is a noteworthy error in Schumpeter's analysis, which is repeated to a less substantial degree in my preceding discussion.

LOWER RETURNS TO ENTREPRENEURS AND INVENTORS: INCENTIVES FOR THEIR ACTIVITY

It is clear that Schumpeter called for positive economic profits to the entrepreneur, at least in any growing economy: "Without development there is no profit, and without profit there is no development" (1936, 184). In contrast, my analysis so far implies that such profits will be zero. The empirical evidence, however, indicates clearly that we are both wrong. In reality, the expectable economic profits of the representative entrepreneur are distinctly negative. How can this be? And what are the implications of these negative economic returns? More specifically, how can we explain this pattern, given the conclusions of Proposition 3.1 and the arguments underlying it? If independent entrepreneurs or inventors cannot expect to earn even the current competitive rate of profit, what can induce them to undertake their activities?

To get at the answers, we must turn to the supply side of independent entrepreneurs and inventors, leaning more on empirical evidence than upon abstract theory. Here and in the next chapter, I will focus on two mechanisms that characterize the relation between the market and the entrepreneurial firm. These can be described as (1) the superstar reward structure and entrepreneurial overoptimism, and (2) the psychic rewards of innovative activity. Before I discuss these mechanisms in detail, let me offer an observation that relates to both of them. As is to be expected, the market provides clear incentives for entrepreneurs to undertake the hazards of radical innovation. As we will see next, however, both of the mechanisms just mentioned entail *financial underpayment* of the average innovative entrepreneur. That is, such entrepreneurs receive lower financial returns than corporate employees with similar education and experience who provide comparable efforts.

Here a few preliminary words must be said to avoid misunderstanding this book's assertions about the supply of entrepreneurial activity. First, I have argued that independent entrepreneurs supply a disproportionate share of breakthrough innovations, but it is not my hypothesis that a large percentage of real-world entrepreneurs employ innovation in the process of creating their new firms. On the contrary, the evidence—imperfect though it is—suggests that most new firms are virtual replicas of firms already in existence, with nothing innovative about them.[13] Second, I am not suggesting that even among that relatively uncommon species—the innovative entrepreneur—the focus is on anything that reasonably can be deemed a *breakthrough* innovation. Casual empiricism indicates that the bulk of the novelties such entrepreneurs introduce are only slightly better "mousetraps." Accordingly, it is not my claim that most entrepreneurs devote themselves to radical innovation or even to any innovation at all. Rather, I propose the converse: that among the (rare) innovations that can be considered radical, a disproportionate share is provided by independent innovators and their affiliated entrepreneurs.

In what follows in this chapter and the next, I will account, first, for the comparative paucity of breakthroughs that emerge from sizeable labs and other facilities affiliated with large, established innovative firms. Second, I will explain why a significant group of entrepreneurs and inventors—albeit, a comparatively small one—is willing to undertake the great uncertainties and the typically enormous personal effort that pursuit of their objectives requires. The issue is not why there are so many that do so, but, rather, why there is a significant set of these adventurers at all.

UNDERPAYMENT OF INNOVATIVE ENTREPRENEURS AS A GROUP: EMPIRICAL EVIDENCE

There is systematic evidence (see, for example, Freeman 1978) that the average earnings of self-employed individuals are significantly lower than those of employees with similar qualifications. The same is presumably true of self-employed innovative entrepreneurs, in particular.

There are at least two studies that support this hypothesis for innovative entrepreneurs. Thomas Astebro (2003) reports, on the basis of a sample of 1,091 inventions, that

> the average IRR [internal rate of return] on a portfolio investment in these inventions is 11.4 percent. This is higher than the risk-free rate but lower than the long-run return on high-risk securities and the long-run return on early-stage venture capital funds . . . the distribution of return is skew; only between 7–9 percent reach the market. Of the 75 inventions that did, six received returns above 1400 percent, 60 percent obtained negative returns and the median was negative. (226)[14]

Perhaps even more striking is the recent work of Nordhaus (2004), which provides evidence showing how little of the efficiency rent goes to the innovator:

> Using data from the U.S. non-farm business section, I estimate that innovators are able to capture about 2.2 percent of the total surplus from innovation. This number results from a low rate of initial appropriability (estimated to be around seven percent) along with a high rate of depreciation of Schumpeterian profits (judged to be around 20 percent per year). . . . [T]he rate of profit on the replacement cost of capital over the 1948–2001 period is estimated to be 0.19 percent per year. (34)[15]

Still more extreme is the phenomenon of open sourcing[16] and shareware in computer programming. Here a great and growing body of complex and valuable material has been created painstakingly. Much of this material evidently has enormous value in economic and other terms, but it has been created and offered to others with modest, if any, restrictions and without financial reward. Thus, a much noted and much valued activity is produced with zero financial reward, a payoff evidently far below what the work could have elicited if performed inside an established business enterprise.

SUPERSTAR MARKET REWARD STRUCTURE, OR THE MULTI-MILLION-DOLLAR LOTTERY

Despite the low financial returns, the relatively frequent focus of independent inventors and their entrepreneur partners on more radical ideas can be attributed to the great wealth and enormous prestige that success in their undertaking appears to promise. We all are familiar with those inventor-entrepreneurs who have become enduring legends: Eli Whitney, James Watt, Elias Singer, Thomas Edison, and the Wright brothers, among others.

The adulation and great financial rewards, *along with their rarity,* transform the innovative entrepreneur's activities into a lottery that offers just a few mega-prizes. Indeed, innovative entrepreneurship is like a mega-lottery—or like those occupations such as acting in films—that offer a limited number of superstar positions. The prize, however, is available only to those who provide successful *breakthrough* innovations. A technological contribution that permits humanity to fly or to send messages through the air may elicit headlines, but a minor improvement in automobile door handles is not likely to receive much attention. Just as multimillion-dollar lotteries have a greater attraction than a thousand-dollar lottery at a local club—even if the latter's terms are better actuarially, the pursuit of breakthrough innovations holds special appeal for independent entrepreneurs.[17]

A well-recognized attribute of lotteries is their built-in unfairness, as measured in actuarial terms. The average payout is sure to be less than the per-ticket-holder take of the lottery operator. There is a similar loss prospect for the representative entrepreneur. In part, the willingness of innovators, like the buyers of lottery tickets, to accept these biased terms is probably attributable to overoptimism or to sheer miscalculation. The empirical evidence supports the hypothesis that inventors and entrepreneurs are characterized by a degree of optimism well above the norm.[18] They are inclined to believe, more than others, that they really are likely to win this lottery's grand prize. The return such individuals expect to receive is apt to be well above its actuarial value.

MONETARY COMPENSATION, PSYCHIC COMPENSATION

That is hardly the end of the story. Each of these activities—innovative entrepreneurship and the purchase of lottery tickets—provides an important payoff of a second sort. Both activities offer distinct psychic rewards, and not only to those who have already achieved success or who even have a real and substantial likelihood of success. The *prospects* of glory, wealth, and fame hold real value, even if they never materialize. They are, indeed, the stuff of which dreams are made. For the entrepreneur, contemplation of imagined success is only part of the psychic reward. In reading the biographies of the great inventors, one is struck by the fascination, the moments of triumph, and even the pleasure of puzzle-solving and experimentation—though punctured by frustration and exhaustion—that accompanied the process of their work.

Moreover, one has to be careful in jumping to the conclusion that the entrepreneur is underpaid. Representative entrepreneurs may be shortchanged financially, but their *total* payoff may be closer to what economic theory would lead us to expect—though part of the payoff takes the non-monetary form of psychic rewards. In effect, it is as if they are paid in two different currencies: partly in dollars, partly in euros. In equilibrium, such two-currency payment recipients could clearly expect their compensation package to contain fewer dollars than someone similarly engaged whose contract calls for payment exclusively in that currency.[19] That this is how markets work is confirmed by casual observation.[20]

This story pertains not only to the entrepreneur, but to the whole economy. The fact that multi-million-dollar lotteries purposely are structured to be actuarially unfair means, as already noted, that the purchasers of tickets in such a lottery will, on average and as a whole, receive back less money than they invest in the lottery. But, arguably, the masses of purchasers who grab up the tickets are not irrational if they receive an adequate payment in another currency: psychic rewards. This scenario helps to explain, in an example from another arena, why, despite the rigors of their training and the difficulties of their work, the typical earnings of professional dancers are so meager.[21] One easily can think of many other occupations with similar attributes.

Dramatic pay disparities between, for instance, the ballerina and the banker cannot be attributed only to the sheer willingness of the recipient of psychic benefits to be exploited financially. The market mechanism enforces this result, as Adam Smith pointed out. Given two occupations—one very distasteful and the other a source of great pleasure—if payoffs and ability requirements are equal, Smith noted, we must expect the workforce to shun the one and flock to the other, driving wages up in the former and depressing them in the latter, as a garden-variety manifestation of supply and demand.[22]

INDEPENDENT INVENTORS AND ENTREPRENEURS AS LOW-COST, BREAKTHROUGH GENERATORS

We have not yet answered the question that launched our discussion of the expected negative financial returns of entrepreneurship: why are independent entrepreneurs disproportionately the suppliers of breakthrough innovation? Fuller discussion of this phenomenon awaits the following chapter, where we also will examine the other side of this coin—the relatively small number of breakthroughs by the large firms that are responsible for the bulk of the U.S. economy's private R&D expenditures. However, we already can surmise the answer. Much of the reward of independent inventors and entrepreneurs is psychic, *a type of payment that entails no cost to the buyer of their services.* Consequently, the giant firms find it economical to outsource the task of radical innovation to these independent actors, rather than attempting to produce such inventions in house.

Facing a make-or-buy decision, oligopoly firms in high-tech industries are induced by independent suppliers' low wages to rely heavily on purchasing or leasing breakthroughs from outside their firms.

PREVIEW: ON THE LONGER-RUN SUPPLY OF INNOVATIVE ENTREPRENEURSHIP

At this point, we are focusing on self-employed inventors and entrepreneurs, to whom the demand function is not directly applicable. However, as I will argue next, the structure of supply in this market is observable and distinctive. Here we will focus on the special attributes of *supply*, rather than demand, in basic distribution theory. The distinctive supply conditions of the different factors of production often are employed as the primary attributes that distinguish one factor from another. For instance, land is fixed in supply, but physical capital is a produced good whose quantity is determined by the profit calculation and earlier investment, while the supply of labor largely is determined exogenously. In contrast, at least in marginal productivity theory, there is virtually no difference among the factors in the way that *demands* for them are determined.

Looking at the market for entrepreneurial activity from the supply side does permit some interesting observations, in addition to those in the immediately preceding sections. Such observations are based firmly on clear historical evidence, but apparently have not yet achieved general recognition. Our analysis of the supply side will find it necessary to re-classify entrepreneurs in yet another way, which will be discussed more thoroughly in later chapters. A moment's thought will confirm that there are many entrepreneurial occupations that contribute little or nothing to an economy's output—or whose activities even reduce it, including, for example, rent-seeking lawyers who design new ways of pursuing remunerative litigation, the warlord organizers of private armies who invent novel military strategies, or enterprising bank robbers who find new ways to break into safes. The distinction between these unproductive or destructive entrepreneurs and productive innovative entrepreneurs offers significant insight into the determination of a society's supply of *productive* entrepreneurs, on whom discussions of entrepreneurship usually focus.

In the nonmathematical growth literature, it often has been asserted that an abundant supply of entrepreneurs effectively stimulates growth, while shrinkage in the economy's cadre of entrepreneurs is a significant impediment to growth. These apparently vital phenomena—the appearance and disappearance of entrepreneurs—have long been left as a great mystery, with hints that they hang on cultural developments in the economy and changes in other psychological and sociological influences that are more or less vague in character. As I have noted elsewhere (Baumol 2002b, chap. 5; see also chapter 9 in this book), a review of the historical evidence suggests an alternative explanation that is less magical or science-fictional in character. This alternative scenario holds that entrepreneurs do not appear suddenly from nowhere or, just as mysteriously, vanish. Rather, entrepreneurs are always with us, but as the structure of the rewards offered in the economy changes, entrepreneurs switch the locus of their activity, moving into arenas where the payoff prospects are most attractive. In doing so, they move in and out of those activities that generally are recognized as entrepreneurial *and productive*, exchanging them with other activities that also require considerable enterprising talent, but may be quite distant from the production of goods and services. When institutions change, the relative payoffs offered by different enterprising activities are modified accordingly, and the supply of entrepreneurs shifts from the now less rewarding to the more rewarding activities. Just as technological change led workers and engineers to reallocate themselves from canal building to railroad construction, and then to still more modern enterprises, entrepreneurs also have reallocated themselves to different occupations, in accord with changes in the structure of payoffs. If we recognize that entrepreneurial talent can be driven to reallocate itself from one category to another by changes in the structure of incentives, it becomes clear that when there is a pertinent change in the institutions that govern the relative rewards, entrepreneurs will be induced to shift their activities among the affected fields of endeavor. When this shift occurs, the set of productive entrepreneurs will appear to expand or contract autonomously. For instance, if institutions change to prohibit private armies and to create a national military force, as happened in Europe between the end of the Middle Ages and the Industrial Revolution, the rewards offered by the creative operation of private military forces are reduced, and entrepreneurs will look elsewhere to realize their financial ambitions. If, simultaneously, rules banning confiscation of private property and enforcing patent protection of inventions are adopted, as happened in England during the same period, those with entrepreneurial talent will shift their efforts to productive and, indeed, innovative activities.

This brings me to my third central result:

PROPOSITION 3.3: Entrepreneurship is a resource that is subject to reallocation between productive and unproductive activities. The supply of *productive* entrepreneurs is heavily influenced by the institutional arrangements that determine the relative payoffs to these two types of activities.[23]

This proposition, which conveys the essence of the supply side of the theory of entrepreneurship, completes our discussion of the behavior of the innovative entrepreneur. We have shown how one can analyze the supply of innovative entrepreneurial effort, the entrepreneur's pecuniary reward, and the theory of pricing of the resulting products. The next chapter will examine corresponding scenarios for large established firms and their innovative activities.

Oligopolistic "Red Queen" Innovation Games, Mandatory Price Discrimination, and Markets in Innovation

Now, here, you see, it takes all the running you can do, to keep in the same place. If you want to get somewhere else, you must run at least twice as fast as that!

—The Red Queen, *Through the Looking Glass*
(Carroll 1902, 38)

Innovation is not a homogeneous product.

—William J. Baumol, "Baumol's Tautologies" (unpublished)

Having gone through the theory of the supply and pricing behavior of entrepreneur-innovators, our discussion turns next to a primary group of purchasers of their products, the innovative oligopolists. After leaving the hands of their inventors, most innovations still have a long way to go before they achieve their market and utility potential. For the most part, promising breakthrough innovations are taken over and developed by "Goliath" firms, and so, to complete the story, I turn next to the R&D-related activities of these large enterprises.

THE MARKET MECHANISM'S INNOVATION ARMS RACE

Elsewhere (Baumol 2002b, especially chap. 3), I have described the R&D activities of the oligopoly firms in the high-tech industries of developed economies as an arms race. Following Schumpeter, I emphasized that these firms regard such things as price and advertising as weapons of *secondary* importance in their competitive battles. Instead, the primary weapon clearly has become the new or improved product that these firms race to introduce before a rival can bring to market an alternative that is equally or more attractive to consumers. No firm in this position dares to fall behind in the race to create new and better products because protracted failure to do so can be fatal. The famously cited quotation from Lewis Carroll's Red Queen, at the head of this chapter, effectively characterizes the situation in which the firm then finds itself—having entered the innovation race, each has no option but to run as fast as it can, if it is to succeed in maintaining its position in the market. This remarkable "Red Queen game" feature of the market is a key attribute of advanced economies and helps to account for their unceasing and unprecedented outpouring of innovations. This game clearly is motivated by something far more powerful than high monetary rewards. After all, when pursuing riches, successful participants eventually are able to rest on their laurels and withdraw from further innovative activity. An innovation arms race, however, permits no rest, lest competitors outperform and thereby kill off the enterprises of those who are less active.

This incredibly effective—indeed, ingenious—arrangement is not invented, designed, or imposed consciously by any person or group. Instead, it is yet another fortuitous product of the market mechanism. Unlike the institutional developments that underlie the Industrial Revolution's initial expansion of productive entrepreneurial activities, which I ascribe largely to historical accident, the Red Queen game of the innovation process is automatically introduced by oligopolistic competition and, therefore, is yet another contribution of the market mechanism itself.

The pertinence of this discussion to our larger analysis is summarized by the four observations below.

- First, the oligopolistic, high-tech firm finds itself unable to avoid frequent and substantial reinvestment in R&D, without which it cannot survive. It also cannot survive if its pricing approach precludes recoupment of these outlays.
- Second, as I have argued elsewhere,[1] relative ease of entry into the innovation process means that even oligopolistic firms have little reason to expect much more than zero economic profits from their outlays on innovation.[2] Here, zero profit means that revenues must just cover *all* of the firm's costs, including the repeatedly sunk R&D outlays that the Red Queen game forces them to incur, as well as any foregone profits that the invested funds could have obtained elsewhere. If profits are more than sufficient to cover all of these costs, additional entrants will be attracted into the activity, and their competition will eliminate the excess of earnings over costs. On the other side of the matter, firms will exit the innovation process if they only can expect levels of earnings that are insufficient to cover their

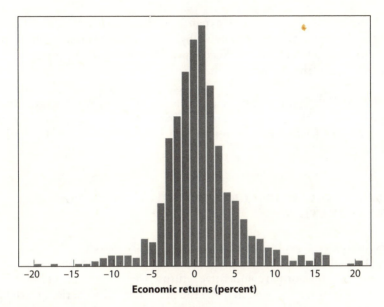

FIGURE 4.1
Average Economic Returns of 1,000 Large U.S. Firms, 1996–2005. (Source: Williams and Kreitzman 2008.)

unavoidable costs. So if these forces do succeed in precluding revenues that either exceed or fall short of costs, zero economic profits must become the norm.

- Third, typical (or average) performance must include the failures, as well as the successes—and there is plenty of evidence that failure is not a rarity. The frequency with which giant firms drop out of the Fortune 500 should surely suggest that failure is a common outcome. Moreover, an ingenious study by Williams and Kreitzman (2008) confirms that it is very close to the norm, as is strikingly demonstrated in figure 4.1, which reports the distribution of economic profits among 1,000 of the largest U.S. firms. The clustering of the earnings near zero is striking.[3]
- Fourth, once the requisite R&D has been carried out, the amount of expenditure on the creation of a new product or process need not be increased any further if there is an expansion in the number of customers for a firm's products. That is, once an innovation's blueprint is available, it can serve one hundred or one million customers, with the latter entailing no additional R&D expenditure. In the economic literature, this is referred to as the public good property of innovation, and it implies that none of the R&D expenses will enter the firm's marginal costs—the additional costs that are incurred when

the number of customers expands. Consequently, equality of price and marginal cost generally will yield revenues insufficient for firms to recoup R&D outlays. Such a price level cannot be expected to be viable for the innovating enterprise.

Before dealing with the pricing issues that face innovative oligopolists, I will consider the supply side of the story—that is, firms' decisions on the amount of R&D financing they will be driven to supply by market forces.

A KINKED-REVENUE-CURVE MODEL OF SPENDING ON INNOVATION

Despite the zero-profit prospect, oligopolists are driven to keep up their R&D spending by an understandable preference for *zero* economic profits, which yield only normal competitive returns, over *negative* profits, investor flight, and insolvency. We can make the technological scenario underlying the investment decision more explicit with the help of a microeconomic construct that is very similar to the old kinked-demand-curve model that explains why prices tend to be "sticky" in oligopoly markets. The underlying mechanism in this model is a fundamental asymmetry in the firm's expectations about its competitors. The issue here is whether or not the firm is likely to want to move its price in either direction from the current level that prevails in the industry. The answer is that it will not want to change price in the scenario envisaged. Instead, it will hesitate to lower its price—for fear that its rivals will match the price cut, leaving the firm with few new customers and dramatically reduced revenues. However, the firm also fears that if it increases its price, its competitors will *not* follow, so that it will be left all by itself with an overpriced product and few, if any, customers. A firm with such beliefs will set its price at the prevailing industry level—no more and no less—and leave it there unless the situation changes drastically.

The essence of the analogous process of R&D level determination is similar: in a market in which innovation is the prime instrument of competition, the firm's expected profit depends heavily on the quality of its anticipated new products and processes, *relative to those of its competitors*, which, in turn, depend on the relative amounts the rival firms spend on R&D. For simplicity, I assume expected total revenue functions are linear in the single variable ($[R&D]w - [R&D]c$), where the first of these terms is the R&D outlay of our maximizing firm, w, and the second term is that of its representative competitor, c. The total cost function also is assumed to be linear, but its variable is only our firm's own R&D expen-

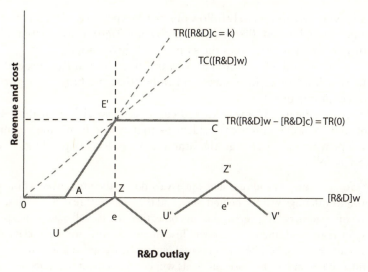

FIGURE 4.2
Oligopoly Equilibrium in R&D Expenditure

diture because the R&D expenditures of rivals surely affect the revenues, but not the cost, of our enterprise. Then we have the two functions, in which total revenue is equal to *TR([R&D]w – [R&D]c)*, and total cost equals *TC([R&D]w)*.

In figure 4.2, we graph this process under two extreme and alternative assumptions about competitor behavior:

CASE ONE. *[R&D]c = k* (constant), so the rival does not change its behavior, no matter what our maximizing firm, *w*, does.

CASE TWO. *[R&D]c = [R&D]w*, so that the rival imitates exactly whatever level of spending our firm, *w*, selects.

Since we can confidently expect total outlay of the firm to rise when its output increases, our firm's total *cost* curve will be upward sloping, no matter what its rival's decision rule. For simplicity, *TCw* is drawn through the origin, but that is irrelevant for this analysis.[4] There are also two alternative total *revenue* curves. The straight line labeled *TR([R&D]c = k)* corresponds to the case where competitors do not respond to our firm's spending decision. In that case, our firm's (expected) total revenue locus also will be upward sloping, as in the figure—the more our firm spends, the more its product can be expected to improve, relative to those products resulting from the unchanged outlays of its rivals. We also must consider

61

the case where rivals precisely follow our firm's expenditure level. This total revenue curve, labeled $TR([R\&D]w - [R\&D]c) = TR(0)$, is a horizontal line because its one variable takes the same value throughout.

Let point e on the horizontal axis be our firm's initial R&D spending, above which all three lines meet, indicating that the firm earns normal (zero) economic profit.

Following the usual logic of kinked-curve scenarios, it is plausible—and supported by some empirical evidence—that if our firm's management considers whether to change the amount of its R&D spending, it will reason as follows:

> If we raise our expenditure and our rivals don't, the attractiveness of their product offerings will fall behind ours, and they will be threatened with severe loss of customers. To prevent this outcome, these rivals will match our spending increase, and, therefore, we will lose money because we will receive only our old revenues, despite our increased outlays. If we spend less, however, we will also lose money because our rivals will be tempted not to reduce spending and, thereby, will be able to steal our customers. As a result, our revenues will fall sharply—probably more than costs.[5]

Two conclusions follow. The first is that the expected total revenue curve (the heavy, kinked line), $AE'C$, will be composed of two segments, each a part of the other two TR lines. To the left of point e, segment AE' corresponds to the revenue curve in which R&D spending by our firm's rivals is constant, while the segment, $E'C$, of the expected revenue curve to the right of e follows the curve where rivals match our firm's outlay rise, so spending by all firms remains equal.

The second conclusion is that our firm, like its rivals, will be driven to continue its current level of spending on R&D, which we can call "the industry spending norm." This is because either a rise in our expenditure or a fall will not just reduce our profits, but actually will cut profits below the competitive level. This is shown by the kinked total profit curve, UZV, whose peak is e. This profit curve lies below the horizontal axis, except where Z just touches the horizontal axis at the current spending point, e. Here competition prevents our firm from earning more than zero economic profits. The total profit curve is obtained by plotting the vertical distance between the kinked, thick total revenue curve, the revenue expectation locus, and the total cost curve.

This is the stationary equilibrium story, which explains how firms in an innovation arms race determine the amount of their R&D spending. It is, however, only a snapshot picture that gives little substantive information. For instance, this explanation does not indicate how equilibrium point e is selected, but only—whatever its magnitude—that it will be sticky.

To find out more, we must proceed from our snapshot to a motion picture in which the portion of figure 4.2 that has already been described is only a single frame. Motion *will* occur if our firm happens to hit upon a particularly promising invention that justifies an increase in its R&D spending from its previously sticky level. As a result, the total profit curve will shift upward and to the right, to the kinked line, $U'Z'V'$, whose peak, Z', lies above point e' in figure 4.2. To protect their market positions, our firm's rivals soon will be forced to increase their spending as well. As a result, the industry norm will rise from e to e' in the graph. *This result is a ratchet mechanism*[6] that acts in a manner similar to the mechanical device that prevents a wound-up spring from suddenly unwinding. It allows spending to increase when changing conditions make it profitable, but permits no reductions, which would cut profits to negative levels.[7]

Thus, we conclude:

PROPOSITION 4.1: Supply of R&D financing in the innovation arms races of oligopolists. Oligopolistic competition with innovation as the primary weapon forces firms to adhere to the industry standard of R&D expenditure, with occasional rises in that norm.

The prior discussion shows how competition forces firms in high-tech industries to keep up with one another in their R&D investments. The investment level remains fairly constant until one firm breaks ranks and increases its spending. Then all of the other firms follow suit. This arrangement normally holds technological spending steady, sometimes permits it to move forward, but generally does not allow it to retreat. Thus, we can expect R&D spending to expand from time to time. Once the new level is reached, however, the ratchet—enforced by the competitive market—prevents firms from retreating to the previous lower level. Such ratcheting is a critical part of the mechanism that has produced the extraordinary growth records of free-enterprise economies. Such enormous growth differentiates these economies from all other known economic systems. In this way, competitive pressures force firms to run as fast as they can in the innovation race, just to keep up with the others.

This scenario surely is not inconsistent with the empirical record of private R&D spending. Figure 4.3, reproduced from chapter 2, shows private spending on R&D in the United States for the bulk of the period since World War II. The graph has two noteworthy features: the acceleration of spending in a roughly exponential pattern and the virtual absence of regular declines in such outlays during periods of recession.[8]

Thus, we appear to have a plausible model of the behavior of R&D spending by oligopoly firms engaged in the competitive innovation process. However, no mechanism for determination of N, the value of the industry's normal level of R&D spending, has been described yet. This

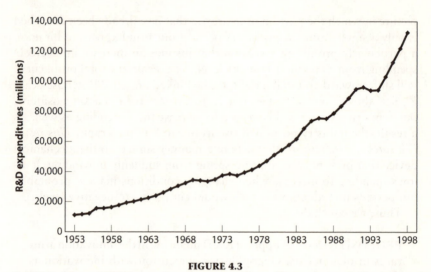

FIGURE 4.3
Real U.S. Private R&D Expenditures, 1953–1998 (millions of 1992 dollars). Note: expenditures are deflated using the GDP implicit price deflator. (Sources: National Science Board 2000; and Economic Report of the President 2001. Reprinted from Baumol 2002b, fig. 6.2, p. 77.)

is because, if our analysis is valid, there is no such mechanism—at least none that is deterministic and yields a unique result. As we have seen, the model has indicated that there is a ratchet mechanism in which competing parties occasionally are tempted to increase their outlays from a previous industry norm to a new, higher norm, with evident disincentives for any return to a lower outlay. Since such a move creates a new industry norm, it is clear that the norm actually is a moving target. Its value has a substantial component that certainly has fortuitous—if not outrightly random—elements. Our theory can describe its qualitative behavior, but not its magnitude, at any particular point in time.

THE DAVID-GOLIATH PARTNERSHIP: MARKET FORCES AND OUTSOURCING BREAKTHROUGHS FROM LARGE FIRMS TO ENTREPRENEURIAL ENTERPRISES

In chapter 3, we discussed the relatively low earnings, on average, of inventors and innovative entrepreneurs. Here I will examine an important implication of that story, which relates to the market mechanism's critical role in disproportionately allocating activity aimed at breakthrough innovation to independent inventors and entrepreneurs, rather than to corporate giants. As discussed in the previous chapter, the underlying mechanism is found in the evidence that part of the reward of independent entrepreneurs and inventors is composed of the psychic benefits they derive from their activity. The fact that these psychic benefits are a tangible reward to the recipient, but generally are *costless to the provider*, is a key aspect of this mechanism. This implies that an innovative entrepreneur who, on average, receives great pleasure, but meager financial rewards, from the activity, nevertheless may be richly rewarded overall. However, the low *financial* payment means that innovations obtained from this source can be purchased cheaply in monetary terms, giving this sector of the economy a marked competitive advantage. That is, according to this analysis, independent inventors and their innovative entrepreneur partners will tend to be the more economical suppliers of breakthrough innovations to the economy. As we know, one of the virtues of markets and competition is their ability to move economic activities toward those suppliers who can provide them most inexpensively. In the case at hand, the low-cost, psychic reward component of the independent innovator's compensation makes it more economical for the large firm, in considering its make-or-buy options, to acquire its breakthroughs from others, rather than provide them in-house.[9] Firms are forced to do so for fear that if they do not engage in such outsourcing, their rivals will. This is one market-based explanation[10] for the disproportionate share of radical innovation stemming from independent entrepreneurs.

Why does the low-wage, competitive advantage of the independent innovator-entrepreneur not extend to less radical innovations—the cumulative, incremental improvements that are giant firms' specialty? At least part of the answer lies in the greater complexity and higher investment costs of creating such innovations. A Boeing 777, for instance, is obviously far more complicated than the primitive device the Wright brothers made airborne at Kitty Hawk. This is no accident—by its very nature, this revolutionary invention, like so many before it, grew ever more complex as it was repeatedly modified and improved. The transformation of the Boeing 747 into the Boeing 777 entailed an army of engineers and designers, which, in turn, required expenditures that made the outlays of the Wrights dramatically insignificant by comparison. Add to this the expensive market research that often precedes or accompanies a major innovative project at a large firm, and it is easy to see why the independent innovator was, and continues to be, at a marked disadvantage in the financing of incremental improvements of inventions that have reached an advanced stage of sophistication.

There is an important additional reason for large firms to outsource innovative activity targeted at breakthroughs: such an arrangement shifts the most extreme risks to the independent entrepreneur. Normally, one would think that large firms are in a better position to deal with risk, as compared with independent entrepreneurs, because they are apt to have larger reserves to fall back on and can afford simultaneously to undertake a number of projects. In short, the law of large numbers certainly would be on the side of large firms. The evidence, however, suggests that this advantage is not enough to lead them to focus on revolutionary invention. Work on breakthrough ideas clearly is beset by great uncertainty. Arguably, it requires a touch of madness to devote one's time and resources to the untried prospects that a breakthrough innovation entails. Indeed, there is reason to suspect that innovative entrepreneurs characteristically are self-selected risk lovers—that is, they are attracted by the prospect of magnificent prizes, despite the low probability of attaining them. This is a much more extreme type of predisposition than that of lottery ticket buyers who, after all, risk little if the few tickets they purchase do not pay off. Rather, the inventor is apt to risk all—including, sometimes, the welfare of his family—in the belief that success in his enterprise is not merely a matter of chance, but is dependent on his own ability and persistence.[11]

In contrast, large firms characteristically seek to avoid risks—or at least to minimize them—because failure in the innovation process can threaten their survival. Moreover, where entry is easy, firms' profits and reserves are apt to be low, making it even more difficult to cover the costs of projects that prove disappointing.[12] The bottom line is that market forces drive large innovative firms to risk-avoidance to the extent permitted by innovative activity, which forces them toward focus on incremental activity, leaving the enormously uncertain pursuit of breakthroughs to independent inventors and their entrepreneur partners. The second central proposition summarizes this reasoning.

PROPOSITION 4.2: Market-driven assignment of the tasks of innovation. The assignment of a large share of breakthrough innovations to independent inventors and entrepreneurs and of incremental improvement to large firms is driven by market forces, such as the effects of psychic rewards on financial costs, the high investment cost of incremental improvements, and the relative risk-bearing propensities of the two groups.

There is no reason to expect the market forces just described to be transitory. If they are enduring, it follows that we can expect the current division of innovative labor between small and large firms to continue. There also is no reason to believe that this distribution will damage the public interest.

ON THE MARKET MECHANISM'S ENFORCEMENT OF PRICE DISCRIMINATION BY INNOVATIVE OLIGOPOLIES

Having dealt with the theory of supply of R&D activity by the large, established firms that engage in substantial innovative effort, let us turn to the second primary topic of this chapter: the theory of pricing by these firms. I will argue next that the discriminatory pricing model of the preceding chapter applies also to the oligopoly innovator—that is, Proposition 3.1 in chapter 3 also applies to these firms. For in this arena, we still can expect the premises underlying that proposition to be valid:

1. Economic profits are zero, so that nonnegative profits are attainable only by means of the vector of prices that maximizes profits.
2. The firm's customers can be separated into groups with different demand elasticities, with trade among these groups not carried out easily.
3. Where price discrimination is feasible, it will normally yield profits higher than those attainable under uniform pricing.

Only the first of these conditions seems different for large, established firms that, for example, may possess monopoly power and so, may earn substantial profits. As noted already, however, with entry into innovative activities largely unobstructed, and the big firms driven by an innovative arms race to constantly repeated investment in the innovation process, it follows that these large firms, too, will be pushed toward normal profits on their R&D outlays. Only the quest for survival will prevent them from abandoning the activity. Consequently, even large firms will be forced to adopt the market-determined discriminatory prices that maximize their profits in order to recoup their R&D investments, as Proposition 3.1 asserts. By Proposition 3.2, those prices will tend to be Ramsey optimal.

This is, of course, exactly the story offered in chapter 3 in order to explain pricing by independent entrepreneurs and inventors. Moreover, this is precisely what the Schumpeterian scenario describes—albeit in a manner that disguises the price discrimination side of the story, which almost exactly follows the explanation of the pricing process just offered for large established enterprises. Here it should be recalled that what is entailed in Schumpeter's analysis is a pattern of pricing that is not discriminatory in the usual sense. Instead, it takes a form that I refer to as *intertemporal* price discrimination. In this scenario, the entrepreneur and inventor recoup the bulk of their outlays of money and effort in the initial period after the introduction of an innovation, when competition is weak or nonexistent. At this point, the seller's demand curve is inelastic, and the profit-maximizing price is high, but as imitators appear, the initial seller's demand curve grows more elastic, and the original price falls. The rest is well known.

It is important for our theoretical structure to note that the stories for the oligopolist and the independent entrepreneur are exactly the same, in terms of formal analysis. In both cases, discriminatory pricing is imposed by market forces, and demand elasticities determine the difference in the prices at which different transactions are carried out, with the number of firms in a submarket serving as a primary determinant of those demand elasticities.

SYNTHESIS: ON THE MARKET FOR INNOVATION

Markets where inventions are bought and sold or offered for rent are hardly a new phenomenon. By the last quarter of the nineteenth century, they were widespread, active, and significant in the United States. Illuminating reports on the history of the patents system by Lamoreaux and Sokoloff (1996 and 2007) and by Khan (2005) describe an industry in which specialist professional brokers systematically sought out producers of a commodity with the aim of convincing them of the profitability of selling or licensing its use to others. At that time, there also were trade publications in which inventors advertised their new products and the opportunities they offered.

Thus, an active market for inventions has existed in the United States for a considerable time, and good descriptions of its activities and its modes of operation are available. The difficulty besetting any theoretical analysis of this material, however, is that the market's structure and the nature of its workings do not fit any of the standard models. Instead, they entail a combination of several well-known models, whose aggregated workings in the arena under discussion here do not seem to have been extensively explored. On the basis of the conclusions proposed in chapters 1 and 2, I will argue that although the innovation market hardly fits the model of pure competition, it is useful to think of it in terms of aggregate supply and demand. Here I propose to treat the supply side as it would be in the standard analysis of monopolistic competition because both forms of competition are characterized by a profusion of active participants who face no daunting barriers to entry and who, to a considerable extent, are organized into small enterprises. The products of these enterprises are heterogeneous, by definition, thus leading to the characterization proposed here for this side of the market. In contrast, I suggest that the demand side of the innovation market is *oligopsonistic*—that is, the buyers of the products sold in the market are dominated by a number of large firms, though they also can include in their population a few or many small rivals.

In sum, the market structure just described tends to be a powerful instrument for promoting innovation and growth in the economy. The Red Queen game, in which each firm in the market must introduce inventions as quickly and frequently as it can, in order to retain its competitive position, which the market structure imposes upon oligopolistic buyers, provides abundant and dependable demand for innovation and induces this demand to grow. On the other side, given appropriate institutional arrangements,[13] the incentive structure that drives entrepreneurs' activities leads to a constantly expanding supply of innovation via the entrepreneur's search for wealth, power, and prestige.

This completes our discussion of the models of the supply and pricing behavior of independent inventors and entrepreneurs, as well as established innovative firms. Clearly, our analysis fits into the basic models of pricing and firm behavior that are part of the elementary theory of the firm. However, this model raises additional issues—notably, about the economic efficiency of the processes it describes. We will turn to this issue next and follow up on the discussion below in the two subsequent chapters.

IMPLICIT WELFARE ISSUES

The constructs discussed in the previous section bring to the fore a particular, theoretical issue related to welfare: what are the public-interest implications of the market-driven pace of innovation? From the point of view of the general welfare, does the free market tend to invest too much or too little money and resources in the process? Indeed, there is considerable discussion in the literature about the welfare implications of the market-driven magnitude of the resources devoted to innovation.

For instance, some of these forces can lead to overinvestment in innovative activities. The process of creative destruction entails a detrimental (i.e., negative) externality—namely, that the products rendered obsolete by the introduction of superior substitutes may belong to individuals other than those who bring the novel product to market. For that reason, entrepreneurs will sometimes find it profitable to introduce inventions that sink rival products before their usefulness has been exhausted, thereby imposing a cost to society that will be borne by others. In this instance, the cost to society will exceed the private cost—the cost borne by those who introduce the new product prematurely.[14] This possibility is supplemented by the argument offered here that the financial cost of breakthrough innovation may be substantially reduced by the psychic rewards derived by the inventors and entrepreneurs who undertake this work. This can artificially cheapen the innovation process, relative to the value of its products, and also can lead to excessive investment.

69

However, the other side of the story still seems to be considerably more compelling. There are huge innovation spillovers—the benefits to people other than those who have created an innovation. This is true particularly of the benefits to society that eventually stem from basic research. The fact that these benefits, to a large degree, are apt to be derived by people other than those who contributed their effort and resources to the research obviously constitutes an enormous obstacle to innovative activity. The evidence indicates that those engaged in innovative activities may receive rewards that are as little as 3 percent of the social benefits (as noted earlier in this chapter). Accordingly, it would seem hard to believe that the market incentives for allocating resources to innovation are not extremely far below those required for maximization of social welfare.

Chapter 5 of this book focuses on this topic. However, it must be made clear that this discussion does not provide any theorems on the optimality of market-driven innovative activity—nor does it provide any rigorous standards by which the issue can be judged. It will offer, however, the perhaps surprising conclusion that these enormous innovation spillovers may not be terribly far from optimal. I argue that this is so because the spillovers themselves have great social value. Consequently, there is a trade-off between the social gains from any enhancement of the financial incentives for innovation and the benefits entailed in the spillovers themselves. As we will see in the next chapter, recognition of this trade-off will lead us to a rather different view of Pareto optimality and its pertinent implications.

APPENDIX

PAYOFF MATRICES FOR RED QUEEN GAMES

It seems evident that this chapter invites discussion aided by game theory.[15] This appendix suggests a possible line of reasoning that can be used to move in this direction. As noted by Professor Elias Khalil (1997), the originator of the concept of the Red Queen game, the simplest form of the game is intimately related to the "Prisoners' Dilemma model." Moreover, Khalil points out, the scenario entails somewhat greater complexity at a slightly deeper level. What follows is my interpretation of these two versions of the scenario.

Here the discussion will focus on determining the magnitude of the firm's innovative activity. For the simplest scenario, we assume that each R&D spending firm has two choices: either to spend N dollars (the current industry norm) or L, a lower level of expenditure. Thus, in an industry composed of Firm A and Firm B, the payoff matrix for Firm A will have the form shown in table 4.1 , where Pa represents A's economic profit

Table 4.1
Payoff Matrix for an Innovation Arms Race, Simplest Form

B's Strategy

		N	L
A's Strategy	N	Pa = 0 Pb = 0	Pa very high Pb negative
	L	Pa negative Pb very high	Pa low positive Pb low positive

payoff, and so on, in accord with the analysis presented in this chapter. Here, as usual, zero *economic profit* means the current rate of competitive profit on equally risky investments (i.e., normal profit).

The prototype payoff matrix shown in table 4.1 is a classic Prisoners' Dilemma matrix. It leads to an equilibrium point with both firms spending at the level of the industry norm, since that strategy pair is a maximin solution and a dominant strategy for each player. As usual, both firms could have done better for themselves if they had been able to collude and agree on a low level of innovative expenditure, where each would have been unthreatened by any likelihood that its competitor would succeed in obtaining an innovative product that would be highly attractive to customers.

The story of the kinked revenue curve, on which we have focused, is a bit more complex. In this scenario, which implicitly entails a repeated game, each firm has a third option. In addition to *L* and *N*, the firm can select *H*, which raises its outlay to an expenditure level that is substantially higher than the initial industry norm. The payoff matrix for that case is shown in table 4.2. Here we do not know all of the entries, but we have inserted those that are directly pertinent to this analysis.

In table 4.2 the maximin solution for both firms is to engage in high R&D spending—for either firm will lose more if its rival selects strategy *H* and the former selects either *L* or *N*, thereby falling behind its rival's product quality and novelty. However, this is a repeated game, and both players know that if one firm lost out in the previous round by choosing *L* or *N* when its competitor adopted *H*, that loser firm will be driven in the next round to select *H*. Therefore, both firms will lose in the long run, relative to what they would have earned if both had adhered to the earlier industry norm.

Table 4.2
Payoff Table for an Innovation Arms Race, Kinked Revenue Scenario

B's Strategy

		L	N	H
	L	*not specified*	Pa negative Pb high	Pa negative Pb fairly high
A's Strategy	**N**	Pa high Pb negative	Pa = 0 Pb = 0	Pa negative Pb fairly high
	H	Pa fairly high Pb negative	Pa fairly high Pb negative	Pa intermediate negative Pb intermediate negative

More specifically, either firm—say, Firm B—must recognize that if it adopts strategy *H*, then in the next round, the other firm can respond by adopting the same strategy as its countermove, thereby depriving Firm B of the potential gains from its initial choice of *H*. Moreover, Firm A's countermove threat is credible, because once A has adopted *H*, Firm B will not have available any other move in the next round that protects it from incurring large economic losses. Moreover, once the two firms have chosen *H*, neither can retreat by itself to a potentially more profitable strategy, *N*. Unless its rival can be guaranteed to undertake the same retreat to *H* simultaneously, the initiator of the retreat will subject itself to losses, and the other firm will have the incentive to persist in its choice of *H*. Thus, the *H,H* outcome will be stable, and if either firm moves to this strategy, the other will have no choice but to follow. The conclusion is that if the two players are rational, then in the absence of some exogenous development that dictates otherwise, such as a costly breakthrough invention, neither firm will find it attractive to abandon strategy *N*.

This is the payoff matrix interpretation of the kinked-revenue-locus equilibrium. Clearly, this has a ratchet mechanism that permits players to be lured into increased expenditure—whether for good reason or as a result of overoptimism. The new level of R&D spending, *H*, becomes the new industry norm for all the players, but once that is done, the structure of the game provides a strong disincentive for any retreat to a lower level of spending. This is, evidently, what is meant by the term "ratchet."

Additional light can be thrown on the matter by a somewhat more elementary approach. Consider an industry composed of identical firms with identical profit functions, $Fi(Ri)$, where Ri is Firm I's expenditure on R&D. *Ceteris paribus*, let Ri^* be Firm I's profit-maximizing R&D expenditure, and let Rm^* be the average profit-maximizing expenditure in the industry, where we assume $Rm^* = Ri^*$ for all i.

Next, let $G(Ri - Rm)$ be a Red Queen management-reward function for the industry, with $G' > 0$, $G(0) = 0$. If all firms initially adopt their individual profit-maximizing outlay level, Ri^*, we will have $G(Ri^* - Rm^*) = G(0)$. If we let Gi represent the partial derivative of $G(.)$, with respect to Ri, it will pay Firm I to increase its expenditure, so long as $Gi = (Gm)dRm/dRi > 0$—that is, so long as the rivals follow Firm I's move only to a moderate extent, if at all. Thus, there will be a constant temptation for the management of firms involved in a Red Queen R&D game to exceed the R&D level that would emerge if its reward were simply proportioned to the firm's profit. Only if $Gi = (Gm)dRm/dRi$, as we assumed in the discussion of figure 4.2, will $Ri = N$, for all i, be the solution, $Ri = N$, which will be perfectly sticky. Clearly, the implication is that a Red Queen reward system for compensation of management will tend to stimulate (some) enhancement of innovation activity.

This discussion suggests that a Red Queen arrangement has two growth-enhancing features that differentiate it from a system of rewards based on the player's own performance, irrespective of the performance of others. First, the Red Queen game leads all players to enhance their reward-seeking efforts when one of them does so. In contrast, in a scenario where each player simply selects the values of her decision variables that maximize her own payoff, a move by another player need not elicit any corresponding change in her behavior. Second, the ratchet property of a Red Queen game tends to prevent any retreat when a growth-enhancing move has been adopted by the group of players. Obviously, retreat is much less complicated where no such ratchet mechanism is present.

This brings us to the essential feature of a Red Queen reward arrangement: its magnitude depends on the difference between the achievement of the player in question and the achievements of her competitors. It is this feature of the arrangement that transforms the players' behavior into a competitive *race*.

PART II

Welfare Theory: Technology Transfer, Imitation, and Creative Destruction

Optimal Innovation Spillovers:
The Growth-Distribution Trade-off

*[If] everyone received the full measure of his marginal
product and no joint inputs existed, the benefits generated by
great entrepreneurs and inventors would accrue entirely to them.
There would be no "trickle-down" of progress to the masses. . . .
The trickle-down of benefits is a merit of capitalism in the real
world, and it works insofar as the distribution of income departs
from the strict standard of reward for personal contribution to
production.*

—Arthur Okun (1975, 46–47)

Chapter 3 reported evidence from Nordhaus (2004) that, unlike the static
case, the externalities of the innovation process are enormous, with consequences that are arguably beneficial to the general welfare, despite their
well-known impediments to economic efficiency. This chapter will provide
the underlying argument for this assertion and will attempt to show that
the net benefits of innovative entrepreneurship are not only positive, but
also gigantic. Indeed, they account for the bulk of the enormous growth
in the general population's standards of living during recent centuries. In
itself, this is surely reason enough to redirect welfare theory away from
its stationary focus.

This chapter picks up with the issue of optimality that concluded the
discussion in the previous chapter: given the apparently enormous spillovers that emanate from the innovation process and its other, attendant
externalities, how far is the economy from an R&D outlay level that can be
deemed to approximate optimality? The possibly surprising answer that I
offer here is that our economy may not be all that distant from optimality.
The evidence, as we have seen,[1] indicates that in any relatively wealthy
economy, a very substantial proportion of today's GDP—very likely more

than 90 percent in the United States, for instance—is composed of innovation spillovers. This means that the bulk of the benefits of innovation go to people who have not contributed to the creation and effective utilization of the inventions. Yet despite their inefficiency implications as disincentives for innovation, it will be argued that these spillovers may well be desirable, on balance. For if poverty and inequality are to be dealt with effectively, it is to these spillovers that we ultimately must look.

In addition to pointing out the resulting conflict between efficiency and distributive goals, this chapter will demonstrate how theoretical analysis can incorporate this trade-off into a more formal and informative structure. As part of this discussion, I will offer two key, interrelated conclusions, which I outline in the next two paragraphs.

First, I note that the distributive implications of innovation spillovers are critically important for the general welfare, particularly if we accept the reduction of poverty as a significant social goal. I will argue that a very substantial proportion of GDP in the world's economically advanced nations is composed of innovation spillovers, which, in turn, are not devoid of benefits to society. Indeed, one of the virtues of these spillovers is their enormous magnitude. It is to these substantial spillovers that we must attribute the bulk of our recent progress toward reducing the poverty and inequality of earlier time periods, when these social ills were far beyond anything currently experienced in today's prosperous economies.

Second, I will argue that formal welfare economics tends to evade issues related to income distribution. Its excuse is a hypothetical process, the lump-sum transfer, which is taken as the theoretically ideal instrument of redistribution. This procedure calculates the requisites of an equilibrium that is economically efficient—regardless of any attendant maldistribution of income and wealth. Then any shortcomings on that score are assumed to be rectified—or at least rectifiable—by lump-sum transfers that, by definition, do not modify—and, hence, do not worsen—the equilibrium that the preceding calculations showed to be perfectly efficient. I will take the position that, in reality, lump-sum transfers are generally impossible to achieve.[2] In particular, the assumption that they can be used to undo the redistributive effects of a program that eliminates the innovation externalities that harm economic efficiency is virtually self-contradictory. Because lump-sum transfers are often impossible, for reasons discussed below, they cannot constitute a beneficent solution to the problem created by the unavoidable trade-off between distributive goals and the requirements of economic efficiency.[3] As part of my analysis of the resulting conflict, I will point out that there are—perhaps frequently—what amount to Pareto-optimal outcomes that violate the efficiency conditions presented in the economic literature. In such a situation, an economy's total wealth is lower than it might have been in a regime of perfect efficiency. In exchange, however, the community experiences less economic inequality and less poverty.

How does the subject of this chapter relate to the activities of the innovative entrepreneur, on which this book focuses? The answer is that entrepreneurs are apt to play a key role in generating the spillovers in question, since they have no general reason to care who uses an invention and who (aside from themselves) receives its profits—whether it is someone who made essential contributions to the innovation process or, at the other extreme, someone who had nothing to do with it. Entrepreneurs can be found in any segment of the market in which there are earnings to be gathered, and, therefore, they can be the generators of at least some part of the spillovers. Moreover, they have no compunctions about delivering the benefits of an innovation to any promising customer—whether or not that customer has done anything to deserve them—so long as that recipient is willing to provide attractive compensation.

Before getting to the body of the discussion in this chapter, I must offer an important caveat. In emphasizing the role of entrepreneurs in the innovation process, I do not mean to imply that they alone play an important part. There are, of course, other indispensable inputs—notably, the labor and capital stock used in the creation and production of the inventions. There are also many (replicative) entrepreneurs and many workers and owners of capital who contribute little or nothing to innovation. Indeed, this is probably true of the preponderance of the members of each of these groups. Despite this pattern, the living standards of these entrepreneurs and workers, as well as the real wealth of these capitalists, have, on average, risen spectacularly during the past two centuries.[4] The bulk of these gains—the spillovers on which this chapter will focus—surely can be attributed, in large part, to innovation.

NON-LUMP-SUM, PARETO-OPTIMAL LEVELS OF INNOVATION SPILLOVERS

It has just been asserted, and presently will be explained more fully, that there is an inescapable and widespread trade-off between efficiency and equity, so that, if productive efficiency is improved, distributive equity is apt to worsen. Accordingly, a discussion of Pareto optimality that ignores distribution arguably is, to modify the old cliché, like a performance of *Julius Caesar* from which the conqueror of Gaul is absent. Therefore, I will base my discussion on a modified Pareto optimality concept that I call non-lump-sum (NLS) Pareto optimality—that is, optimality for a world in which lump-sum redistribution is impossible and in which distribution is taken into account.

I will use this concept to examine the consequences of nonzero spillovers (externalities) from innovation, with the conjecture that the plausible range of optimality may include spillovers that are very large. This, of course, conflicts directly with the standard view in the economic literature that only zero externalities are consistent with an optimal allocation of investment to innovation activity. As Nordhaus (1969) noted, "External economies are an important aspect of the production of knowledge. The greater the externality, the more inefficient is the final equilibrium" (39).

My argument that a zero spillover level in innovation is not generally optimal rests on the observation that, while zero spillovers are likely to be a requirement for the maximization of the *total* wealth of the community, they also may result in an extremely unequal distribution of that wealth. This entails the continuing impoverishment of substantial sectors of the community. As I will demonstrate in this chapter, there is no unambiguously optimal level of spillovers. Instead, there is a range of values of what I call the *spillover ratio*—that is, the share of the benefits of innovation that goes to people who did not contribute to the innovation process—within which, *all values of the ratio are NLS Pareto optimal*. Thus, all of them may be considered second-best Pareto optima because they are subject to a constraint that rules out hypothetical, but totally infeasible, redistributive arrangements.

My analysis takes off from a pathbreaking paper by Paul Romer (1994), which introduces a more profound view of the spillovers generated in the innovation process. Romer observes that gains in real wages, which result from innovation and are spread throughout the economy, must constitute spillovers, since they consist, in large part, of social benefits, rather than private benefits that accrue exclusively to participants in the innovation process. Indeed, it can be argued that the bulk of the unprecedented and widespread rise in the developed world's living standards since the Industrial Revolution could not have occurred without the revolution's innovations. Consequently, a very substantial share of the benefits of innovation—in the form of spillovers—must have gone to people other than the innovators themselves.[5]

Romer studied the role of these differences between private and social benefits—the spillovers of innovation—in impeding innovative activity and discussed the difficulty innovators face in covering their sunk costs and the reduction in innovative activity and output that occurs as a result. In this chapter, I will retell this part of the story, placing emphasis on another side of the matter: the inevitable trade-off between the number of innovations actually produced and the standard of living of the majority of the population. In this scenario, as innovation raises overall GDP, any increase in the typical worker's standard of living constitutes a rise in the spillovers from innovation. This, in turn, depresses the flow of further innovation.[6] Thus, the more the general public benefits from such growth in GDP, the slower that growth must be.

This is more than just an embellishment of the old story of the trade-off between output and distributive equality. The mechanism under discussion here is very different from the one most often considered, in that it does not involve the disincentive to work that results from a reduction of the marginal return to worker effort. Instead, I will focus my discussion on an issue at the heart of the capitalist growth process: the private payoff to innovation—how it is divided and how it affects the structure of incentives.

ON POVERTY IN THE ERA PRECEDING THE INDUSTRIAL REVOLUTION

The amount of purchasing power at stake in the redistribution that occurred in recent centuries is truly enormous. Indeed, it is difficult to comprehend the scope of the resulting differences in living standards, but this section will suggest what is entailed.

This discussion rests on an observation that Romer (1994) offered in passing: if the innovators of recent centuries had not lost *any* of the benefits they generated—that is, if spillovers had been zero, real wages today would be barely higher than their levels before the Industrial Revolution![7] Indeed, it is almost impossible to imagine how great a difference these spillovers have made—though I will attempt to illustrate it. U.S. per capita GDP in 1820 is calculated to have been less than one-seventeenth of what it has been in more recent times. According to the best available estimates, even as late as 1870, real per capita GDP is estimated to have been less than one-eleventh its recent level (Maddison 2001, 126). If one assumes the most extreme case—that the spillovers from innovation could somehow have been reduced to (anywhere near) zero, the living standards of the vast majority of the citizens of today's rich countries would have stalled at pre–Industrial Revolution levels. One can hardly argue that it would be socially preferable to achieve a total GDP far higher than today's, through maximal incentives for innovation, while simultaneously condemning most of the world's population to near-medieval living standards. That, however, is the world that a zero-spillovers premise depicts. Here, I will digress to offer a few illustrations that suggest what those earlier living standards were like.

Understandably, one may reject as irrelevant ancient history the apparently substantial fall in English real wages from the mid-fifteenth century until the time of Shakespeare, some 150 years later (Phelps Brown and Hopkins 1956). But developments related to the Industrial Revolution certainly are pertinent here. The era before the Industrial Revolution, which ended in the middle to late eighteenth century, was characterized by living conditions so miserable that we find them difficult to comprehend. Even the wealthy and powerful, who enjoyed ostentatious clothing, exotic foods, and armies of servants, suffered for lack of the technology of human comfort, which had not been invented yet.

Two examples illustrate this point. The first is a description of the 1732 journey from Berlin to Bayreuth undertaken by Frederick the Great's favorite sister, Wilhelmina, who was pregnant at the time:

> Ten strenuous, abnormally frigid days were spent upon roads, bad enough in summer, now deep with snow. On the second day the carriage in which Wilhelmina was riding turned over. She was buried under an avalanche of luggage. . . . Everyone expected a miscarriage and wanted Wilhelmina to rest in bed for several days. . . . Mountains appeared after Leipzig had been passed . . . Wilhelmina was frightened by the steepness of the roads and preferred to get out and walk to being whacked about as the carriage jolted from boulder to boulder. (Wright 1965, 142)

A second illustration of the standard discomfort experienced by even the rich and powerful before the Industrial Revolution is the oft-cited report by the Princess Palatine, Louis XIV's German sister-in-law, that in the winter of 1695, wine froze in the glasses of guests dining with the king in the Hall of Mirrors at Versailles (Braudel 1979–86, 1:299)!

Statistics and other pieces of evidence tell a story that is consistent with such anecdotes. Using genealogical records, Fogel (1986) estimates that between 1550 and 1700, the life expectancy at birth of members of the British nobility—slightly over 30 years for both males and females—was virtually the same as that of the population as a whole. Indeed, the average longevity for the general male and female population slightly exceeded that for members of the peerage for a substantial part of this period. Soon after that, however, things began to change. Early in the eighteenth century, indoor heating was revolutionized by inventions such as the Franklin stove. At the beginning of the nineteenth century, railroads were born and, through these advances and others, the upper classes in Victorian society soon enjoyed historically unprecedented levels of comfort. It is no surprise, then, that during this period, the life expectancy of the nobility leaped upward and ahead of the rest of the British population.

At this point, the less affluent began to catch up, but they still had very far to go, as Rosenberg and Birdzell (1986) note:

Western economic growth. . . benefited the life-style of the very rich much less than it benefited the life-style of the less well-off. . . . The very rich were as well-housed, clothed and adorned in 1885 as in 1985. . . . In fact, the innovations of positive value to the rich are the relatively few advances in medical care, air conditioning, and improvements in transportation and preservation of food. (26–27)

One only can begin to suggest the shocking levels of poverty to which a world without the spillovers from innovation would have condemned the lower-income classes. Indeed, histories of Europe confirm that for many centuries before the Industrial Revolution, the vast majority of the population struggled simply to exist. For instance, most families spent nearly half of their food budgets on "breadstuffs," which commonly took the form of gruel that was consumed in life-sustaining quantities. In France as late as 1790, according to Palmer, "The price of bread, even in normal times, in the amount needed for a man with a wife and three children, was half as much as the daily wage of common labor" (1964, 49).

Devastating famines, a fact of life in centuries preceding the Industrial Revolution, threatened Europe as late as the beginning of the nineteenth century. Fernand Braudel's *Civilization and Capitalism, 15th to 18th Century* documents the depths of human misery in Europe before the Industrial Revolution:

A few overfed rich do not alter the rule. . . . Cereal yields were poor; two consecutive bad harvests spelt disaster. . . . Any national calculation shows a sad story. France, by any standards a privileged country, is reckoned to have experienced 10 *general* famines during the tenth century; 26 in the eleventh; 2 in the twelfth; 4 in the fourteenth; 7 in the fifteenth; 13 in the sixteenth; 11 in the seventeenth; and 16 in the eighteenth. . . . The same could be said of any country in Europe. In Germany, famine was a persistent visitor to the towns and flatlands. Even when the easier times came, in the eighteenth and nineteenth centuries, catastrophes could still happen. . . . The poor in the towns and countryside lived in a state of almost complete deprivation. Their furniture consisted of next to nothing, at least before the eighteenth century, when a rudimentary luxury began to spread. . . . Inventories made after death, which are reliable documents, testify almost invariably to the general destitution . . . a few old clothes, a stool, a table, a bench, the planks of a bed, sacks filled with straw. Official reports for Burgundy between the sixteenth and the eighteenth centuries are full of references to people [sleeping] on straw . . . with no bed or furniture, who were only separated from the pigs by a screen. . . . Paradoxically the countryside sometimes experienced far greater suffering [from famines than the townspeople]. The peasants . . . had scarcely any reserves of their own. They had no solution in case of famine except to turn to the town where they crowded together, begging in the streets and often dying in public squares. (1979–86, 1:73–75 and 283)

The regular famines and widespread starvation that had occurred in Europe at least once per decade, on average, began to disappear by the nineteenth century. Still, famines continued occasionally well into the nineteenth century—and not only in Ireland. Thus, in relatively wealthy Belgium, "During the great crisis of 1846, the newspapers would tell daily of cases of death from starvation. . . . At Wynghene, cases became so frequent that the local policeman was given the job of calling at all houses each day to see if the inhabitants were still alive" (de Mees 1962, 305).

The description of the horrors of the existence of the lower-income classes before the Industrial Revolution can go on and on, but the point is clear. It is they who had the farthest to go to improve their circumstances. And close the gap they did. There is no better way to demonstrate these advances than to report figures showing how much the purchasing power of an average worker's hour of labor has increased over the course of the twentieth century. For example, the Federal Reserve Bank of Dallas (1997, 5–17) has estimated that the wage required for "earning our daily bread" now can be earned in less than one-third the labor time it took in the early twentieth century. In 1919 the average worker labored 13 minutes in order to earn enough to buy a pound of bread, compared to just four minutes in 1997. Moreover, the work time required to buy a three-pound chicken in 1919—more than 2.5 hours—had fallen to just 14 minutes by 1997. In 1910, 345 hours of work time bought a kitchen range and 553 hours of work time bought a clothes washer. By 1997, those numbers had dropped to 22 and 26 hours, respectively. There are many other eye-opening comparisons. The purchase of a calculating device in 1916 required 494 hours of labor time, but only 46 minutes in 1996; a 1954 color television required 562 hours of work, but just 23 hours in 1997; and the purchase of a 1908 Model T automobile necessitated 4,696 hours of labor, versus just 1,365 hours for a 1997 Ford Taurus.

These observations return us to the central point of this chapter. If poverty and its elimination are major components of the general welfare, as the preceding discussion indicates, then these considerations cannot be left out of any analysis of the deviations from or proximity to optimality of the economic arrangements. For that reason, the spillovers from innovation, which arguably encompass the bulk of the welfare improvements since the Industrial Revolution, cannot be treated as merely undesirable impediments to technical advance. Instead, these must be recognized as primary contributors to the reduction of poverty and, therefore, as a source of enormous benefit to the general welfare. In the next section, I will explain how theory can begin to tackle the resulting issue—the trade-off between total production and equitable distribution—using the two previously defined concepts, the NLS Pareto optimum and the spillover ratio.

THE RANGE OF NON-LUMP-SUM (NLS) PARETO OPTIMA

As a first step, I will use a graph to describe the locus of NLS Pareto optima that emerge in a world in which lump-sum distributions are ruled out. To simplify, I assume that the employed population is divided into two groups: those who contribute to the innovation process (Group I) and the other members of the workforce (Group II). We also let Y be some index of the community's total net output. The vertical axis in figure 5.1 displays a scalar measure of these total welfare benefits, Y, that are currently attainable by the two-group economy.[8]

Here I should note that the former group includes not only the inventors themselves, but also those that invest in the activity, and the innovative entrepreneurs who ensure that the end products of the innovative process are put to effective use. The horizontal axis of the graph measures Z, the *share* of the total benefits that accrue to Group I, from left to right. The share of the benefits to Group II $(1 - Z)$, is measured from right to left along the same axis. In the absence of lump-sum transfers, incentive compatibility constraints on individual behavior imply that the maximum, Y, depends on Z, and that the maximum will be attained if there is no feasible contract able to separate the incentive to work from the level of compensation. Point e denotes the (Z, Y) combination at which Y is maximized. At this efficient point, OE_{max} is the share of the benefits that accrues to Group I, so that $1 - E_{max}$ is Group II's share. In the absence of lump-sum transfers, any other distribution—that is, any other value of Z—must reduce Y because of the resulting decline in allocative efficiency, ignoring the incentive compatibility constraints. For simplicity, I assume that the remaining distribution share values, Z, yield values of Y that are bounded from above by a smooth, hill-shaped welfare frontier. This heavy, solid curve, $AYeB$, which, for brevity, I will call *Curve Y*, marks the upper boundary of the economy's feasible outputs.

Next, it is easy to derive from the overall benefit-distribution frontier, Y, the two corresponding upper frontiers for Group I and Group II. With Z, which represents the *proportion* of output that accrues to members of Group I, these two total output shares are given by the expressions, ZY and $(1 - Z)Y$, for Group I and Group II, respectively. These immediately yield two corresponding curves, labeled *I* and *II*, which report the maximum benefits obtainable by the corresponding groups at each level of Z. *Curve I* starts at zero at the left end of the graph, where $Z = ZY = 0$, and then asymptotically approaches Y, as it moves toward the extreme right,

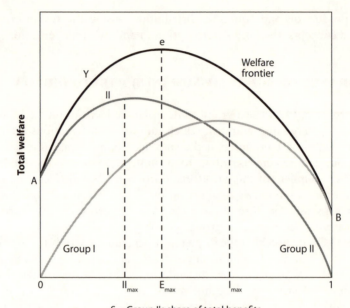

S = Group I's share of total benefits

FIGURE 5.1
Locus of Non-Lump-Sum Pareto Optima. (Reprinted from Baumol 2002b, fig. 8.4, p. 147.)

where $Z = 1$, so that $ZY = Y$. The same procedure, but moving from right to left, yields *Curve II*. We can expect both curves to be concave near maximum, $Y(Z = E_{max})$, as well as to the right of E_{max} for Group I and to the left for Group II—so long as Y is concave.[9] Therefore, we can assume that the curves for Group I and Group II both have interior maxima that occur at share levels, $Z = I_{max}$ and $Z = II_{max}$, respectively.

It can readily be shown to follow that $I_{max} > E_{max} > II_{max}$, so that Group I's maximum must lie to the right of Group II's. To see that this must be so, note that at E_{max}, $Y' = 0$, $d(ZY)/dZ = Y > 0$ and $d[(1 - Z)Y]/dZ = -Y < 0$, so that Group I's benefits increase as one moves to the right of E_{max}, and Group II's benefits increase as one moves to the left of E_{max}. Therefore, at each of the maxima for the individual groups, there must be some loss of overall efficiency because Y must be below its maximum, e. This also will be true throughout the range between the two maxima for the two groups—with the exception of the single point at $Z = E_{max}$, where Y attains its maximum value. Except at that point, there will be a trade-off between efficiency and virtually any desired distribution of the benefits.

The range between the maxima for the two groups is a region in which it clearly is impossible (along the efficient frontier) to benefit either group without harming the other. In other words, the frontier points within this range indisputably are all NLS Pareto optima. Such a range must always exist where the efficient point, e, is an interior maximum of Y, the measure of social welfare, and where the Y frontier is hill-shaped. For, then, any change in distribution *must* favor some group(s) of individuals at the expense of others, since the change also must decrease Y, the total size of the pie available for distribution.

The range of NLS Pareto-efficient optima need not be small. Indeed, it can include the entire Y frontier because it is at least theoretically possible that *both* parties can have corner maxima. To see this, we calculate the requirement for such a maximum for Group I, where the relationships are assumed to be suitably differentiable, so that we require for an interior maximum of Group I that $dZY/dZ = Y + ZY' = 0$. That is, $Z = -Y/Y'$.[10] To the right of the maximum of Y, we can expect to have $Y' < 0$. Thus, the Group I-maximizing Z will be positive. As Z increases, we can expect $-Y/Y'$ to decline monotonically. If, at $Z = 1$, we have $-Y'/Y > 1$, Z will equal $-Y/Y$ only to the right of $Z = 1$, yielding a corner maximum for Group I, as just asserted. The corresponding possibility arises for Group II. If both of these possibilities occur, then *any* distribution at the frontier will have the Pareto property that one group can benefit only at the expense of the other. More to the point, *any* frontier magnitude of Y—that is, any output level selected because the corresponding income distribution is considered particularly desirable—will then be NLS Pareto optimal, no matter how great the sacrifice by Y that is entailed.

Normally, that extreme situation is unlikely. Where the scenario is different, there will be segments at both ends of that frontier, such that from any point contained in these segments, Pareto-improving moves that benefit *both* parties will be possible. Where the maxima for the two parties happen to fall close together, the range of NLS Pareto optima will be small, yielding a small range of optimal distributions of Y. As we have just seen, the optima of the two groups must lie on opposite sides of the maximum, Y. Thus, all of these optima will be close to the value of Z that maximizes Y, and consequently, only a small sacrifice of Y will be consistent with optimality.

Finally, it is important to note that where there is a broad range of NLS Pareto optima, one needs some sort of social utility or social welfare function to select those that are preferred. Suppose, then, that such a function exists and that it places a high value on equality of income distribution. In this instance, the function may very well not select a point near the center of the graph. For $Z = 0.5$ assigns exactly half of Y to each of the two groups, but if Group I contains a thousand individuals, while

Group II contains 500 million, the resulting distribution hardly would be satisfactory to egalitarians. Rather, a value of Z closer to Group II's maximum point—call it $Z = Z^*$—would surely be more desirable. Moreover, if the selected value of Z were slightly larger than Z^* and gave more to Group I than Z^* does, the chosen Z would be NSL Pareto optimal and, thus, consistent with a high value of the social welfare function—even though this entails a substantial sacrifice of Y by society as a whole. Much of the remainder of this chapter will focus on this type of case.

MARGINAL COST, TOTAL COST, AND THE ADOPTION OF SOCIALLY BENEFICIAL INNOVATIONS

Before constructing a more formal model of the socially optimal level of spillovers from *total* innovation, I will review an important issue that, as Romer has noted, goes back to Dupuit: the role of *total cost*, relative to that of *marginal cost*, in "lumpy" decisions in which one cannot choose to do just a very little bit more or a very little bit less—for example, the choice between devoting scarce resources to building an entire bridge or the launching of an entire innovation process. Where such an activity has substantial fixed and sunk costs, or where scale economies make small-scale entry infeasible, one cannot rely on marginal analysis because marginal data relate only to small adjustments.[11]

This means that, when deciding between allocating available resources to construction of a bridge, or instead launching a large-scale R&D project, the criterion to consider is whether or not the *total yield* from the project will exceed the *total cost*. A profit-seeking firm will not undertake an innovation unless the total revenue is expected to be greater than the total cost, and society should not undertake an innovative project unless its total benefits are expected to exceed total costs. In other words, the choice in such a situation cannot be determined by the usual *marginal* analysis.

The legitimate argument that conventionally links this situation to the spillovers of innovation is straightforward. It suggests that there are many prospective innovations that promise total net social benefits but, nevertheless, will not be carried out by private enterprise—even if *marginal* spillovers, at whatever margin is relevant, are all zero. In fact, there are many potential innovations whose prospective total benefits, including their contributions to consumers' surpluses, are greater than their total costs. However, no one will find these innovations profitable to carry out because a considerable proportion of their total benefits would go to persons other than the innovator (in the form of spillovers). In this chapter, I will carry on with the story from this point and provide a somewhat different ending.

A MODEL AND GRAPHIC ANALYSIS OF
OPTIMAL SPILLOVERS

Next I provide a formal analysis of the relation between the spillover ratio and optimality, adopting two premises to facilitate the discussion. The first is that production uses only two inputs—labor and innovation—so that income earners are divided into innovators and (noninnovating) workers. In the second premise, I assume that, with a given labor force, the production frontier can be shifted outward only by innovation.

Let S represent the spillover ratio—that is, the share of the benefits of innovation that do not accrue to the innovator, relative to the total benefit contributed by innovation. Consider two scenarios. In the first, the value of S is assumed to be fixed exogenously. In the other scenario, it is treated as a modifiable parameter.

This model follows Romer (1994) in recognizing that there is a vast set of potential innovations that offer society different amounts of total net benefit over and above their sunk costs. Each such innovation, I, also requires a sunk expenditure, $C(i)$, where i is the index assigned to invention I, as described below. Assume that both benefits and costs can be translated into money terms and that the total gross benefit, $B(i)$—the value before the deduction of sunk costs—is given by the discounted present value of the stream of the benefits, minus the unsunk costs expected from invention I from now to eternity.

Maximization of the direct benefits from innovation clearly requires that, at any given time, the economy carry out every recognized prospective innovation, I, for which $B(i) - C(i) > 0$. Given the spillover ratio, however, private enterprise will undertake only those innovations for which $B(i) (1 - S) - C(i) > 0$. This means that the beneficial innovations, J, for which $C(j)/(1 - S) > B(j) > C(j)$, will be lost to society. This is, roughly speaking, where the story stands in much of the literature.

To take this story further, I will utilize two simple graphs. Figure 5.2 depicts the relationship between the benefits from innovation and the share of innovations that are actually carried out from among all of the innovations considered possible by prospective innovators. It shows how spillovers limit the number of prospectively useful innovations actually undertaken.

In figure 5.2, we assume that the spillovers are a fixed percentage (for example, $S = 0.75$) of the total future benefits of an innovation. The potential innovations recognized as worth carrying out are taken to constitute a continuum—or can be approximated by one. We also assume that the sunk investment required to carry out a single innovation is fixed at level C.[12] The horizontal axis, which extends from zero to unity, represents the share of currently recognized innovation possibilities that actually is

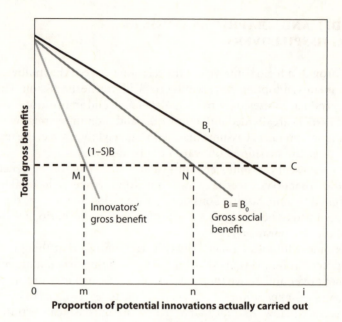

FIGURE 5.2
Spillover Ratio, Optimality, and Equilibrium. (Reprinted from Baumol 2002b, fig. 8.1, p. 128.)

carried out. Innovations are indexed *in descending order* of incremental gross benefit, B. Here gross benefit is defined as the discounted present value of all current and future gains an innovation provides, minus the discounted value of all current and future costs other than the sunk costs needed to produce that innovation. The descending order of benefits, then, means that $B(i) > B(j)$ iff $i < j$. For simplicity of presentation, the gross benefits curve, B, is taken to be linear. By construction, B must have a negative slope throughout because of the way in which the potential innovations are ordered here. With S a given constant, one also can draw in the innovator's gross benefits curve, $(1 - S)B$. Point N, where the B and C lines intersect, represents the point at which all recognized innovations that currently promise a net gain to the economy are exhausted. That is, at N, the economy has adopted every recognized innovation with benefits that exceed its sunk costs.[13] However, private enterprises will be unable to go beyond point M, with its much lower output of innovation, because spillovers, SB, will prevent such enterprises from covering the sunk costs of any additional innovations.[14] This implies that the level of innovation can be much below the socially efficient level, n.[15]

Next consider what happens in figure 5.2 when there is a change in the spillover ratio. If line B remains fixed in its initial position, B_0, as S increases, the line, $(1 - S)B_0$, will move steadily lower and become steadily steeper, with the curve rotating clockwise. However, this overlooks the possibility that, at least up to a point, the spillovers themselves will contribute to productivity and innovation and, hence, to the total benefits the economy derives from innovation. There are at least two ways in which this can occur. First, the spillovers from innovation can facilitate further innovation. They may do so by cutting down the need for and the expenses involved in the design of duplicative technology by competing firms. Moreover, to the extent that technical advance is cumulative—with one step facilitating the next, as is certainly true in many fields, today's technological advance by one firm lays the groundwork for tomorrow's advance by different firms. Second, the spillovers can increase the number of inventors who are able to work effectively, given the earnings provided by the new technology.[16] Zero spillover, as the term is interpreted here, means that the labor force is condemned to very low nutrition and educational levels—perhaps equivalent to those that prevailed before the Industrial Revolution. The evidence indicates, however, that the transfer to workers of some of the benefits of innovation, in the form of improved nutrition and education, can contribute materially to labor productivity. Consequently, as S increases above zero—say to S_1—at least initially, line B can be expected to shift upward or rotate counterclockwise by an amount sufficient to yield a private benefit line, $(1 - S_1)B_1$, which lies above B (see figure 5.2). However, when S becomes sufficiently large, further increases in S can be expected to lower and flatten the line, $(1 - S)B$, monotonically.

These relationships and their implications yield more interesting insights with the aid of figure 5.3, which focuses on the effects of changes in the *spillover ratio*. In this figure, the horizontal axis represents S, the size of the spillover ratio. Like i on the horizontal axis of figure 5.2, this ranges between $S = 0$ and $S = 1$. The upper curve, B^*, is the integral of $[B(i) - C]$ from $i = 0$ to the profit-maximizing value of i in figure 5.2, where $(1 - S)B(i) = C$.

In the region to the right of n in the graph, the slope of the B^* curve must be negative, since, by construction, $dB^*/di = B - C > 0$ and, as in note 14 of this chapter, $di/dS = B/(1 - S)B' < 0$, so

(5.1)
$$\frac{dB^*}{dS} = \left(\frac{dB^*}{di}\right)\left(\frac{di}{dS}\right) = \frac{(B-C)B}{(1-S)B'} < 0.$$

We will assume that the $B^*(S)$ curve is normally concave, as drawn. We also observe that, to the right of the point where further invention yields no additional profit, the curve will coincide with the horizontal axis.

The negative slope would persist throughout the graph if innovation were the only direct input to productivity growth, or if innovation were

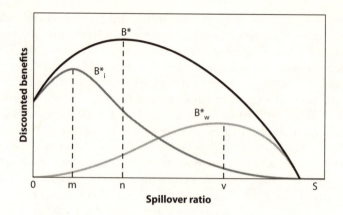

FIGURE 5.3

Benefits as a Function of Spillover Ratio. (Reprinted from Baumol 2002b, fig. 8.2, p. 130.)

not facilitated by spillovers from other innovations. In reality, however, productivity growth is apt to be enhanced, up to a point, by the spillovers from innovation, which facilitate and stimulate further innovation, and by a labor force that benefits from better nutrition and education (which are severely reduced as the value of S approaches zero). Thus, the left-hand end of the graph represents a state of affairs in which workers are ill-fed and ill-educated and where innovation benefits very little from other innovations. As S begins to rise above zero, the B^* curve also rises. That is, toward the left, $dB^*/dS > 0$, so that this portion of the B^* curve has a positive slope. All of this together yields the shape of the B^* curve depicted in figure 5.3, in which the unique maximum at $S = n$ marks the point at which current investment in innovation maximizes the net total gain to society.

The rest of the story differs for the two classes into which our illustrative society is divided: the innovators and the workers. However, it is the same story told earlier in the section within this chapter entitled "The Range of Non-Lump-Sum Pareto Optima." For example, the benefits added by innovation going to the workers are shown by the B^*_w curve, which is given by the expression SB^*. That is, the workers' benefit is equal to the total social benefit, B^*, multiplied by the share, S, that goes to these non-innovators.[17] This lower curve must start off at zero at its left-hand end, where $S = 0$, and approach the B^* curve as S increases toward unity, with the two curves meeting at or before the extreme right, where S equals or is close to unity. B^*_w has the derivative

(5.2) $$\frac{dSB^*}{dS} = B^* + SB^{*\prime},$$

which is positive at the maximum, n, of the upper curve, B^*, where $B^{*\prime} = 0$. This means that v, the maximum workers' benefit, B^*_w, must occur *just to the right of* n, the maximum of B^*. Although the total size of the social output pie is decreasing, this occurs because, slightly to the right of the maximum of B^*, the workers' share of that shrinking pie increases sufficiently to make them better off, on balance. Eventually, however, the size of the social output gain shrinks so much that further increases in S are damaging even to workers. The workers' benefit maximum requires $B^* = -SB^{*\prime}$, which has a straightforward interpretation, in terms of the total benefit pie and the size of the workers' slice. B^* is the workers' gain from a unit increase in their *share* of the pie, while $SB^{*\prime}$ is the workers' loss from the accompanying decrease in the *total size* of the pie, $B^{*\prime}$. For the usual reasons, maximization requires this marginal loss to equal the marginal gain.

The graph also depicts an innovators' benefits curve, B^*_i, represented by the equation, $B^*_i = (1 - S)B^*$. This curve's relation to the B^* curve is perfectly analogous to that of the workers, except that the behavior of the innovators' curve, from right to left (as $1 - S$ increases), corresponds exactly to that of the workers' curve as one goes from left to right—that is, as S increases. Thus, $S = m$, the maximum[18] of B^*_i, must always lie *to the left of* n, the maximum of the social gain curve, B^*.

Several substantive conclusions follow from this discussion. First, it is clear that innovators can be expected not to obtain their maximum reward if they receive *all* of the benefits that their innovations can yield—that is, if spillovers are zero. Rather, their gain is maximized at $S = m > 0$. Moreover, innovators' preferred value of S may be even higher than this if, for example, they derive some utility from altruistic egalitarianism or if higher wages provide other benefits to innovators, such as reducing crime and, thereby, increasing their safety. Similarly, the welfare of workers will be reduced if *all* of the benefits of innovation go to them in the form of spillovers because then, of course, there will be little or no innovation, and little or no benefit will be available to accrue to them. Workers are better off if $S = v$, which corresponds to the maximum point on their benefits curve. They also may derive indirect gains from a value of S that is somewhat lower than v, if greater innovator wealth leads to outcomes, like increased donations to hospitals that benefit workers.

Thus, point n, where productive efficiency is maximized, is *not* likely to be preferred by either party because, while n is a possible compromise between the two groups, it is hardly the only available compromise position. Every point in the entire range, $m < S < v$, is a possible solution because any change from a point within that range harms one of the groups, while benefiting the other. That is, the corresponding range of a utilities-possibility frontier, which easily can be derived from our model, must have a negative slope throughout. Thus, rather than there being a unique and clearly definable global optimum, *there is a range of S values that are all NLS Pareto optimal.*[19]

PIGOUVIAN SUBSIDIES, CONSUMERS' SURPLUSES, AND LUMP-SUM TRANSFERS

The preceding analysis naturally prompts us to consider whether or not, at least in theory, one can have it both ways. In other words, is it possible to provide incentives for the socially optimal amount of innovation and subsequently redistribute the resulting gains, thereby making all parties better off? But even if all socially beneficial innovations could somehow be obtained through the market, the lump-sum transfers needed to distribute the benefits to the general population, without distorting the equilibrium, would remain a figment of the theorist's imagination. In the appendix to this chapter, I will seek to show why, *in general*, there can be no such thing as a lump-sum transfer in the real world. In the particular case of innovation, the unreality of the proposal is far more striking. If, as suggested by the evidence, spillover ratios substantially exceed 0.85 (see below and Nordhaus 2004), their elimination would provide a huge addition to innovators' current earnings. If the remainder of the population subsequently were to be compensated by ostensibly lump-sum transfers, the resources for the payout would have to come from the newly mega-rich innovators who, at least initially, would receive the bulk of the economy's GDP. These innovators could not fail to notice that most of their innovation payoffs were being taxed away, and surely, this would eliminate virtually all of the supposedly enhanced incentive to increase the amounts of resources and effort they invest in the innovation process. In this sense, the idea that lump-sum transfers are pertinent to the problem—even in theory—is tantamount to assuming the problem away.

Another attribute that makes innovation spillovers different from other beneficial externalities, as Romer (1994) rightly emphasizes, stems from the sunk costs of the innovation process. Even if the prices of the products of innovation are adjusted to cover the marginal costs of supplying them, the sunk costs generally will not be covered. Moreover, even if Pigouvian subsidies are added to those prices in order to cover all of the pertinent *marginal* costs, this will not cover the remaining costs, and thus, private enterprise will not be willing to invest in every socially beneficial innovation. Here, the obvious test of social desirability is whether or not the total benefits of the innovation, *now and in the future*, can be expected to cover the product's *total* costs—both sunk and marginal.

The bottom line, then, is that there is no way *in reality* to escape the trade-off between the incentives required to elicit the optimal level of investment in innovation and the desire for the resulting rise in real productivity to benefit everyone—not only innovators.

HOW LARGE ARE THE SPILLOVERS?

As indicated in chapter 4, the total size of the spillovers from innovation is hardly negligible. If one provisionally accepts the conclusion that the bulk of the rise in per capita GDP in the world's most prosperous countries, as well as the rise in productivity since the Industrial Revolution, *ultimately* could not have occurred without innovation, it is possible to arrive at a very crudely estimated lower bound for the spillover ratio. For this purpose, it may be noted that per capita GDP has increased almost 12-fold in the United States since 1870, according to estimates by Maddison (2001). This rise in U.S. GDP per person implies that eleven-twelfths, or nearly 92 percent, of current GDP was contributed by innovation carried out since 1870. However, the total contribution of innovation surely is even greater than that, since pre-1870 innovations, such as the steam engine, the railroad, and many other inventions of an earlier era, still add to today's GDP. Moreover, the difference between the increase in labor productivity, which is estimated by Maddison to have risen 14-fold since 1870, and the substantially smaller increase in GDP is attributable, in good part, to enhanced leisure—a benefit also made possible largely by innovation.

We can carry this reasoning somewhat further by estimating what share of GDP went to investors in the innovation process. During the period from 1870 to 2007, the economy's total investment income accounted for less than 30 percent of U.S. GDP. However, investment in innovation is only a relatively small part of total investment. In 2006, for instance, R&D expenditures made up less than 14 percent of total investment in the United States (U.S. Bureau of the Census 2007). If the return on innovation investment were the same as the return to investment of other types (after adjusting for risk), the return to innovation would have been 4.2 percent of U.S. GDP ($30 \times 0.14 = 4.2$) in 2006. Therefore, returns to innovators could not have been much more than 10 percent of GDP. It follows, then, that S, the spillover ratio, may well have been as high as 0.9 or, as Nordhaus's calculation indicates, considerably higher. That is, some 90 percent of innovation benefits, or more, may have gone to people who made no direct contribution to innovation. The startling implication of all of this is that *the spillovers of innovation—direct and indirect—are very likely to be more than half of the growth in current GDP*.[20] For our story, the precise figure does not matter. What is noteworthy is that the spillover ratio seems to be surprisingly large.

Before concluding our discussion of innovation's contribution to growth, one important qualification must be noted. For our purposes here, contributions to economic growth from all sources other than innovation have been omitted from the discussion. This is not, however, because these contributions have been negligible. No such assumption is intended, nor is this or any related premise critical for my main argument. It is clear, for example, that enormous contributions have been made by education and other forms of investment in human capital. Still, the enormous expansion of outlays on education and physical productive capacity in the world's industrialized countries, by itself, would not have been possible without the resources provided by the innovation that emerged during the era of the Industrial Revolution. That initial burst of innovation constituted a necessary condition for the economic expansion that has occurred since the eighteenth century. If new technology in agriculture, mining, and manufacturing had not appeared during the Industrial Revolution and in the centuries that immediately preceded it, per capita income levels arguably would have remained at miserably low levels, and significant increases in investments in plant, equipment, education, or the health of the labor force would not have been possible. Moreover, among the economies' different inputs, each improved and expanded input is apt to enhance the quantities and the productivities of the others. In formal terms, this can be expressed by noting that, among input variables, the cross-partial derivatives of national output growth are undoubtedly substantial. For example, innovation surely stimulates educational expenditure—both by providing the necessary resources and increasing the returns to education, which, in turn, facilitates innovation. Accordingly, innovation must be considered the ultimate source—both direct and indirect—of most of the investment in human and physical capital that, along with the innovation itself, surely is responsible for most of the growth in production, production per capita, and productivity that followed the Industrial Revolution.[21]

CONCLUDING COMMENT: RELEVANCE FOR REALITY AND THE GENERAL WELFARE

Most discussions of the consequences of the Industrial Revolution stress that its main social benefit was its ultimate contribution to the living standards of the population as a whole, including improvements in health, longevity, education, and the reduction of poverty, among others. These main spillovers from innovation are the focus of this chapter. Surely, few of us would be prepared to argue that it would be optimal to multiply the wealth of the world's richest innovators far above current levels, while condemning the rest of the population to the miserable living standards that were the norm for most of the seventeenth century. That, however, is exactly what zero spillovers would mean.

The range of choices for society under discussion here can be thought of as possible movements along an *efficiency-distribution frontier*, rather than as a choice among alternative and second-best Pareto optima. Here it is important to determine an optimal trade-off between economic efficiency and the variance of income, via spillovers—the only feasible way to achieve substantial transfers.

Most of us *do* recognize the beneficial spillovers contributed by innovation. Moreover, we all seem to agree that this enhancement of general living standards is a very desirable outcome. Accordingly, perhaps without realizing that we were discussing the *spillovers* of innovation, we have concluded that they are a very good thing. It follows, then, that even if they had increased innovation, zero spillovers certainly would have been far from optimal.

Here the reaction of at least some economists, who contend that disinterested academicians cannot take a defensible stand on the desirability of the state of income distribution, simply will not do. Virtually no one aspires to a world in which innovators receive incomes in the trillions of dollars (putting Bill Gates's wealth into the shade), while the remainder of the community languishes in seventeenth-century poverty. There is, of course, a value judgment involved here, but only cowardice will induce us to disown it. My own judgment on this issue is summed up in George Bernard Shaw's dictum that there is no crime greater than poverty. If we accept this, we also must reject the conclusion that spillovers—particularly if they are substantial—are incompatible with optimality in the growth process. If we concede the validity of this last conclusion, what remains for discussion is a matter of haggling about the appropriate degree of the spillovers' deviation from zero. Accordingly, it surely is not ridiculous to conclude that the most desirable value of S is very much larger than zero—perhaps even not far from its current value.

Of course, those innovations that have never been launched as a result of the spillovers do constitute a loss to society. The point, however, is that there is an inescapable trade-off here between two desirable phenomena: the increase in innovative activity versus the diversion of the benefits of innovation in a manner that helps to bring society out of medieval poverty, spread education and health care, and finance the "better life" not just for the fortunate few, but for the population as a whole.

This chapter provides a possible step toward a formal theory of income distribution policy, by presenting an introduction to the analysis of the choice between low and high spillover ratios. I argue that progress in this arena requires us to abandon the issue-dodging assumption that distributive shortcomings can be cured by lump-sum transfers. More to the point of this book, I have shown here that, over a broad range of levels of R&D activity, any substantial increase in R&D activity is apt to be obtainable only at the social cost entailed in some deterioration in the distribution of income. In that sense, *all* such levels of R&D spending, and the corresponding broad range in the value of spillover ratios, must be deemed to lie within the range of NLS Pareto optimality. That is, any increase in the incentive to innovation within that range entails deterioration in income distribution, while any improvement in distribution brings with it an enhanced disincentive to innovation. Thus, neither move can be deemed a Pareto improvement because the accompanying benefits can be attained only at a substantial cost to society.

It follows from this that intertemporal welfare theory—in which the allocation of resources to innovation is so important and the implications for issues, such as eliminating poverty, are so profound—must be substantially different from the static welfare analysis. Chapter 6 will continue with this theme.

APPENDIX

ON THE IMPOSSIBILITY OF REPEATED AND PERVASIVE LUMP-SUM TRANSFERS

Fairy tales indisputably have their value, but there are times when it is more appropriate, instead, to seek out information grounded firmly in reality. The theorist's recourse to mythical lump-sum transfers as a mode of redistribution that can preserve economic efficiency, for instance, is more legend than fact. In this appendix, I will show why such transfers cannot occur in ordinary, real-world circumstances.[22] This is not just another tedious and counterproductive plea for greater realism in economic models, as an end in itself. Rather, as this chapter has sought to show, much of substance and importance can be learned by dropping this key assumption. For once it is recognized that income redistribution cannot be achieved without sacrificing some economic efficiency,[23] one is led to study the nature of this trade-off and how its cost to society can be minimized.

Of course, it is sometimes analytically convenient and basically harmless to assume that lump-sum transfers are possible and can be carried out systematically. However, as I have indicated, analyses of other important issues can be substantially distorted by such a premise—if it is, in fact, untrue.

It is easy to show why, in reality, lump-sum transfers often are not possible. First, let us recall the definition of the term. A lump-sum transfer refers to an income or wealth transfer that has *absolutely no efficiency-damaging incentive effects.* That is, those people from whom the transfers derive must not wish—or be able—to do anything that damages the economy's efficiency, in order to reduce the magnitudes of their losses. Similarly, the recipients of the transfers must not be able to change their behavior in a manner that impedes efficiency, following their windfall.

However, even a once-and-for-all transfer cannot be expected to be free of any distortion in incentives, if we suppose that it depends on any aspect or consequence of market activity. This problem is even more severe, where such transfers are repeated many times. Thus, the likelihood of distortion is particularly great if the ostensibly lump-sum transfers are to be adopted as a long-lived corrective of any objectionable distribution consequences resulting from a pattern of resource allocation required for efficiency.

Consequently, the problem besetting theoretical recourse to lump-sum redistribution is straightforward. Where a supposedly lump-sum transfer is intended to correct an undesired distributive effect, those whose activities are deemed to have given them excessive income or wealth must be primary candidates to serve as providers of the resources to be transferred, while those considered inadequately endowed with income and wealth will be the recipients. In such a repeated game, members of each group soon will learn that their economic activities, which contributed to their pretransfer wealth or income levels, condemn them to the role of transfer payer or, alternately, ensure that they will be the recipients of such payments. This provides a clear incentive to the payers to cut back on the activities that force them into that position. At the same time, recipients have an incentive to do the reverse.[24]

Nevertheless, such a transfer theoretically can be lump sum if its effects include no externalities or deviations from perfect competition. The Arrow-Debreu theorems state that if the economy is perfectly competitive and there are no externalities, a change in the distribution of wealth will lead to a new equilibrium that also can be Pareto optimal. Thus, all prices and allocated resources can be changed in a manner compatible with the new Pareto optimum.

This is what the theory asserts. Reality, however, is generally different. Here I need not remind the reader that real markets are not perfectly competitive, and that, as has been shown in this chapter, externalities in the real world—the spillovers from innovation, in particular—are far from zero. Instead, what is far more important for this discussion is the fact that the very act of reducing an externality—whether marginal, average, or total—is tantamount to redistributing real income between the recipients of those benefits and the agents whose activities generate them. For, by definition, an externality is simply a redistribution of all or part of the costs or benefits yielded by an activity to those who are not directly involved in that activity—as when the smoke emitted by a factory increases the laundry bills of its neighbors. Consequently, if a decrease in externalities is necessary in order to increase efficiency, clearly there will be a redistributive effect. Similarly, any measure that undoes that distributive effect must automatically re-create the externality. Such offsetting changes in distribution must patently affect efficiency—thus, by definition, they cannot be lump sum.

In short, the difficulty is this. Suppose one starts with an acceptable income distribution, made possible by the spillovers (externalities) of innovation that prevent efficiency. In order to achieve optimality, one must eliminate the externalities and then correct any new, undesired redistribution effects that result. However, the very act of distributive modification indirectly re-creates these externalities because, at the end, those who were better off as a result of the externalities still end up with re-created spillovers—the very benefits for which they made no payment and to whose creation they made no contribution.[25] Meanwhile, those who initially were deprived by the externalities of part of the benefits generated by their activities still suffer the same damage as before. Thus, the externality is reconstituted by the redistribution—this time, via a two-stage process, externalities plus taxation, rather than by a direct one.

We must conclude that a completely equitable distribution of income via the spillovers of innovation must reduce productive efficiency drastically, just as unfettered pursuit of absolute efficiency via the elimination of all externalities would benefit only a select few and hold down the living standards of the many. Like inseparable Siamese twins, each of these twin goals—efficiency and equitable distribution—can be singled out for promotion to an extreme *only at the expense of the other*. Consequently, maximization of the economy's total product, along with restoration of a spillovers-based, commendable distribution via lump-sum transfers, is inherently a self-contradictory notion.

Enterprising Technology Dissemination:
Toward Optimal Transfer Pricing and the
Invaluable Contribution of "Mere Imitation"

*Every country must be much benefited, which by means of early
translations, possesses itself of the fruits of the labours of foreign
nations.*

—Claude Berthollet (1791)

In the previous chapter, I argued that, unlike most externalities, the spillovers of innovation make important contributions to the general welfare.
Next I will turn to a mechanism that facilitates the generation of these
externalities, arguing that here again the market mechanism generates
general and substantial economic benefits. It must be emphasized that
this entails no claim of anything like optimality.[1] However, I do maintain
that the market systematically leads firms to disseminate their proprietary
innovations voluntarily and energetically, in the process benefiting the
recipients—other firms, inventors, and sometimes even final consumers
who put the novel items to use for their own purposes. Of course, proprietors of intellectual property who permit others to use it, generally do so
in the hope of financial reward. Indeed, the sale of intellectual property,
or permission to use it, is often lucrative for those entrepreneurs who seek
novel uses for the property or novel ways to market it.

There is, then, a substantial class of entrepreneurs who arrange to
transfer new technology and disseminate it to new markets or firms,
in order to advance the recipients' productive activities. These entrepreneurs may deal in inventions that cannot be considered truly novel,
but they also do not engage in humdrum copying of enterprises that
are widely extant and commonplace. Rather, they specialize in recognizing new markets or new uses for an innovation. There are at least
two reasons why this can be considered an innovative step. First, the

very recognition of an appropriate and promising new market is an act of discovery. Second, very often in the process of transfer, intellectual property is adapted to local conditions and needs, and even materially improved.

Technology transfers between producers, among markets, and between one country and another are surprisingly commonplace. They are also critically important for economic progress. For instance, although Japan and the United States are the world's leaders in innovation, as indicated by volume of patenting, both still must import a substantial proportion of the remaining innovations from elsewhere in the world. Indeed, in order to keep pace with other countries, every advanced economy on the planet must obtain from elsewhere the preponderant share of the innovative ideas that it uses.

In addition, like the innovation process itself, a substantial proportion of technology transfers and exchanges has been taken over and routinized by large business firms as a regular business activity and a key part of their pursuit of profit. There are markets in technology licensing, and many business firms have entered into contracts and formal networks that facilitate cooperation, information trading, and licensing, by the network's members, of each other's intellectual property.[2]

This chapter has a number of purposes. First it will indicate more explicitly what induces firms *voluntarily* to make their proprietary technology available to others—even direct horizontal competitors. Second, it will explore the social costs and benefits of such technology transfers, indicating how the market carries them out. Third, the chapter will examine the welfare implications of technology exchange networks. Finally, it will investigate the associated pricing issue: what is a socially desirable fee for the owners of intellectual property to charge those who seek to acquire licenses for its use?

THE KEY DILEMMA: THE TRADE-OFF BETWEEN THE INCENTIVE FOR INNOVATION AND EASY TECHNOLOGY TRANSFER

In addition to the efficiency-income distribution trade-off examined in the previous chapter, there is another significant conflict inherent in any rules that affect the use of intellectual property. It has to do with the trade-off between, on the one hand, the provision of effective incentives for investment of labor and other valuable resources in the difficult and risky activities required for successful innovation and, on the other, facilitation of the rapid dissemination and adoption of new products and processes, while phasing out those that are obsolete. Incentives for innovators' efforts are offered by arrangements that impede their new ideas from being used by others. On the other hand, encouragement of growth via rapid and effective replacement of the obsolete evidently requires rapid *dissemination* of improved techniques and products, as well as their widespread adoption by firms other than the original innovator. However, these two desiderata appear to be in conflict. After all, rapidity and ease of dissemination can threaten innovators' monopolies over the use of their intellectual property and, hence, their reward.

Clearly, then, *both* the abundance of invention and the rapid elimination of obsolete technology play a necessary role in generating substantial growth. However, success in the latter generally can be achieved only at the expense of the former. The more quickly all suppliers' inventions can be made available to a market for use, the smaller the reward that the possessor of the intellectual property in question can hope to obtain. Although these effects are not always recognized, we will see that patent rules throughout the world generally are designed with the aim of promoting both of these apparently conflicting goals.

This chapter will examine a number of such issues that arise in the arena of technology transfer. As is evident from the list below, some of these issues are theoretical, while others are not.

1. How substantial is the voluntary licensing of intellectual property for business usage, and does this activity entail significant licensing of property protected by patent or copyright law to the owners' direct competitors?
2. In a society in which licensing to others by the proprietors of innovative intellectual property rarely is imposed by legal institutions, what induces owners to engage voluntarily in such licensing transactions?
3. When, as happens frequently (as will be shown in this chapter), a number of firms form what is explicitly or implicitly a network for sharing information on intellectual property and its cross-licensing, what are the welfare implications?
4. What are socially appropriate license fees—that is, prices that do not impede competition or damage welfare in other ways—for the use of new and proprietary technology?
5. How do all of these concerns impinge on the dilemma that was just described—the social trade-off between generously compensating those engaged in innovative activity and ease of rapid dissemination of new technology? We will see that the free market has alleviated the problem to a considerable degree.

PRELIMINARY OBSERVATIONS ON THE MARKETING
OF ACCESS TO PROPRIETARY INNOVATIONS

The observations listed next provide the foundations for our examination of the magnitude of voluntary technology dissemination, the types of industries involved, and the reasons why it pays for firms to undertake such activities.

1. A piece of intellectual property—that is, a patented invention—is, in essence, just another input into one or many production processes. However, it is one that temporarily has a single proprietor. In this abstract sense, a particular property is like an electric utility's power transmission facility that other, nearby generating firms would like to access. The owner of a patent, like the owner of the transmission facility, will find it profitable to let others use the property, *but only at a suitable price*. In particular, the provision of access will be profitable if the license fee is more than sufficient to make up for any foregone profit the proprietor would have been able to earn by retaining the input for its exclusive use.

2. Because firms differ in their abilities and in the activities at which they are relatively efficient, some will be better at innovative activity, while others will be superior in the use of inventions as inputs to final-product supply. This can lead to specialization in which inventor firms profit by licensing or selling their inventions to other firms that are more effective users. Clearly, this can contribute to economic efficiency. Indeed, there are entrepreneurs who specialize in seeking out such opportunities and seeing that they are utilized.

3. Because of the public-good[3] attribute of information, it may cost the proprietor of intellectual property virtually nothing to license the property to others. If so, any revenue from selling access to an innovation, unlike the sale of a manufactured item, will constitute a pure addition to the licensor's profit. This is not to say that access is generally costless to the licensee. On the contrary, it may require expensive retraining of staff, acquisition of new equipment, and even some degree of reorganization—all of which can be very expensive. These costs are not borne by the licensor, but such a license is likely to have an opportunity cost, as it allows the licensee take business away from the licensor.

4. As is well known, firms can acquire the essence of intellectual property by industrial espionage, by reverse engineering, or by using available information to create substitutes that differ sufficiently from the original to immunize the imitator from legal countermeasures. Indeed, when an invention is patented, the pertinent technical information becomes public, thus facilitating such "hostile replications." However, what I elsewhere have called "friendly transmission," in which use of the invention is permitted by mutual consent on mutually acceptable terms, normally can be

carried out far more rapidly and at a far lower cost because the owner of the intellectual property facilitates the transfer of information, training of the licensee's personnel, or any number of other strategies. This often makes it worthwhile for a company that wants to use such an invention to agree to pay for access, rather than undertaking a hostile acquisition.

5. In an industry in which technical change is frequent and substantial, delay in putting out a new product or in the adoption of a new process may mean that the product or process will be obsolete before it reaches the market. This is yet another powerful inducement for firms to acquire access by friendly means, which generally are much faster. However, this incentive also implies that, by licensing, the owner of the invention may give up little of the competitive advantage derived from being the first to put the invention to use. If, as the evidence suggests, it often requires something on the order of a year before the licensee can get the licensed invention up and running, the licensor then retains a year without competition in its use of the invention.

6. Contrary to appearances, patents play a crucial role in encouraging the *dissemination* of technology. Rather than denying use of technology to others, the primary role of a patent often is to ensure that the inventor can obtain satisfactory compensation for its use by others. In this way, patents help to internalize the pertinent externalities of innovation by simultaneously encouraging investment in innovative activity *and rapid dissemination of the novel products of that activity*. As we will see, patent laws in many countries are explicitly designed to stimulate both invention and dissemination.

"MERE IMITATION" AS INNOVATIVE ACTIVITY

In the process of voluntary technology transfer just described, many firms are both recipients and producers of the innovative product. This role often is regarded as essentially un-innovative. Yet, as I will argue next, it is critical for the technical progress of both developing economies and the most advanced of industrialized economies.

Predictably, most of the innovation that a relatively small industrial economy can expect to introduce comes not from the country's own R&D activities, but from those of other countries. However, this should not be regarded as a deficiency. In a world in which almost all major technological development takes place in some 25 countries and where technology licensing and trading is increasingly common, it is a tautology that even the average innovating country should expect some 24/25ths of its new technology to come from abroad, if it is to avoid falling significantly behind rival countries.

Here it is important to note that the imitation process is the source of a significant misapprehension: the notion that it has few or none of the attributes of a truly innovative activity. However, this is simply incorrect. History is replete with examples of substantial improvements contributed by imitators. In part, these improvements were elicited by the need to adapt technology to local conditions in the new market: differences in size of a market, in the nature of consumer preferences, in climatic conditions, and in the character of available complementary inputs. Stephenson's Rocket, the pioneering locomotive that made its historic first run in 1829, provides an apt example. In that same year, a locomotive was imported from England into the United States; then, in the following year, Peter Cooper ran his Tom Thumb, a locomotive with three times the traction power of the Rocket. That is, Cooper contributed to the original invention and did not stop with the provision of a mere copy. More recently, the same was true in the widely noted transfer of innovative products, such as television sets and computers, to Japan, where they were not merely replicated, but considerably improved—thereby contributing to both consumer benefit and market competitiveness. Thus, there is nothing inherently inferior about a process of organized imitation of foreign technology. Indeed, as De Camp, a historian specializing in the history of innovation, has observed, "Every invention contains some borrowing and every borrowing some invention" (1990, 20). Moreover, because innovation is important for economic growth, every economically advanced nation can be expected to take part in innovation or to seek permission to use the intellectual property of others. Indeed, those that do not innovate or borrow run the risk of falling behind. Thus, in order to be an effective user of such foreign technology, it is important for a country to ensure that it is both a skilled imitator and an effective innovator.

What Schumpeter described as the act of imitating the work of the original inventor also is characteristically an inventive act in itself, which entails adaptation, improvement, and discovery of new uses. Moreover, subsequent modification of an original invention—typically carried out via routinized procedures—often contributes far more to output and productivity than was yielded directly by the original, breakthrough invention. In chapter 2 of this book, I noted that market forces have led to a division of labor in the innovation process that contributes efficiency by leaving the origination of breakthrough innovations to independent inventors and entrepreneurs, while subsequent developments and improvements of breakthrough inventions are undertaken by large corporations. In order to function, however, this subdivision of innovation-related tasks requires the transfer of technology from small, originating firms to the larger developers of the inventions. This is yet another way in which the transfer of technology contributes critically to the process of innovation and growth in an economy.

TECHNOLOGY MARKETS AND THEIR PREVALENCE

Individual inventors and entrepreneurs have long engaged in selling and licensing their intellectual property, and an active market in such property goes back at least to the decade after the American Civil War.[4] Today, cross-licensing and other means of transferring or exchanging technical and other innovative information on a substantial scale are standard activities in many large enterprises. Arora, Fosfuri, and Gambardella (2001) list a sample of "leading deal makers in markets for technology," which includes companies such as Microsoft, IBM, AT&T, Monsanto, Motorola, Bell South, Daimler-Benz, Eli Lilly, Eastman Kodak, Sprint, Philips Electronics, Siemens, General Motors, Honeywell, Boeing, Fiat, Ford, General Electric, Hitachi, Toshiba, Dow Chemical, Johnson & Johnson, and many others (34–37). The authors report the results of a survey of 133 companies by a British consulting firm, which indicate that 77 percent of the companies studied had licensed technology from others, while 62 percent had licensed technology to others. Nevertheless, they report that "when compared to internal R&D, . . . licensing is a fairly modest activity in terms of budgets involved. The survey estimated that expenditures for licensing technology from others amount to 12 percent, 5 percent and 10 percent of the total R&D budgets of North American, European and Japanese respondents, respectively" (30–31). Arora also estimates that the size of the 2002 market for technology was about $66 billion in North America alone.[5] In light of the preceding argument, it seems surprising that, in the aggregate, R&D licensing remains fairly modest. Perhaps this is because, in addition to licensing R&D, many firms forge explicit, interfirm alliances that mandate cooperation in the creation and improvement of technology and sharing of the resulting new or modified technology.[6]

In sum, for many firms, participation in technology markets is critically important. The sale of access to polypropylene technology constitutes a major activity of the Union Carbide Corporation, for instance, and IBM has signed technology exchange contracts with every major manufacturer of every significant computer part. Indeed, about 20 percent of IBM's total profits are derived from the sale of licenses. Moreover, according to the U.S. National Science Board, between 1991 and 2001 American, European, and Japanese firms arranged some 5,750 strategic technology alliances. The profusion of licensing and interfirm alliances has led to the formation of the Licensing Executives Society, which reports a membership of nearly

10,000 from more than 60 countries. In sum, it is clear that voluntary dissemination is no isolated and unusual phenomenon, although, in the aggregate, it still seems to be fairly modest.

INCENTIVES FOR THE VOLUNTARY AND RAPID DISSEMINATION OF INVENTIONS

Some firms do guard their proprietary technology and strive, with the aid of patents, secrecy, and other means, to prevent other firms—notably rivals—from using their new products and processes.[7] However, this protective stance can be unfortunate for economic progress, as consumers who purchase from other firms are forced to accept obsolete features in the items they buy (Rey and Tirole 1997). Firms that deny each other access to proprietary improvements in their common product can survive by marketing their somewhat differentiated outputs, but each firm's product is rendered inferior, in terms of what is currently possible technologically, by the obsolete features that the firm is forced to retain.

Happily, this is hardly the norm. On the contrary, as noted in the previous section, voluntary licensing of access to proprietary technology is widespread in the economy. The question is why. The primary incentive, of course, is profit. Many firms derive substantial income from the sale of such licenses. The logic is straightforward. Suppose Firm A invents a new widget and expects to make a net profit of X dollars per widget, of the new type that it produces. If rival Firm B licenses its widget technology from Firm A for a fee of Y dollars $(Y > X)$ for each unit of the new widget it is able to sell, then Firm A obviously can be better off letting Firm B do so, even if every widget sold by B means one less sale for A. Of course, Firm B generally will be able to afford such a high fee only if it is a more efficient *producer* of widgets than Firm A—though it may be an inferior inventor. In this way, the price mechanism encourages both licensing and efficient specialization. Inventive activity will be undertaken primarily by the more effective inventor, while production of the resulting innovation will be undertaken predominantly by the more efficient producer. Such unreciprocated licensing does take place; in practice, smaller enterprises that lack the financing and personnel to carry out extensive R&D typically sell licenses to large firms that are in a position to undertake such activities.

There are a number of other incentives for such profitable and voluntary exchanges in the free market. The most straightforward reason, which is most frequently offered by businesspersons, is the very high cost of R&D activity. By entering into a sharing network, this burden can be divided and reduced for each participant. Given the public-good attribute of the resulting information, it is far less expensive (per user) to provide such information to several firms than to supply it to only one.

Risk reduction is another reason for the voluntary exchange of R&D. In any given year, a firm's R&D division may fail to come up with any significant breakthroughs. Firm A, for instance, fears that this will happen to it in a year when its rival, Firm B, achieves a significant breakthrough—and vice versa for Firm B. Since product and process improvement are a matter of life and death in high-tech industries characterized by vigorous oligopolistic competition, technology-sharing agreements serve as effective insurance policies, protecting each participant from such a catastrophe by ensuring that each participant firm has access to the latest technology created by any member of the group.

A further, and less obvious, reason for voluntary R&D dissemination entails the trading of technology because it protects the firms in the technology-sharing network from entry by new competitors. Consider, for example, an industry with 10 firms of identical size—each with similarly staffed and funded R&D divisions. If those 10 firms form a technology-sharing network, each will then have available to it the discoveries of its own R&D establishment, as well as those of nine other firms. Now, suppose an eleventh firm wants to enter the market, but is not invited to join the network. Having only the products of its own R&D division at its disposal, while the other firms each obtain the outputs of 10 R&D establishments, the entrant can find itself at a severe competitive disadvantage.

From the viewpoint of society, the technology-sharing consortium has its pros and cons. Provided that anticompetitive conspiracy is absent, such networks can stimulate innovative effort by helping to internalize the externalities generated by each firm's innovative efforts. That is, such consortiums offer each member firm some compensation for the innovation it has created—the benefits of which otherwise would have gone to other (external) users without reward to the creator. Indeed, if—as frequently is the case in such exchanges—each firm makes compensation payments, based on the value of the innovation in question, to any other member of the network whose innovations are of a market value significantly superior to its own, then all of the firms have a direct incentive to offer the network a menu of the most valuable innovations they can create. Moreover, such networks also tend to be welfare-enhancing, as I will discuss in detail later in this chapter.

However, there are dangers against which the authorities must be vigilant. Such networks can serve as vehicles or as camouflage for anticompetitive behavior. For example, the network's contract discussions could serve as a disguise for price fixing by the network's member firms, thereby eliminating any downward pressure on prices created by competition. Alternatively, the firms can enter into an agreement for mutual restriction of their R&D expenditures, in which each firm knows that if it limits its innovative efforts, it can rely on its rivals to do the same. Or the contracts could be offered in a discriminatory manner that limits the benefits offered to new entrants or denies them access altogether.

Similar perils for the public interest arise in yet another of the reasons for voluntary technology sharing: "patent thickets" and the widespread patent pools that have been formed to deal with the "thicket" problem. The meaning of the term "patent thicket" can be illustrated by a complex piece of equipment, such as a computer. Each component of the computer characteristically is covered by a surprisingly large number of patents—a thicket of patents—many of which are owned by a considerable number of different firms that are likely to be direct competitors in the final-product market. For example, an estimated 90,000-plus patents related to microprocessors were held by more than 10,000 parties in 2002 (U.S. Federal Trade Commission 2003, 9). This puts many of these firms in a legal position that can enable each to bring the manufacturing processes of the others to a halt. The most effective way to prevent the catastrophic consequences this possibility threatens for each firm is the formation of a patent pool, in which each firm makes the use of its patents available to the pool's member firms (and also to outsiders, in order to avoid intervention by antitrust authorities). There are many such pools in the United States, with widely varying membership rules and license fee arrangements, as well as other differences that are not germane here.

The U.S. Department of Justice and the Federal Trade Commission have recognized both the benefits of coordination in this arena and the attendant danger of anticompetitive collusion. In 2000, their jointly issued *Guidelines for the Licensing of Intellectual Property* explicitly discussed the substantial pro-competitive benefits of licensing, which include the coordination of research efforts and trading of proprietary technology. The fact that licensing has become sufficiently important to merit such attention by the antitrust agencies is, in itself, significant.

HISTORICAL ANTECEDENTS: PATENTS AS INSTRUMENTS FOR DISSEMINATING INTELLECTUAL PROPERTY

As already noted, despite the common misunderstanding of patents as an institution designed to inhibit technology transfer, the opposite is closer to the truth. This is indicated by the universal disclosure requirement that forces the patent applicant or recipient to make all of an invention's relevant technical information public. Indeed, as I stressed earlier in this chapter, from its very beginning, the patent was designed primarily for the purpose of eliciting transfer. Indeed, when it was originated, the patent's primary role was to *encourage* intercountry technology transfer via larceny from a foreign source. It is often reported that patents were introduced in the fifteenth century in Renaissance Italy. However, the birth of patents actually seems to have occurred in England at least as early as 1331, when John Kemp, a Flemish weaver, was given a patent[8] monopoly to pursue his trade in England (North and Thomas 1973, 1470). As is the case today, a patent granted a monopoly over production and sale of an item to the recipient(s) for a specified period. Initially, however, patents were granted *not to the creator or inventor of the IP at issue, but to a foreign producer who could steal the idea from his own country and export its use to England.* A French workman who had mastered a trade initially carried out only in France, for instance, would be offered a patent as an incentive to come to England and set up a competing trade there. Thus, early patent use was not designed to offer protection to *creators* of IP, but instead, functioned as an incentive for transferring the IP. As North and Thomas (1973) note, this use of patents was hardly rare:

> This policy of encouraging foreigners to bring in new innovations from the continent was extended to many other areas [aside from weaving]; mining, metal working, silk manufacturing, ribbon weaving, etc. Of the fifty-five grants of monopoly privilege made under Elizabeth, twenty-one were issued to aliens or naturalized subjects. These included privileges for making such products as soap, machines for dredging and draining land, ovens and furnaces, oils, leather, grinding machines, salt, glass, drinking glasses, force pumps for raising water, and writing paper; as well as for introducing processes for tempering iron, milling corn, extracting oil from rape seed and dressing, drying and calendaring cloth. (153–54)

Patents—in the modern sense—were adopted into English law in the Statute of Monopolies of 1626, as a way of limiting the monarch's misuse of patents to reward favorite subjects or for other purposes not in keeping with the requirements of effective intellectual property management.[9]

THE WELFARE IMPLICATIONS OF TECHNOLOGY-SHARING ALLIANCES

A technology-sharing arrangement among patent-holding firms can generate welfare benefits by permitting wider and more rapid use of innovations—as long as the sharing of information does not undercut the incentive for R&D investment or lead horizontal competitors to engage in monopolistic behavior. For example, colluding competitors could agree to cut their expenditures on innovation to save effort and expense, as already noted.[10] To investigate some possible benefits of such technology sharing, a mathematical model will be used to demonstrate that information-sharing networks tend to *increase* the profit-maximizing oligopolist's spending on innovation, if the innovations of a network's firms are complementary.[11] Moreover, the cost savings that network membership entails actually increase the profit-maximizing output per firm.

Before presenting the first two propositions of my central result, Propositions 6.1 and 6.2, I should emphasize that neither of them implies that a technology network yields a socially optimal outlay on innovation by the firm. It still remains true that the externalities of innovation can lead to outlays that generally are not optimal, at least in the efficiency sense of the term. I will argue here only that the technology network tends to move matters in the right direction. The network internalizes part of the externality by enabling innovating Firm A to obtain a substantial reward for its own innovation effort, in the form of cheaper and quicker access to the innovations of other enterprises that are beneficiaries of its technology. Specifically, we have the following proposition:

PROPOSITION 6.1.[12] If a network has a fixed number of profit-maximizing firms that supply a single product and invest in cost-reducing R&D, and if each firm in the network behaves like a "Cournot oligopolist"—i.e., there is complementarity among the research outputs of the technology-sharing firms, then an increase in the number of network members will increase each member's outlay on innovation, as well as its output of the final product. This, in turn, will shift each member firm's total cost function downward.

Here I assume that the number of firms in the industry is expected by each firm to be fixed, so that an increase in $n + 1$, the number of network members, is expected to entail an equal reduction in the number of non-members. The Cournot assumption means that each firm will expect the total output of the remainder of the industry to be unaffected by a change in n. For convenience, n will be treated (unrealistically) as a continuous variable. It is also important to note that the variables in the model refer to *expected values*, so that all of the calculations become *ex ante* in character.

The same results hold if the inventions are very weak substitutes, so that the rate at which costs are reduced when an additional member joins the consortium is positive, but relatively small. Thus, we also can prove, analogously, the following:

PROPOSITION 6.2.[13] Under the assumptions of Proposition 6.1, if each network member expects every other member to make exactly the same decisions that it does,[14] any increase in n, the number of firms that share the results of each other's R&D, will shift each firm's production cost curve downward. When n rises,[15] *each* information-sharing firm will increase its output. If the marginal-cost-reducing returns to x, the firm's investment in R&D, are increased by the availability of more technical information from other network members (complementarity in their innovations), a rise in n will increase the firm's R&D outlays.

It is important to observe that the results of Propositions 6.1 and 6.2 also must apply to the *formation* of a new technology network. This follows because the decision of n firms to create a technology-sharing network can be interpreted simply as an increase in the number of its members from zero to n—and the result follows directly. Thus, the creation of a new technology-sharing network can increase spending on innovation, increase output, and reduce cost.

TOWARD WELFARE OPTIMALITY IN LICENSE FEES

Even among the members of a technology-sharing network, licenses normally are not given without charge. Rather, a price is set for permission to use a firm's intellectual property. This immediately raises the question: what is the magnitude of that price that best serves the public interest? Lawyers and courts usually employ a standard asserting that a license fee should satisfy what is referred to as a RAND—reasonable and nondiscriminatory—fee criterion. However, even lawyers admit that RAND-compatible license fees are not well defined and that the rule, therefore, is hardly operational.

I will argue here that there is only one license fee formula that actually satisfies the requirement that precludes discrimination among licensees. Moreover, I will show that this fee provides the appropriate incentive for voluntary licensing and promises to be beneficial to both the licensor and the licensee. It does so by ensuring that licensees can obtain whatever profits are made possible by any superiority their firms may possess in efficiency in utilizing the intellectual property in question, while simultaneously ensuring that the license fee provides the licensor with at least as much profit as could be obtained through refusal to license. Of course, the latter conclusion means that the license fee rule preserves for the licensor any unwarranted supercompetitive profit it could obtain by exercising monopoly power. I will argue, however, that the proper cure for that problem should be sought by measures circumscribing such unwarranted power in the first place—rather than by distorting the efficient licensing fee. If supplemented by the prevention of monopoly power, the fee should be set at the cost that would emerge in a perfectly competitive market for access to the intellectual property in question—that is, if there were a large multiplicity of suppliers of the required license. Finally, I will argue that license fees that follow the formula provided below help to reconcile the basic growth dilemma of innovative activity—the conflict between availability of incentives for the inventive activity and those that encourage rapid dissemination of its results. For, by making dissemination profitable, the intellectual property holder can be rewarded without denying others access to the property in question.

For these purposes, I will employ a formula[16] derived from the literature on economic regulation, which provides substance to the commonly advocated RAND criterion. This formula rests on a license-fee-determining principle called the efficient component-pricing rule (ECPR), which I will show to be both necessary and sufficient for determining a license fee that is competitively neutral and, therefore, reasonable and nondiscriminatory. As will be indicated next, the prices determined by the rule also possess significant efficiency properties. These properties are relevant to the allocation of the innovation's use among competing producers of final products, as well as to the division among firms of the task of creating the technology in question and using it to make final products.

When an innovation has been offered for license, there generally will be firms that consider using it as an input to produce final outputs similar to those of the patent holder. The question is, once given a license to use that intellectual property, what share of that final output should be produced by each of these firms? Or, if that output will be produced by a single firm only, which of the firms should get the job? License fees will influence that allocation, and, consequently, the efficiency of the industry's activities obviously will be affected.

In particular, the royalty rate will affect innovators' and licensees' allocation of the relevant tasks. The lower the fee, which is commonly expressed as a percentage of the price of the final innovation-using product, the more of the final product we can expect the licensees to supply, as a reduction of the license fee cuts the licensees' relative production cost. Similarly, if license fees are negotiated separately with each licensee, the allocation of final output production among those firms will be affected. In this case, a socially optimal set of fees will be one that permits efficient allocation of the supply of the final product among the competing providers. Below we will see that a price that meets this efficiency requirement will yield the formula proposed here as a method of providing substance to the RAND criterion. Moreover, I will argue that this is the only license fee that does so.

This efficiency problem is most difficult when the holder of a patent or other intellectual property (IP) also is the supplier of some or all of the final products that the invention is used to manufacture. In this instance, the IP holder competes directly with other suppliers of identical or close-substitute final products. A license fee that is too high will handicap the IP holder's more efficient competitors, whereas, a fee that is too low confers a competitive disadvantage to the IP owner—even if that firm is the more efficient supplier.[17] The issue, then, is whether or not a pricing rule exists that prevents either type of inefficiency. Without such a rule, the social costs of the use of inventions can increase by a substantial margin.

THE ECPR FORMULA FOR ACCESS PRICING

The pricing principle that I propose here is referred to as the *efficient component-pricing rule* (ECPR), or the *parity principle*. To explain this principle, let us assume that the industry contains a number of firms that manufacture the same product. One of these firms creates an invention that serves as an input to the manufacture of the final product. This invention is so good that no firm denied its use will be able to survive. According to the ECPR principle, the price the IP-holder firm should charge its rivals for the use of its innovation is the same price the firm implicitly charges itself for its use of the IP in the manufacture of its own final product—minus the additional costs of the other inputs that go into the patent-holding firm's final product. The parity principle tells us that this is the price that must be charged to its final-product competitors by the exclusive owner of any patented input, if its fee is not to be discriminatory. Determining the price that the IP holder charges itself is the key problem, as no such price is reported openly and, even if it were, its accuracy hardly would be trusted by others.

The logic of the proof—that the parity-pricing formulas (given below) satisfy the requirement that the IP owner charges others the same amount it implicitly charges itself—is not difficult to understand. We need a reasonably straightforward test to ensure that the fees are not discriminatory prices—that is, to determine whether or not the licensor is charging others prices such that the resulting costs to all the users are the same. If the IP owner also uses the innovation in the same way as its rivals, the cost of that use by the IP-owning firm itself also must be the same. The following observation provides that test. If (and only if) two different producers of widgets, Firm A and Firm B, pay the same license fee for the technology they employ, but Firm A's other costs per widget are $6 higher than those of Firm B, which just breaks even if it sells widgets at a price of $20, then

115

Firm A will loose money if it charges less than $26 per widget. If the difference between the prices at which the two firms can afford to sell a unit of the final product is exactly equal to the difference between the costs of the remaining inputs they require to provide that final product, then both firms must be paying the same price for use of the invention. Accordingly, the invention's price cannot be discriminatory between the two firms. So if Firm A is both the owner and a user of a licensed invention, it will sell use of the IP to itself at the same price that it sells that input to a rival final-product provider, if and only if, at that input price, the rival can afford to sell the final product at a price that differs from the IP holder's by precisely the amount that the rival's remaining-input cost differs from the IP owner's. If the competitor's remaining-input costs are X cents lower per unit of final product output than the IP owner's, then both are paying the same price for use of the IP—if the rival can afford to provide the final product exactly X cents more cheaply than the IP owner can.

All of this can be described formally, using explicit formulas[18] to derive an efficient license fee. Here, we use the following notation:

$P_{f,i}$ is the IP owner's, I's, given price per unit of final product.
$minP_{f,c}$ is the competitor's, C's, minimum viable price of final product.
P_i is the price charged for a license to use the IP, per unit of final product.
$IC_{r,i}$ is the incremental cost to the IP owner of the remaining final-product inputs, per unit of final product.
$IC_{r,c}$ is the corresponding figure for the competitor.
IC_i is the incremental cost to the IP owner for use of the IP by itself or by others.

As I will demonstrate in the appendix to this chapter, the efficient component-pricing rule requires that the licensing price satisfy either—and, hence, both—of two equivalent rules. The first is expressed in the formula

(6.1) $$P_i = P_{f,i} - IC_{r,i}.^{19}$$

Alternatively, and equivalently (as will be shown), the ECPR price of the bottleneck input must satisfy

(6.2) $\quad P_i = IC_i +$ the IP owner's final-product profit per unit.

Equation (6.1) tells us that ECPR establishes a tight link between the price, $P_{f,i}$, that the IP-owning firm charges for its final product and the price, P_i, that it charges its rivals for the license to use the relevant IP. If incremental production costs do not change, efficiency requires that an increase in one of these prices must be matched, dollar for dollar, by an increase in the other. In addition, equation (6.2) tells us that the efficient price of the license is the direct incremental cost to the owner of the IP resulting from other firms' use of the invention, plus the associated opportunity cost. This opportunity cost is the patent holder's loss of profit due to the IP being licensed to a rival, which can take final product business away from the licensor. Thus, the second form of ECPR asserts that the price of the license should equal any direct incremental cost incurred in supplying it to a competitor, plus any incremental opportunity cost incurred as a result of that transaction.[20] Standard economic analysis tells us that this is a proper way to set the price—that is, the price of a license should equal marginal (incremental) cost, including marginal (incremental) opportunity cost.[21] This last observation confirms that the ECPR price—because it equals the incremental direct cost, plus the incremental opportunity cost—is the price that would prevail if the market for the licenses in question were, in fact, competitive. In this case, the task is to prove the following:

PROPOSITION 6.3: The "Level Playing Field" Theorem. The parity price for use of a bottleneck input, such as a legally protected innovation is both necessary and sufficient in order for the "playing field" to be level. This means that the maximum difference between the remunerative prices of the perfect-substitute final products of the IP owner, I, and its final product competitor, C, is exactly equal to the difference in the firms' remaining incremental costs (other than the license fees).

The parity-pricing formula (6.2) completes the proof that parity pricing of an IP license is a necessary and sufficient condition for a competitively neutral license fee, as called for by a RAND commitment. Moreover, it follows that ECPR is necessary for economic efficiency in the provision of a final product by competing suppliers. If this rule is violated, a less efficient supplier of the remaining inputs can win the competition for the business of supplying those inputs—instead of the task going to a more efficient rival. That is, violation of the ECPR rules permits a less efficient supplier of the final product to undercut more efficient competitors. It follows that, at the ECPR price for the task of producing the final product, market forces will allocate the task of supply to the most efficient producers—whether or not the provider of the innovation input is among them. This proof can be extended to cases with three or more competing firms.

It is important to note that the ECPR formula (6.1) does not preclude discriminatory pricing of a final product that uses the pertinent IP as an input. Thus, the formula constitutes no threat to a meritorious discriminatory regime, such as one that offers reduced prices to the indigent—although it is equally inoffensive to discriminatory prices that are less desirable.

More remarkably, ECPR pricing makes it possible for any efficient entrant to compete in every segment of the pertinent market, whether or not its customers are the recipients of a subsidy. To demonstrate this, we note that ECPR requires strict compliance with its basic formula—final product by final product and *from one sale of the final product to another*. In particular, this requires the price charged by the IP owner to vary with the terms on which each unit of the final product is sold by that firm. Specifically, suppose the license fee is X dollars per unit of a relevant final product sold, wherever the price of the final product sold by the innovation owner is $50 per unit. Then, ECPR requires the license fee to fall to $X - \$4$ on any final product sales the licensor makes at a unit price of $46. This is precisely what the ECPR competitive neutrality formula, given by equation (6.1), tells us. All other factors being equal, then, the license fee to a final product competitor must vary from one use of the IP to another by precisely the amounts that the licensor's corresponding final product prices vary. Similarly, if two different final products have equal incremental costs, but the price the IP owner charges for one of the products is $0.2 more than the price of the other, the competitively neutral license fee for the two uses also must differ by exactly $0.2.[22] That is, *any discrimination in the IP owner's final product prices must be mirrored precisely in its IP license fees*, as formula (6.1) implies. As a result, a competitor will earn exactly the same markup on the sale of the final product—whether it is sold to customers who are charged specially high prices or to buyers who face prices that are particularly low. Thus, the competitor who can operate profitably in any one segment of its market when paying the ECPR license fee also can operate with the same profit per sale in *every other* market segment.

In sum, ECPR license fees offer entrants and other rivals of the bottleneck owner the same ability to compete in each and every market in which the IP owner offers products. Unless their entry or survival is threatened by the inefficiency of their *own* operations, these competitors will not find themselves excluded from any branch of the regulated industry. In particular, they will not be driven to seek markets or market segments that offer special "cream skimming" (overpricing) opportunities, as all of the IP owner's outputs promise the same rates of return, under ECPR, to equally efficient entrants.

ECPR AS "INDIFFERENCE PRINCIPLE" AND ITS ROLE IN VOLUNTARY LICENSING

The parity-pricing rule sets a price that benefits the patent holder by selecting the license fee that is just sufficient to recover the incremental opportunity costs resulting from licensing an invention to rival final-product suppliers.

This is, in other words, the price that just makes up for the profit reduction caused by the enhanced competition from the licensee. As a consequence, the patent-holder firm is (at least) as well off financially if some, or all, sales are made by rival suppliers of the final product, who pay the ECPR license fee for use of the requisite IP. For this reason, ECPR sometimes is called the "principle of indifference." That is, ECPR sets the royalty rate at the level that makes the innovator firm, at worst, indifferent to producing the IP-using final product itself or by licensing production of the same quantity of final product to a rival firm. Indeed, whenever a rival final-product producer is more efficient than the IP owner, the latter is protected from loss by licensing at the parity price—and even stands to gain by licensing if, as a result of the licensee's superior efficiency, sales of the final product increase with each unit sale by the licensee adding the same fee that covers per-unit opportunity cost to the licensor. In this way, the IP owner never will lose out to a rival under an ECPR license fee. For if licensees are neither more nor less efficient than the IP proprietor, the latter will earn the same—whether or not it licenses the input. Alternatively, if no prospective licensee is as efficient as the IP owner, no rival will be able to afford the license, as the public interest requires, thereby leaving final product supply exclusively to its most efficient provider, the IP owner. Thus, we conclude that an ECPR price should not impede voluntary dissemination to efficient users by a rational owner of intellectual property.

ECPR AND PRICING OF INPUTS IN UNREGULATED COMPETITIVE MARKETS

For the reasons described above, it is easy to see that access to intellectual property would be priced at the ECPR level in an unregulated and effectively competitive market. Accordingly, the rule follows the requirements of the competitive market model for regulation and antitrust activity. To understand this, assume that the pertinent licensing market is competitive because it offers a considerable number of alternative intellectual property inputs that are good substitutes for one another and entail similar costs. However, even in these circumstances, no firm owning such IP would be willing to offer access to it to anyone, if it is in a competitive market and if the price does not compensate the proprietor fully for any profit she foregoes as a result of the transaction. In other words, the license fee in an effectively competitive market never will be set below the ECPR level. Nor will it ever be significantly higher than ECPR. This is because, in this hypothetical competitive market, rival owners of substitute intellectual property will find it profitable to license it at any price that is even an iota above the ECPR level, since that price still will exceed the amount that leaves them indifferent to undertaking the transaction or refusing to do so. Competition from this source, then, automatically will drive the license fee down (at least, approximately) to the ECPR level, as asserted. Thus, the correspondence of the ECPR price and the price of a license to make use of proprietary technology in a hypothetically competitive market provides further evidence of the efficiency properties of the parity prices.

ECPR DOES NOT CURB MONOPOLY POWER

It is important to note a frequent criticism of ECPR: the claim, which has considerable validity, that parity pricing preserves any monopoly profits that may be present and extends their reach from the exploited, final consumer to the licensee user of the pertinent input. This argument is straightforward. ECPR requires input pricing to include any opportunity cost that the licensor incurs, if the licensee is enabled by the licensing transaction to take business away from the input owner. If the owner has any monopoly power, however, and uses it to extract monopoly profits from its own sales of final product, then any loss of such a sale must entail forgoing the monopoly profit on that sale. Since the opportunity cost component of the parity price "makes the input owner whole," by restoring any profits foregone in the transaction, the parity price will restore any monopoly-profit component of the final product's price that the competition of the licensee otherwise might have eliminated.

The defenders of ECPR recognize that this criticism is just and have stated repeatedly that legitimate use of ECPR must take it into account. However, many take the position that modification of input license fees is not the proper way to deal with the problem. Indeed, this follows from the level-playing-field theorem, which tells us that any deviation from the parity price is an invitation to inefficiency in supply—that is, in the firm that the market will select for the role of final-product supplier. The monopoly profit problem is indeed real, but its source can be found in whatever monopoly power exists in the final-product market and the resulting excessive prices of the final products, rather than in the prices of input-use licenses. Thus, in order for ECPR to serve the public interest, ideally it must be included in a regulatory package that also contains measures that eliminate the monopoly profits on the final product by mandating price ceilings or enacting other rules that constrain the setting of final-product prices. Such a package is the surest way to protect consumers from exploitation, prevent the allocative inefficiencies that monopoly prices introduce, and ensure efficiency in the roles assigned to licensors and licensees. We can conclude, then, that ECPR alone is an ineffective means of eliminating monopoly profits. Bear in mind, however, that this surely is not the purpose for which the instrument was designed. Indeed, the rule could just as easily be criticized for its inability to cure venereal disease or eliminate water pollution.

In the case of copyrights and patents, the answer to the criticism that ECPR preserves monopoly profits is even more direct. After all, a central purpose of these instruments is to ensure the opportunity for individuals, such as composers and inventors, who are successful in their creative endeavors to earn appropriate incentive rewards, via payments that legally are permitted to exceed what is required for mere recovery of the costs incurred in the creative process. Accordingly, in the United States, the courts have held that the incomes generated by patents or copyrights cannot automatically be deemed to entail monopoly earnings. What some have identified as monopoly profits can be interpreted simply as socially desirable incentives for innovation, which are protected by patents and copyright laws in cases where the source of the earnings is novel intellectual property classified as an "innovation." Moreover, in an earlier chapter, we showed that the expected earnings from inventive activity, in reality, are often less than enough to yield zero economic profits over the economic lifetime of the invention. Thus, even if some innovator earnings are considered to entail a monopoly earnings component, they surely constitute virtue—rather than vice. If ECPR preserves these earnings when patented or copyright-protected materials are used as inputs, generally there is no reason to deplore this result.

ECPR: WHERE DOWNSTREAM COMPETITORS PROVIDE IMPERFECT SUBSTITUTES

In discussing the attributes of ECPR, we have assumed that a licensor's downstream rivals supply products that are perfect substitutes for those produced by the licensor itself. This leads to the presumption that every x units of increased sales by a rival will reduce the licensor's quantity of final-product sales by precisely x units. In turn, this underlies the mathematically derived conclusion that the ECPR price precisely covers the licensor's opportunity cost resulting from licensing—that is, the profit that the licensor foregoes when she allows a rival to use her firm's IP to produce a competing product.

What if, however, a rival's product is an *imperfect* substitute for the IP owner's final product—so that an x-unit expansion of final product sales by the licensee only cuts the licensor's sales by, say, $0.6x$? In this instance, the opportunity cost incurred in the licensing process also would be correspondingly lower—only some 60 percent of the profit earned by the licensor on sales of x units. In turn, competitive neutrality would require the license fee to be reduced similarly. Here the license fee should be set according to equation (6.2), where the opportunity-cost component is 40 percent lower than the IP owner's profit per unit of final-product output.[23] This lower fee still provides compensation that is sufficient to insure that permitting others to use its IP to produce competing final goods will not reduce the licensor's earnings.[24] Moreover, at a certain point, administrative concerns, as well as the legal principles of relevant market definition, suggest that a sufficiently imperfect substitute can be deemed no competition at all—thus, relieving the IP holder of RAND nondiscrimination obligations for that particular use.

The theoretical optimality properties noted above still hold for our modified ECPR rule. For the license fee just described is precisely the price that would be charged in a perfectly competitive market for licenses, in which a large number of imperfectly substitutable IP inputs compete for licensee customers. That is, the price of a license would be exactly equal to any incremental cost entailed in the provision of the license, plus any *actual* opportunity cost entailed in granting it.[25] Therefore, the calculation of the ECPR license fee should be modified in the manner just described. The result is a generalized ECPR fee that is more difficult to calculate and monitor, but appears to offer all of the advantages of ECPR described in this chapter.

CONCLUDING COMMENT: HOW THE MARKET MECHANISM ALLEVIATES THE CONFLICT BETWEEN EASY DISSEMINATION AND INNOVATORS' REWARDS

I have just argued that ECPR mimics the prices of inputs, such as intellectual property, that would emerge in a fully competitive market, where the license fee would be set to cover the direct marginal cost of providing the input, plus any marginal opportunity cost entailed in its provision by the IP owner to the licensee. For all practical purposes, this is identical to the parity-pricing formula.[26] Since the public interest is served by competitive market pricing, the same also must be true of parity pricing.

In this chapter, we have seen arguments suggesting that the ECPR license fees are consistent with the interests of all immediately affected parties. The process entailed in this story can be interpreted as one in which the patent or copyright owner, in effect, reaches a "make or buy" decision on the final-product inputs not covered by copyright. As usual, this is because it pays the IP-owning firm to buy, rather than make, those other inputs if—and only if—their seller is the more efficient supplier, and so provides the inputs for less than it would cost the patent-holding firm to make the inputs itself. In effect, ECPR gives the task of supplying those remaining inputs to the licensee only if it is the more efficient provider.

The other main point that emerges from this discussion is that, *with the aid of the patent system and innovative entrepreneurs*, the market mechanism has introduced powerful incentives for rapid dissemination of novel products and processes, without creating a major disincentive for investment in the innovation process. This is surely no minor contribution to technical progress and growth. For while the free market has not eliminated the conflict between encouraging innovative effort and facilitating dissemination, it has adopted practices that ameliorate the problem to a considerable degree. These practices include the creation of technology markets, in which inventors willingly offer the use of their intellectual property to others, in return for a *quid pro quo* that rewards inventors and their entrepreneur partners, while actually facilitating and speeding the use of the intellectual property by others. Under such an arrangement, society effectively has it "both ways"—technology imitation benefits both the imitator and the inventor and, through the resulting stimulus for growth, also provides a valuable benefit to society.[27] Once again, this attribute markedly distinguishes dynamic welfare theory from its standard stationary variant.

APPENDIX

PROOFS OF PROPOSITIONS 6.1, 6.2, AND 6.3

PROOF OF PROPOSITION 6.1

Let the profit function of a typical network member (Firm 1) be given by

(A6.1) $$\pi = R(y, Y) - f[x + \alpha X(n)]C(y) - x,$$

where $R(.)$ is Firm 1's total revenue, $C(.)$ is Firm 1's total non-R&D cost in period zero, y is Firm 1's final-product output per period, and Y is the total output of all other firms in the industry, which Cournot assumes to be constant. The variable, x, is the innovation expenditure of Firm 1, $X(n)$ is the sum of the expenditures on innovation of the n other members of the network, α is a constant, $(0 < \alpha < 1)$, representing the cost of "friendly" technology transfer, and D is the Jacobian determinant of the derivatives of π.

Then, by assumption, we expect

(A6.2) $$R_y \equiv \frac{\partial R}{\partial y} > 0, \ f_x < 0, \ f_n < 0, \ \text{and} \ C_y > 0.$$

By the second-order conditions,

(A6.3) $$D > 0, \ \pi_{yy} < 0, \ \pi_{xx} < 0.$$

Finally, we define complementarity between x and $X(n)$, where $dX/dn > 0$, as

(A6.4) $$f_{xn} < 0$$

that is, a rise in $X(n)$ increases the marginal cost saving yielded by a rise in x, which represents Firm 1's expenditure on innovation.

Therefore, the first-order maximization conditions for equation (A6.1) are

(A6.5) $$\pi_y = R_y - fC_y = 0, \ \pi_x = -f_x C - 1 = 0.$$

Setting the total differential of each of these equal to zero, in order to determine what changes in y and x are needed to restore equilibrium after an exogenous change in n, we obtain

(A6.6a) $$d\pi_y = \pi_{yy} dy - f_x C_y dx - f_n C_y dn = 0$$

(A6.6b) $$d\pi_x = -f_x C_y dy + \pi_{xx} dx - f_{xn} C dn = 0.$$

Thus,

(A6.7a) $$\frac{\partial y}{\partial n} = \frac{(f_n C_y \pi_{xx} + f_{xn} C f_x C_y)}{D} \text{ and}$$

(A6.7b) $$\frac{\partial x}{\partial n} = \frac{(f_x C_y^2 f_n + \pi_{yy} f_{xn} C)}{D}.$$

By equations (A6.2), (A6.3), and (A6.4), it follows directly that equations (A6.7a) and (A6.7b) are both positive.

Moreover, the effect of a rise in n on Firm 1's total production cost for a given volume of output, y, is

(A6.8) $$\frac{dfC}{dn} = Cf_n + Cf_x \frac{\partial x}{\partial n} < 0.$$

PROOF OF PROPOSITION 6.2

For simplicity, rewrite the profit function of a member of the technology network as

(A6.9) $$\pi = R(y) - f(z)C(y) - \frac{z}{n}, \ C' > 0, f' < 0,$$

where $z = nx$ is the total outlay on R&D by all of the members of the network, combined. In turn, differentiating with respect to z and y, we have the first-order maximum conditions,

$$(A6.10) \qquad -f'C - \frac{1}{n} = 0, \quad R' - fC' = 0.$$

Equating to zero the total differential of the LHS of each equation yields

$$(A6.11a) \qquad \pi_{zz}dz - f'C'dy = \frac{-dn}{n^2}$$

$$(A6.11b) \qquad -f'C'dz + \pi_{yy}dy = 0.$$

We now obtain our comparative-statics results directly, using inequalities corresponding to equations (A6.2), (A6.3), and (A6.4):

$$(A6.12) \qquad \frac{dz}{dn} = \frac{-\pi_{yy}}{n^2 D} > 0, \quad \frac{dy}{dn} = \frac{-f'C'}{n^2 D} > 0.$$

Recalling that C is the initial total cost function for the firm and that f is the function indicating the proportion by which that cost is reduced by invention, we also have $\partial fC/\partial n = (\partial fC/\partial z)(\partial z/\partial n) = f'C\partial z/\partial n < 0$, so that the firm's production cost, fC, is, *ceteris paribus*, a decreasing function of n. We can complete our proof by substituting $x = z/n$ in equation (A6.9) and then, by repeating all of the preceding steps, can obtain the result that $\partial x/\partial n > 0$, iff f'' is negative, zero, or positive and sufficiently small. This can be interpreted to mean that the innovations are complementary, independent, or very mild substitutes. That is, in all such cases, technological information exchange actually will stimulate each firm's outlays on innovation.

The result that, under the premises of either Proposition 6.1 or Proposition 6.2, an expansion in the number of members of the network reduces production cost is not, by itself, conclusive evidence that efficiency is thereby increased. For, with a given y, it is still conceivable that spending on R&D will increase by more than the cut in production cost. When n increases, if the resulting rise in the firm's innovation outlay, x, does not exceed the reduction in its cost contributed by access to the technology of the new network member(s), this, obviously, will not happen. However, if a larger value of x were selected voluntarily by the firms, this presumably would indicate that the yield of the incremental R&D outlay more than covers this enhanced expenditure. Certainly, this must be true if the markets are perfectly competitive or contestable, and there is at least a presumption that the same conclusion holds in a considerably broader range of market conditions. This demonstrates that an increase in the number of members of the network presumably will be welfare increasing.

PROOF OF PROPOSITION 6.3

As noted earlier in this chapter, we use the following notation:

$P_{f,i}$ is the IP owner's, I's, given price per unit of final product.

$minP_{f,c}$ is the competitor's, C's, minimum viable price of final product.

P_i is the price charged for a license to use the IP, per unit of final product.

$IC_{r,i}$ is the incremental cost to the IP owner of the remaining final-product inputs, per unit of final product.

$IC_{r,c}$ is the corresponding figure for the competitor.

IC_i is the incremental cost to the IP owner for use of the IP by itself or by others.

As asserted in the text, I will demonstrate here that the efficient component-pricing rule (ECPR) requires that the licensing price satisfy either—and, hence, both—of two equivalent rules. The first is expressed in the formula,

(A6.13)
$$P_i = P_{f,i} - IC_{r,i} .$$

Alternatively, and equivalently (as will be shown), the ECPR price of the bottleneck input must satisfy

(A6.14) $P_i = IC_i +$ the IP owner's final-product profit per unit.

As asserted in Proposition 6.3, "The parity price for use of a bottleneck input, such as a legally protected innovation, as given by (A6.13) or (A6.14), is both necessary and sufficient in order for the 'playing field' to be level."

The level playing field is defined by

(A6.15)
$$\min P_{f,c} - P_{f,i} = IC_{r,c} - IC_{r,i} ,$$

where $minP_{f,c}$ is the lowest compensatory price the competitor can afford to charge for the final product. Equation (A6.15) requires that this minimal competitor price should differ from the patent owner's price by exactly the amount—positive or negative—by which the competitor's remaining costs differ from the IP owner's. The lowest price that is financially viable for the competitor is given by

(A6.16)
$$\min P_{f,c} = P_i + IC_{r,c} .$$

That is, the competitor's price must cover the IP licensing cost, plus the remaining cost of supplying the final product—including the cost of the required capital, made up of depreciation and normal competitive profit. In comparing the two equations, we see that the level playing field condition (A6.15) will be satisfied if and only if

(A6.17) $$P_i = P_{f,i} - IC_{r,i}\ .$$

This is the parity-pricing formula (A6.13), and we see that it is both necessary and sufficient for a level playing field. Q.E.D.[28]

The parity-pricing formula (A6.17) is also identical to the opportunity-cost variant of the rule, (A6.14), since, by definition,

(A6.18) $\quad P_{f,i} = IC_i + IC_{r,i} + I$'s profit per unit of final-product,

or, by equation (A6.17),

(A6.19) $\quad P_i = P_{f,i} - IC_{r,i} = IC_i + I$'s profit per unit of final-product. Q.E.D.

The Entrepreneur and the Beneficial Externalities of Creative Destruction

The bourgeoisie cannot exist without constantly revolutionizing the instruments of production . . . [A]ll fixed fast-frozen relations are swept away, all new-formed ones become antiquated before they can ossify.

—Karl Marx and Friedrich Engels,
Manifesto of the Communist Party (1976, 487)

The process necessarily revolutionizes the economic structure from within, incessantly destroying the old one, incessantly creating a new one. This process of creative destruction is the essential fact about capitalism.

—Joseph Schumpeter, *Capitalism,
Socialism and Democracy* (1947, 83)

We have so far focused on the role of the innovative entrepreneur in the introduction of novel products and processes into the economy and the resulting stimulus of economic growth. We have also discussed the costs and benefits of the manner in which this process is carried out by large firms and small start-ups, alike. There is, however, another component of the welfare consequences of the innovation process that deserves considerable attention: the replacement of products and processes that innovative activity renders obsolete. The question is whether or not the older technology still could have had a useful life, and whether its replacement occurs too soon or, alternatively, whether society would have benefited if it had occurred even earlier. In this chapter, I will argue that such replacement often takes longer than might be expected, with the old items continuing to operate alongside the new for some considerable time. Second, it will be noted that the owners of the intellectual property for the older product are often not the proprietors of the new technology's IP. Hence, the latter may force abandonment of the earlier models prematurely, at cost to society, because the owners of the new IP have little concern about the resulting losses to the proprietors of the old. However, it is important to recall that there are other impediments to innovative activity—notably, the large share of the benefits that go to others, which tend to hold back innovative activity, keeping it below the optimal level for society. Because the phenomena discussed in this chapter drive matters in the other direction, the net result may be a gain to the general welfare. However, the incentives for the rapid dissemination of new technology that were discussed in the previous chapter may help to offset this problem by offering the owners of those products and processes prematurely displaced by the innovation process easier and quicker access to new products and processes.

Schumpeter's felicitous term, "creative destruction," is exceptionally useful because it offers both a clear message and stimulating ambiguity. Its clear message is the fact that innovation and growth force obsolete technology to be swept away without hesitation or remorse. Marx and Engels's earlier discussion of the macroeconomics of industrial growth in the *Manifesto of the Communist Party* introduced this argument:

> The bourgeoisie . . . has put an end to all feudal, patriarchal, idyllic relations. It has pitilessly torn asunder all the motley feudal ties. . . . The bourgeoisie cannot exist without constantly revolutionizing the instruments of production. . . . Conservation of the old modes of production in unaltered form was, on the contrary, the first condition of existence for all earlier industrial classes. (1976, 486–87)

Schumpeter, an unapologetic admirer of Marxian growth analysis, simply extended the idea to the related microeconomics issue—the replacement of obsolete products, processes, and firms by their more up-to-date and superior successors.

To the extent that it avoids informing us about the desirability of this process of replacement of the old by the new, the concept of creative destruction remains ambiguous. Indeed, by itself, it offers no basis on which to judge how far the process should go in order to serve the public interest most effectively. Without creative destruction, Schumpeter surely implies, we would be condemned to stagnation and forced to forgo the improved living standards offered by technical progress. However, even he must have recognized that, at least in a few cases, there is much to be said for some of the old ways, which progress sweeps aside just as effectively as it destroys those past products and techniques that are patently inferior to their replacements. The implications for the general welfare are important to both the academic literature and policy. They lead us to consider the obvious questions: does the economy engage in too much or too little creative destruction, and how can one tell?

129

Until recently, most economists writing on this subject, from the viewpoint of economic efficiency, held that the substantial spillovers of innovation[1] probably cause considerable underinvestment in innovative activities because, as we have seen, much of the benefits of innovation goes to people other than those who have devoted the effort and resources required to create it. However, more recent writers—notably Aghion and Howitt (1998)—have raised the opposite possibility. They argue that because the inventors and entrepreneurs who create the pertinent innovations and those who suffer the resulting destruction are often *different* individuals or groups, the process entails an externality that tends to induce overinvestment in innovation by inventors and entrepreneurs. That is, an individual considering investment in the design of a better mousetrap may ignore the social cost that will be entailed in the resulting obsolescence of earlier-model mousetraps because they are supplied by others, who will bear the resulting financial loss. No part of that loss will fall on the provider of the new model. Moreover, because entrepreneurs and inventors typically earn less than their equally qualified counterparts employed by large firms, it is conceivable that the products of innovative activities are underpriced and, therefore, excessively cheap for the purchaser. At the same time, although they serve as disincentives for innovative activity, spillovers from innovation and ease of disseminating technology are great benefits to society.[2] Accordingly, it is difficult to determine whether innovation and change under capitalism are too scarce—or excessive.

I will argue that the one set of externalities stemming from creative destruction tends to offset the other, the spillovers of innovation benefits. In doing so, they produce, on balance, a result that is, as I suggested in chapter 5, not too bad, in terms of economic efficiency. Indeed, in that chapter, I argued that innovation spillovers are the source of vast benefits for society. These benefits, however, are counterbalanced by their accompanying disincentives for innovative activity. The externalities stemming from creative destruction—and the stimulus for innovation that they provide by exempting innovators from much of the damage entailed in rendering earlier technology obsolete—strengthen this conclusion. Indeed, these latter externalities may be doubly beneficial—not only in offsetting some of the disincentive effects of innovation spillovers, but also in permitting the preservation of those spillovers' beneficial consequences.

CREATIVE DESTRUCTION AND INVESTMENT EFFICIENCY IN INNOVATION

I already have noted the standard view, which holds that inefficiency is introduced into the innovation process by the externalities that prevent the assignment of an adequate quantity of resources to it.[3] This is because the process is characterized by substantial spillovers that yield a large proportion of the benefits to people who did not participate in the innovation. These beneficiaries may include the general consuming public and even an innovator's direct competitors. In this way, the rewards to the innovator are reduced—perhaps severely, and the resulting innovative activity can be expected to be less than optimal.

More recently, as theorists have sought to formalize more elements of the growth process, they have returned to Schumpeter's notion of creative destruction, observing that this feature of innovation also generates externalities that, unlike innovation spillovers, tend to stimulate overinvestment in the innovation process—beyond the level that is socially optimal. That is, these externalities damage the interests of rival suppliers not party to the innovative activity by prematurely consigning their perfectly usable products to obsolescence. Consequently, innovation generates a considerable social cost that is not borne by the innovators, who, in turn, can be expected to disregard this cost and invest more in innovation than is justified by the resulting social cost. In short, the supply of innovation activity may be excessive, rather than inadequate, as previously believed.

What is common to both of these positions is the conclusion that innovation is a source of externalities, while allocative optimality is possible only if these spillovers—beneficial or detrimental—are zero, or at least zero on balance. My position, however, is very different. In this book, I have argued—contrary to accepted views—that zero spillovers are incompatible with optimality. Moreover, I have provided evidence that innovation spillovers, in the form of benefits to people other than the innovators, are surprisingly large—perhaps too much so. Thus, the externalities associated with creative destruction constitute a countervailing influence that may be socially beneficial in two ways. First, these externalities may help to offset the depressing effect of spillovers on innovation activity. Second, as we will see here, there seems to be no reason why such externalities should weaken the desirable distributive consequences of innovation spillovers.

SOMEWHAT-LESS-DESTRUCTIVE CREATIVE DESTRUCTION: HETEROGENEOUS PRODUCT RACES

Let us first consider whether or not the creative destruction story, as recounted here without nuance, is something of an exaggeration. That is, accounts of the scenario, in which the appearance of a new and superior product drives *all* suppliers of older, substitute products out of the industry, may be apt to overstate the problem of premature abandonment of older products and processes. In this story, even if the now-obsolete products remain workable and retain some particular elements of superiority, the market mechanism fully destroys their market, so that even items that still possess some residual value are denied to the economy.

Investment theory has long taught us, however, that if such replacement occurs prematurely, it can reduce the discounted present value of the stream of net benefits promised by the innovative products. We know, for example, that a firm that uses a piece of equipment that can be replaced by a new and superior substitute is apt to be ill advised to scrap its old equipment immediately—regardless of its remaining life and operational features—and replace this with the novel alternative. Instead, if much good life remains in the old machine, it will likely be profitable to delay its replacement.

Moreover, substitutes tend to be imperfect. Even if they have marked advantages over the older product, the novel substitutes also may have both absolute and comparative disadvantages (e.g., problems in learning to use the novelty), as well as technical problems that remain to be worked out. Much of the literature on competition among innovators interprets the process as one in which there is a single prize, and the winner takes all. Therefore, the inventor who reaches the patent office first, as when Alexander Graham Bell beat his rival in the invention of the telephone by several hours, becomes the sole possessor of the legal right to profit from the invention.

Of course, there are inventions of this sort, particularly when the new products or processes that rival inventors are vying to create are homogeneous—essentially identical. This is apt to be true of technical advances whose sole purpose is to reduce the cost of a homogeneous final product. In this instance, the innovation that provides the greatest cost saving clearly will outcompete any rival, leaving no place in the market for an inferior cost-cutting substitute.

Inventions, however, are generally not so homogeneous. Instead, competing firms' research and development laboratories often turn out innovations that are imperfect substitutes for one another. One may be superior to the other in some features, but inferior in others, while another may be only marginally inferior and, therefore, salable at a slightly lower price. In such cases, the race offers many prizes. The winner receives the highest payoff, but those who come in close behind obtain compensation commensurate with the value of their performances.[4]

In a highly competitive market, the relationship among the payoffs to the different innovators in the race can be analyzed with the help of the standard Ricardian rent model. In such markets, competition forces imperfect substitute innovations to be priced so as to offer purchasers of their services exactly, or at least approximately, the same value in net benefits. Thus, if purchasers are homogeneous, the difference between the rent payments to the suppliers of any two (imperfectly) substitutable innovations must be equal to the difference in the benefits they provide to buyers.

This result follows from the behavior of product buyers, as well as from that of profit-seeking investors in innovation. It demonstrates that investment in the innovation process will be increased only if doing so is expected to raise the probability of winning a more valuable prize, such as claiming the second-largest, rather than the third-largest, profits. However, suppose that, as in a regime of perfect competition, free entry into the innovation process reduces expected net profits to the same competitive level for all participants. In this case, expected revenues will be higher for inventions only if their costs are higher. Consequently, the expected gross earnings from the slightly inferior invention that earns the "second-place prize" should exceed those of the "third-place prize" by precisely the incremental cost necessary to advance that product from third- to second-place quality. That is, the price of every variant of some piece of technology will be proportional to its cost, so that none of the variants earns more than the competitive level of profits.

Ricardian rent theory tells us that the prices of products of different quality in fully competitive markets always will be set in this way. It also teaches us that such a differential rent arrangement should be consistently efficient in allocating resources among activities that are expected to produce heterogeneous substitute innovations. Indeed, Tse (1996) provides a formal argument demonstrating this result—albeit, for a rather more restricted set of circumstances. If entrants into the innovation race face no barriers, it follows that these arguments are fully valid.

This conclusion about heterogeneous innovative products that are substitutes applies equally to the older substitutes that are threatened by creative destruction. Typically, these products are not driven quickly from the market by the appearance of substitute technology. Sailing ships, for instance, continued to be built and used long after the steamship's workability had been demonstrated. Indeed, competition from steamer ships provided an incentive for the design and production of sailing vessels whose speed, capacity, and economy far surpassed earlier models. Similarly, horse-drawn vehicles continued to operate for some time in competition with early automobiles. Indeed, one can understand the reluctance of the milkman to give up his horse, which knew every customer's location along the route and did not have to be told where to go next. Today, we see the same story illustrated by costly high-definition TV sets, whose relatively sparse sales have continued for some time, alongside the abundant sales of conventional sets. As Ricardo's analysis makes clear, in perfect markets, price differences must reflect performance differences among substitute products. Consequently, the destruction of an older item can be a protracted process, which, in turn, reduces the social cost of the premature weakening of the market for those products.

REPRISE: THE BENEFITS OF INNOVATION SPILLOVERS

Chapters 5 and 6 of this book provided two important reasons that explain why zero innovation spillovers may not be optimal. The first, as noted in chapter 5, is the trade-off between the increased flow of invention and the distribution of some of the benefits of such inventions to others, thus increasing *overall* living standards. As I argued in that chapter, there is no single level of spillovers that is unambiguously optimal. Instead, there is a range of values of what I call a "spillover ratio"—that is, the share of the benefits of an innovation that go to people other than its investors. Within this ratio, *all values are Pareto optimal in the absence of any possibility of lump-sum transfers.* Thus, all of the values of this ratio may be considered second-best Pareto optima—subject to a constraint that rules out hypothetical, but totally infeasible, redistributive arrangements.

Chapter 6 emphasized a second spillover that is critical for the general welfare: the social benefits of the rapid and unimpeded transfer of technology to those who can make good use of it. In this, the earnings that the markets in technology licenses offer to IP owners help to secure a balance between the incentives for innovative activity and ease of dissemination. These markets, however, clearly do not eliminate all of the associated obstacles to economic efficiency.

In these scenarios, any invention-based increase in the average worker's standard of living constitutes a rise in the spillovers from innovation, which, in turn, depresses the flow of further innovation. Thus, the more the general public benefits from such growth in GDP, the slower innovation must grow. Reducing the impediments to the transfer and dissemination of technology, for instance, entails such a trade-off. Far from being a minor concern, these two externalities are enormous, in terms of the values involved and their welfare implications. Indeed, this trade-off between the private and social payoffs to innovation and the speed with which new technology and new products become available has significant consequences for the growth process, as we have seen. This is because innovation spillovers, entailing easy and uncompensated dissemination of technology, clearly are disincentives for innovative effort. As a result, these forces apparently tend to reduce innovation below the socially optimal level. In contrast, the externalities of creative destruction are an incentive for the enhancement of innovative effort. In other words, if these first two forces lead to social loss, it can be argued that the externalities that accompany creative destruction constitute a net social benefit because they tend to offset—though probably only partially—any insufficiency of innovative activity that results from innovation spillovers.

CONCLUDING COMMENT: DO THE "NEGATIVE EXTERNALITIES" OF CREATIVE DESTRUCTION PRODUCE ALLOCATIVE BENEFITS?

If creative destruction were the only source of externalities, they plausibly would lead to excess investment in innovation, above the amount required for economic efficiency. As I have demonstrated in this chapter, however, creative destruction is hardly the only source of externalities capable of distorting the volume of innovative activity. In fact, it is plausible that the externalities resulting from creative destruction are relatively modest, in comparison with the enormous beneficial spillovers of innovation. As I have noted here, unlike other innovation-related externalities, creative-destruction externalities serve as incentives for the overinvestment of resources in innovation processes. This is because the property values destroyed by the invention and supply of new and superior alternatives often damage only the competitors of the most current innovators. Instead, those who supplied the products rendered obsolete by the new innovation experience the greatest reductions in income. The three conclusions below follow from this.

1. Creative destruction externalities offset beneficial spillovers and usually can be expected to bring the economy at least somewhat closer to the desired level of efficiency and the optimal quantity of innovation activity.
2. If creative destruction externalities are, indeed, the smaller of the two types of externalities, their effect is hardly likely to be an *over-correction*. That is, the net result will be an increase in innovative activity that is insufficient to achieve optimal efficiency—however, the resulting allocation of resources still may be non-lump-sum Pareto optimal.[5]
3. Creative destruction externalities entail an increase in the provision of innovation above the quantity that would be provided if inventor-entrepreneurs bore all of the social costs entailed. Consequently, the desirable distributive benefits to those who are not engaged in creating innovation are apt to be increased.

The forces of destruction to which Schumpeter drew attention are, indeed, creative. On balance, they provide valuable benefits to the community—though they also can generate socially damaging externalities. However, I argue that these externalities do not threaten the validity of Schumpeter's conclusion that the process of creative destruction is inherently beneficial—very likely, substantially so.

PART III

Institutions, Payoffs, and the
Entrepreneur's Choice of Activity:
Historical Origins

Economic Warfare as a "Red Queen" Game: The Emergence of Productive Entrepreneurship

Pecunia Nervus Belli [Money is the sinew of war].

—Common saying in Renaissance Europe

There were, Louis XII of France was told by one of his coun-selors, three things a king required in order to fight wars: "first, money; second, money; and third, money."

—Colin Jones (1994, 130)

In this chapter and the next, I turn to the mechanism that determines the supply of innovative entrepreneurs. In chapter 8, I will describe the nature of the incentives that, in recent centuries, have induced entrepreneurs to engage in innovative and, more generally, productive activity. I also will investigate how those incentives came into widespread existence after a long absence. Then, in chapter 9, I will offer evidence suggesting strongly that individuals with entrepreneurial propensities generally allow their activities to be guided by these incentives. In particular, I will seek to explain why innovative entrepreneurship was so rare for most of human history—until it burst forth in the centuries leading to the Industrial Revolution. I will argue that this chronological exploration offers critical insights for growth policy today.

Rather than providing formal economic theory, chapters 8 and 9 focus on the origins of the productive entrepreneur as a mainstay of growth and innovation in the modern market economy. The evidence I will offer is entirely historical, and for that, an apology is required. I cannot claim any qualifications as a historian, and I have not searched any ancient documents in the attics of palaces or churches. Instead, my evidence is drawn from secondary sources created by historians who are qualified to do such research.

Although the inclusion of historical evidence in an economics text is perhaps atypical, such material is about as good as any other evidence available to test my argument that the productive entrepreneurs on whom this book focuses are a modern phenomenon that appeared when the institutions that make modern capitalism possible were established. Indeed, this chapter's central theme builds on an observation, associated with the work of Douglass North, that such entrepreneurs were introduced and their numbers encouraged by the appearance of institutions that invited and supported their goals. Moreover, the institutions that stimulated the volume of productive entrepreneurship have invited further expansion in the number of innovative entrepreneurs because the successful promotion of inventions and discoveries created additional opportunities for entrepreneurs who followed later.[1] My argument goes one step further, however, in suggesting that the introduction and evolution of these institutions was no mere accident. Rather, these institutions emerged from the needs of kings during the Middle Ages and Renaissance who faced the pressures of the "Red Queen" game[2] imposed on them by their near constant military activities.

This chapter and the next seek to explain the relationship between that game and the emergence of productive entrepreneurship. As part of this account, I will provide historical evidence for this hypothesis. Although unavoidably anecdotal, this evidence, nevertheless, seems compelling. Indeed, the sheer drama of the stories I will recount here suggests the power of the forces that can be unleashed by a Red Queen game.

REDISTRIBUTIVE VERSUS PRODUCTIVE
WEALTH ACCUMULATION

A cursory reading of history indicates that individuals motivated by the energetic pursuit of wealth were present in almost every society. Because power and prestige often accompanied wealth, those who were successful in this quest often became leaders of their societies. Of course, not everyone engaged in this game. Such ambitions clearly were unimaginable to a medieval serf, for instance, while monasteries expressly claimed to favor poverty (and some actually acted accordingly). Still, for those in power—Roman emperors, medieval kings and barons, and at least some of the popes—wealth was a substantial component of their objectives in life.

We can consider there to be two ways in which individuals can accumulate riches: they can obtain a larger slice of the pie or they can somehow arrange for the pie itself to become larger, in the process ensuring that they receive a significant portion of the expanded pie. I refer to these two modes of activity, respectively, as "redistributive wealth-seeking" and "productive wealth-seeking."

There are several observations, noted below, that help to explain the industrial revolutions of the past few centuries and their unprecedented pace of innovation and economic growth.

1. Redistributive activity is, by far, the more obvious way to accumulate riches.

2. Only in the past few centuries have there been changes that discouraged redistributive wealth-seeking and provided substantial incentives for the productive accumulation of wealth.

3. The volume of innovative entrepreneurial activity tends to be substantially larger in an economy whose institutions favor such entrepreneurship, as the resulting innovations provide additional opportunities for such activity. In contrast, redistributive entrepreneurship, whose activities are destructive, tends to reduce the output of the economy, as well as the opportunities for productive occupation because many of the activities of these entrepreneurs are designed to hinder others by means ranging from rent-seeking litigation to physical violence (both military and civilian).

4. Because redistributive activity characteristically *reduces* an economy's production—often drastically—this form of entrepreneurship can be considered a negative-sum game. That is, even though it has winners, society as a whole loses out as a result of such activity.

5. Effective democracy tends to force rational governments that want to stay in power to adopt rules that encourage productive activity and discourage redistributive activity, since productive entrepreneurship permits every group to be better off, while redistributive entrepreneurship *must* harm some groups and lead them to oppose the currently governing administration.

6. The changes that led to the creation of these new institutions, which arguably underlay the British industrial revolution that spurred a reorientation of enterprising effort toward productive activity, are still largely absent in many of the world's poorest economies. Moreover, these institutions remain highly imperfect even in the wealthiest nations, such as the United States, where a substantial amount of redistributive wealth-seeking activity continues.

This list contains the beginnings of a prescription for policy that could help the world's poorest nations to catch up with more prosperous countries. Alternatively, the most successful economies can look to these observations for guidance on preserving their growth performance in the future.

ON THE HISTORICAL DOMINANCE OF THE
REDISTRIBUTIVE APPROACH

As already hinted, redistributive activity is the obvious route to personal prosperity. If, for instance, a redistributive wealth-seeker has no cows and a weaker neighbor has six, she would take a club, hit the neighbor on the head, and make off with four of the animals—or perhaps all of them. In contrast, productive methods of wealth gathering involve a fair amount of subtlety and uncertainty. Suppose you set out to invent a better seed for the grain with which you feed your herd of cattle. The work is very hard, the outcome highly uncertain, and, perhaps worst of all, even if your efforts are successful, it may well transpire that others will obtain most or all of the benefits of your innovation. In the absence of any special inducements or protective arrangements connected with productive wealth-seeking, any rational wealth-seeker most likely will choose the redistributive path to riches.

History is replete with the evidence of the role of redistributive entrepreneurship.[3] Julius Caesar accumulated vast riches through his success in aggressive warfare. Ransoms and the spoils of war were his primary instruments. In ancient Rome, productive activity—with the exception of agriculture—was considered degrading and was generally left to freedmen—former slaves who bore a social stigma for life—who, if successful, sought to buy their way out of such shameful activity.[4] The condottieri, mercenary soldiers of Renaissance Italy, like the modern warlords of Somalia and Afghanistan, also used violence, or its threat, for this purpose. Even the Medici family, which accumulated a great fortune by productive contributions to banking and traffic in merchandise, soon found this entrepreneurship an unsatisfactory way to keep up the influx of wealth and turned to other directions, including the creation of two popes[5] and two queens of France—all members of the Medici family.

Only very recently has productive activity—notably, the activity of putting inventions to work—widely become *both* lucrative and honorable and, therefore, widespread. Until recent centuries, the role of the innovative entrepreneur, who recognizes a promising invention, oversees its improvement, markets it, and ensures its wide utilization, was beset by daunting uncertainties and was neither honored nor lucrative. Instead, a successful innovation was more likely to be prohibited in response to the demands of conservative trade guilds or simply expropriated by a monarch trying to raise funds for warfare. Such observations help to explain why, in the Soviet Union, for example, despite its well-educated engineers and scientists, new technology rarely achieved broad utilization unless it had evident military or political value.

THE CONSEQUENCES OF REDISTRIBUTIVE ACTIVITY
FOR THE ECONOMY'S OUTPUT

Redistributive entrepreneurial activities have taken many forms throughout history and continue to do so today. I have already alluded to aggressive warfare and, with it, the acquisition of booty and the extraction of prisoner ransoms.[6] The organization and operation of private armies, for instance, generally did not occur by accident—the entrepreneur-captains of such armies often were not content to await demand for their services and frequently sought ways to stimulate the market for warfare. Bribery and more general forms of corruption—arguably the most salient impediment to growth in many of the world's poorest countries—offer another important example of redistributive entrepreneurial activities. Indeed, all of these activities feature clever entrepreneurs who must constantly think of new and imaginative ways to take for themselves the fruits of the activities of others.

Redistributive entrepreneurship takes still other forms, including those that economists refer to as "rent seeking"—that is, those that extract fees for services that offer no produced output in exchange. Landlords, who create no new land when they rent property to others, are perhaps the best example of such entrepreneurial activity. In earlier days, one of the most noted forms of rent seeking involved ingratiating oneself with the monarch, who was expected to give land, patents of monopoly, and other valuable gifts to his or her favorite subjects. Later, in nineteenth-century America, financial manipulation of the country's railroads or its gold supply (the attempted cornering of which was almost carried out successfully via bribing President Ulysses S. Grant's brother-in-law) brought enormous wealth to those captains of industry now known as the robber barons.

Today, redistributive activity is carried out by mafias operating in or hailing from virtually every region of the world—from South America to Europe and Asia. Perhaps more noteworthy—though less obvious—is the massive litigation in the courtrooms of prosperous countries, carried out (often in innovative ways) by firms seeking to acquire legal monopolies (e.g., for the supply of electricity to a city) or by producers battling one another in the courts, rather than in the marketplace.[7] A particularly egregious form of such activity entails misuse of antitrust laws to undermine competition, rather than to preserve it, as intended. A frequent occurrence in the United States, such litigation happens when one firm finds that its inferior products or inefficiency condemn it to lose out to rivals in the marketplace. The firm then takes its competitive battle out of the marketplace and into the courtroom, complaining falsely or on questionable evidence that a rival has engaged in "predatory behavior"—that is, behavior that is illegal because it does not bring profits to the firm that undertakes it, unless that firm's rivals are destroyed or materially weakened. Such litigation has become a common form of rent seeking, with the company that brings the case to court profiting in at least one of the following three ways. First, the plaintiff can obtain a ruling that prevents the rival from competing as vigorously as before—for example, the rival may be directed by the court to raise its prices. Second, if the accusing company wins, the rival may be required by the court to pay a large amount of money to the victor, as compensation for the supposed damages the victor has suffered. Third, the combatants may reach an "out-of-court settlement," in which the allegedly misbehaving firm surrenders and pays a bribe to its accuser, in exchange for agreement by the accuser to withdraw its legal complaint.

Two important points should be emphasized here. First, while redistributive activity was the common form of wealth seeking in earlier eras, it is by no means a thing of the past. Second, while such activity clearly does not add to the productive output of an economy, its full consequences are often far worse: it can hamper production or actually destroy substantial portions of an economy's output. The most obvious example is wealth-seeking military activity that destroys crops and facilities and kills members of the labor force. This hardly needs further explanation. But there are also costs—often substantial—associated with many other redistributive activities that are less violent. A substantial portion of this cost is the "opportunity cost." For instance, the clever and well-educated lawyer who devotes a career to litigation designed to subvert the antitrust laws could otherwise have used those talents for productive purposes.[8] Moreover, because these cases often involve damage claims amounting to billions of dollars (sometimes several years' income for the accused firm), the managements of such firms are distracted from their legitimate activities and forced to defend themselves against attack. Similarly, the economies of developing countries are deprived of productive talent that is often in extremely short supply when an educated individual finds that the most lucrative option is to become a bureaucrat and, thereby, the recipient of bribes. Moreover, as is well recognized, the corruption process often has more direct efficiency costs, incurring delays in urgent business decisions, multiplying the expense of the required paperwork, and, in many cases, prohibiting actions that could enhance efficiency by business firms under the bureaucrat's jurisdiction. For example, in a number of developing countries, the cumbersome, slow-moving process of compliance with regulations and the bureaucratic procedures required for setting up a new firm for business constitutes a major impediment to the exercise of productive entrepreneurship.

It is not difficult to think of additional examples that confirm the contention that the effects of enterprising redistributive activity on production are far from neutral. Such activity entails failure to take advantage of opportunities to stimulate production and is also characteristically damaging—frequently, severely so—to a nation's economic growth. Thus, I conclude that *redistributive entrepreneurship is indeed a negative-sum game. The total return to society when the playing of this game is pervasive is generally far lower than what would have been the sum of the returns to the members of society if that game had never been played.*

MEDIEVAL WARFARE AS A RED QUEEN GAME AND THE BIRTH OF INSTITUTIONS THAT PROMOTE PRODUCTIVE ENTREPRENEURSHIP

We turn next to investigation of the forces that led a substantial proportion of the entrepreneurs in the world's economies to reallocate themselves from redistributive to productive activities. I will argue that a major role was played by the Red Queen game of the European monarchs and their nobles in the Middle Ages. A Red Queen game, as was explained in chapter 4, is a competitive scenario in which every player's success requires her to match or exceed the current efforts or expenditures of rivals, so that each is forced by the others to bid ever higher, and all participants find themselves forced, as in Lewis Carroll's felicitous phrase in *Through the Looking Glass*, to do "all the running you can do, to keep in the same place" (1902, 38). Economics provides many examples of these games, but the focus here will be on medieval arms races—in short, what the monarchs found themselves forced to do, in order to keep their territories intact in the face of that prototypical redistributive activity, royal land grabs by neighboring kings. I contend that the Red Queen scenario describes what underlies one of the most significant economic upheavals in history: the introduction of institutions that provided effective incentives for entrepreneurs to shift their efforts from redistributive to productive activities. The evidence I offer here focuses on a period well before the Industrial Revolution: the late Middle Ages and the early Renaissance. I will argue that the arms races of this period—patently Red Queen games—played a critical role in the birth of the institutions that underlie the more recent turn to productive entrepreneurship and entrepreneurial capitalism.

The key role financing plays in successful warfare is a crucial part of my argument. It can also be shown, as an analogous example, that a powerful contributor to the French Revolution, which arguably opened the way for more rapid economic growth in that country, was the arms race under successive Bourbon kings and British monarchs.[9] These military endeavors had disastrous consequences for French finances and, as a result, forced that fateful summons of the Estates General, whose assemblage was perhaps the first step in that revolution.

Historically, when a nation has achieved a spectacular record of military success, it generally can be attributed to one (or more) of three sources: inspired generalship, a technical breakthrough not yet mastered by the enemy, or substantially superior funding and resources. Alexander, Gustavus Adolphus, Marlborough, and Napoleon are clear examples of the first source of victory. The second is exemplified by the apparent availability only to the Normans of a special stirrup that permitted a spear-carrying rider to strike with the great force of his mount's charge, without giving up his spear by throwing it. This innovative weapon is said to have carried the day at the Battle of Hastings.[10] Similarly, the longbow is judged to have been critical to the English rout of the French forces at Crécy, Poitiers, and Agincourt. There are similar stories entailing suitably designed cannons, as with the harassment of the Spanish Armada in the English Channel. More frequently, however, the source of victory has been substantial funding superiority, as clearly has been documented in Renaissance warfare, the U.S. Civil War, and the military portions of the more recent U.S. engagements in Yugoslavia, Afghanistan, and Iraq. Indeed, it is arguable that without such economic superiority, great generalship, for instance, usually is doomed to fail, as it did for the brilliant Confederate general Robert E. Lee in the American Civil War.[11]

The source of the Red Queen game's power is clear. In an arms race or any analogous situation, the game's very process ensures that the resources invested are almost always inadequate. If, for instance, one participant devotes increased quantities of resources to moving its military power ahead of that of its rivals, those rivals will only be forced to beg, borrow, or steal in order to pour more resources into the fray. Therefore, outlays that once seemed adequate will quickly fall short of the new quantity of resources required to compete. In sum, the players of the game are condemned, without relief, to be short of the resources they need.

THE PAUPER KINGS: HOW IMPOVERISHED MONARCHS WERE FORCED TO CHANGE THE "RULES OF THE GAME"

The hypothesis I offer here is that the military activity of the later Middle Ages forced the adoption of the institutions that made innovative entrepreneurship attractive, which, in turn, contributed substantially to the British industrial revolution of the eighteenth century. As just recounted, the main occupational activity of the medieval monarch was, arguably, aggressive warfare.[12] Certainly a king's status and the success of his reign were based, to a large degree, on his effectiveness in military enterprises. This drove every king of that period into an arms race in which the ante was constantly raised. Here too, innovation—albeit in military technology—was relentlessly raising costs. Wooden castles, for instance, were replaced by stone castles, which were not only more costly to build, but were also far more costly to besiege. Moreover, the spectacular success of the longbow in battles such as Crécy, Poitiers, and Agincourt required that chain mail armor be replaced by plate armor, an expense that fell largely on the nobles. Later, the introduction of gunpowder and artillery in the mid-fourteenth century increased the cost of fortification. Perhaps most important, sociopolitical changes led many kings to decrease their armed forces' reliance upon vassals, who received little or no monetary compensation for military service. Instead, the kinds assembled paid armies—often purely mercenary troops—which added sharply to royal expenses.

The essential point here is that such costly military innovations were not simply a set of fortuitous events. Rather, they were the predictable consequence of the Red Queen game that spawned them. As a result, kings were almost always seriously short of funds. For whenever they managed to scrape up enough money to carry out their military enterprises, the already tight arms race merely ratcheted up another notch. Thus, the kings were perpetually underfinanced, heavily in debt, and unable to find willing lenders. As some historians have put it, they were "pauper kings."

One consequence of the kings' perpetually troubled finances was that the rights of the individual began to be incorporated into the law,[13] as *the monarchs' desperate straits forced them, usually reluctantly, to offer inducements to those from whom they sought funds and other forms of support.*[14] For instance, the kings had to accede to the demands of their relatively powerful and more affluent subjects for protection against arbitrary exactions and abuse. At first, these benefits went only to the magnates, which included the fewer than ten earls and less than one hundred barons in England at the time of the signing of Magna Carta and the birth of Parliament. Perhaps a century later, such benefits were extended to the towns and the commons—essentially, the upper middle class, the knights, the landowners, and wealthier town residents. Moreover, the kings, in their desperation for funds, were sometimes forced to turn to commerce, rather than taxes and booty, as a source of funds, thereby making the profession respectable for members of the English nobility. All of this arguably laid the foundations for the future free-market economy and its remarkable productivity and growth.[15]

History provides many instances that support this hypothesis, but I will confine myself to several of the most critical: King John and the Magna Carta; John's son, Henry III, and the growth of parliamentary control over finances of the realm, along with the first representation of the commons in Parliament; and the case of Edward IV, who ventured into commerce toward the end of the Wars of the Roses. However, these are merely a select few examples among many other cases in point.

KING JOHN AND THE MAGNA CARTA

John came to the throne after the death of his brother, Richard I. In addition to all of England, John inherited French territories considerably larger than those of the Capetian king of France, Philip Augustus. This inheritance was not without complications, however. According to Philip, John's Angevin empire was, in fact, part of Philip's kingdom of France, making John Philip's vassal. When John, on the basis of his claimed independent powers, refused to let one of Philip's French nobles appeal a decision of John's to the French court, Philip used this conflict as an excuse to attack John's territories.

Thus, like his brother and father before him, John was embroiled in French combat. Meanwhile, he also faced military problems in Wales, Scotland, and Ireland. Desperate for funds, he resorted to expedients, such as taxing noble widows, who were forced to pay in order to "buy" immunity from enforced remarriage, and requiring heirs to make large payments before they were allowed to obtain their bequests. Even religious institutions were not immune from John's exactions. This behavior, together with the king's unwillingness to accept the appointments of Pope Innocent III to high posts in the church, led the pope to excommunicate John. At first the king tried to weather the papal storm, but the threat of baronial revolt led him to make an about-face[16] that culminated in the adoption of the Magna Carta in 1215. This charter—compelled by the fiscal consequences of John's and Philip Augustus's Red Queen game—protected the nobility from the sorts of financial exactions and related abuses that have just been described. In return, the nobles agreed to cease their attacks on the king.

HENRY III, SIMON DE MONTFORT, AND THE OXFORD PARLIAMENT

John's son, Henry III, was also notoriously short of funds, as he was forced to expend effort and money in defending what was left of his father's Angevin territories in France. In addition, he was inveigled by the pope to intervene in Sicily in quarrels between the papacy and the Sicilian monarch, Holy Roman Emperor Frederick II. As was to happen again so many times, these circumstances led Henry to adopt financing measures that elicited the anger of the barons. In response, they revolted and in a parliament[17] at Oxford in 1258 forced the king to agree to a new charter that enhanced the rights provided in the Magna Carta by further curtailing the means that could be used by the monarch to raise funds. More important, in order to deprive the king of support among the commons, which included many knights and royal officials, the Oxford charter extended to the (upper) commons rights similar to those that the nobles had extracted from the king for themselves. To counter the power of the barons, Henry sought to invalidate his oath by appealing to France's Louis IX, who ruled that the Oxford agreement, extracted by force, was invalid.

In response, the barons rose up once more—now under the active leadership of Simon de Montfort, who had married Henry's sister, become Earl of Leicester, and then, acquired the king's enmity through several unseemly acts of financial treachery. Although he was a religious bigot, brutal, grasping, and arguably concerned, above all, with the position of his own family, Simon was also an effective leader and a powerful warrior. At the battle of Lewes of 1264, he captured Henry and his son, Edward, who was to be the next king. Simon then established, in effect, a personal dictatorship, leaving the king in place as a figurehead. To impart an aura of legitimacy to his regime, Simon called a parliament, *with commoners attending for the first time*. As a result, some now consider Simon to be "the father of Parliament."

The story ends with the escape of Prince Edward from Simon's captivity, his organization of a royalist army, and his victory at the battle of Evesham in 1265, at which Simon was killed. Edward's subsequent reign also was marked by warfare in Wales, Scotland, and France, and, predictably, he was beset by the usual cash shortages. In 1296, under pressure from his nobles, he accepted a new charter, providing guarantees against arbitrary taxation, a key step toward acceptance of the idea that there should be no taxation without representation.

The evolution of the rule of law—from Henry III to Edward I—was perhaps one of the most important contributions to the birth of capitalism. For surely the rule of law is a necessary condition for the widespread exercise of innovative entrepreneurship and investment in production and commerce that underlies free-market economies.

EDWARD IV: WINDING DOWN THE WARS OF THE ROSES

The Yorkist usurper king, Edward IV used many devices to get out of the financial difficulties resulting from his battle for the throne and the ongoing Wars of the Roses. Perhaps the most notable among these measures was his entry into commerce, which previously had been regarded as a disgraceful activity for kings or nobles:

> Edward IV has some claim to be regarded as the first "merchant king" in English history. From the beginning of his reign he sought to improve his finances by indulging in personal trading ventures, *an example followed by many of his great*

men. . . . In his later years he also made use of the royal ships, when not engaged on other business, as commercial charter vessels. (Ross 1974, 351; my italics)

This passage makes clear that Edward IV's example was quickly followed by other nobles, which, in turn, helped to dissipate the shame of such activities. Indeed, by the time of Adam Smith, three centuries later, at the birth of the Industrial Revolution, many members of the higher nobility were avidly engaged in productive and innovative pursuits.

This change in acceptable occupations for the nobility was crucial for the rise of capitalism because it eventually put an end to the perpetual domestic strife that was, arguably, a major impediment to England's economic growth. Perhaps more important, such changes facilitated the inauguration of the then new economy by introducing into fruitful economic activity members of those groups who previously had been the prime troublemakers,[18] but who were still the major holders of wealth and, therefore, were in the best position to finance such entrepreneurial activity. Once again, this change seems to have been stimulated most immediately by the inherently unsustainable finances of Edward IV's military activity during the Wars of the Roses—a problem attributable to the Red Queen game of the ongoing arms races and accompanying and unrelenting shortage of funding that characterized the king's reign. In short, because Edward was forced by his desperate financial straits to turn to despised economic activities, such as commerce, the profession eventually acquired a degree of respectability. Having begun to be accepted into mainstream economic life, commerce would go on to play a key role in fueling the unprecedented economic growth of England's industrial revolution.

CONCLUDING COMMENT

My hypotheses in this chapter reemphasize the role in the rise of capitalism played by appropriate institutions, and their attendant incentives for productive entrepreneurship. As part of this account, I offer three substantial conjectures. First, I contend that the rise of the innovative or productive entrepreneur can be explained by institutional developments and the structure of the payoffs these provided—an idea that has been emphasized by a number of leading economic historians. Second, the rise of innovative entrepreneurship may be considered a historical accident resulting from these government institutions, one that had no close counterparts in portions of the world outside Europe or, indeed, outside a few select countries in Europe. This development, in turn, may help to account for the very limited number of countries in which the industrial revolutions of the past few centuries occurred. Third, in this chapter, I have described a Red

Queen game that is quite different from that engaged in by the innovating oligopoly firms described in chapter 4. Still, both examples—oligopoly firms and medieval warfare—demonstrate the powerful force such a game can exercise, as well as the profound consequences it can bring. Indeed, in the next chapter, I will examine the results of these historical Red Queen games and their accompanying developments for the supply, the role, and the behavior of entrepreneurs.

CHAPTER 9

On the Origins of Widespread
Productive Entrepreneurship

Interviewer: *Tell me Mr. Sutton—why do you rob banks?*
Willie Sutton: *Because that's where the money is.*

—1952

*As much as two thousand years ago the power of steam was not
only observed, but an ingenious toy was actually made and put
in motion in Alexandria in Egypt. What appears strange is, that
neither the inventor of the toy, nor anyone else, for so long a
time afterwards, should perceive that steam would move* useful
machinery.

—Abraham Lincoln, "First Lecture on
Discoveries and Inventions," 6 April 1858

In this chapter we turn to the *supply* of productive entrepreneurship,
having dealt with pricing, welfare, and other associated issues. I will argue
here that, while the total supply of entrepreneurs varies among societies,
the productive contribution of a society's entrepreneurial activities varies
as entrepreneurs decide whether to allocate their efforts to productive
activities, such as innovation, or alternately, to largely unproductive activities, such as rent seeking or organized crime. This allocation is heavily
influenced by the relative payoffs society offers for each set of activities.
In turn, the structure of those payoffs is affected strongly by changes in
economic and legal institutions, such as those described in the previous
chapter. Thus, policy can influence the *allocation* of entrepreneurship more
effectively than it can influence its *total supply*. In this chapter, I will use
historical evidence from ancient Rome, early China, the Middle Ages, and
the European Renaissance to investigate these hypotheses.

DETERMINANTS OF THE ALLOCATION OF
ENTREPRENEURIAL EFFORT

When conjectures are offered to explain historic slowdowns or great leaps in economic growth, the usual group of suspects is rounded up—prominent among them, the entrepreneur. When growth slows, a decline in entrepreneurship takes some of the blame, perhaps because a society's "need for achievement" has atrophied. When unprecedented expansion occurs, such growth is attributed to the mysterious flowering of entrepreneurship.

Building on the material in the previous chapter, this chapter proposes a different set of hypotheses, which hold that entrepreneurs are always with us and always play *some* substantial role in the economy. There are, however, a variety of roles among which entrepreneurs' efforts can be reallocated, and not all of these roles follow the constructive and innovative script that is conventionally attributed to entrepreneurial efforts. Indeed, at times the entrepreneur may lead a parasitical existence that actually damages the economy.

How an entrepreneur acts at a given time and place depends heavily on the "rules of the game"—an economy's entrepreneurial reward structure—that happen to prevail. Thus, I argue that an economy's laws and regulations—not the total supply of entrepreneurs *or the nature of their objectives*—undergo significant changes from one period to another and, in doing so, help to dictate the *allocation* of entrepreneurial resources. Of course, changes in these rules and other attendant circumstances can modify the size and composition of the class of entrepreneurs, but in this chapter, I will focus on the allocation of the changing class of entrepreneurs, rather than its magnitude and makeup.[1]

My basic hypothesis, if sustained by the evidence, has an important implication for growth policy. The notion that our productivity problems reside in the "spirit of entrepreneurship" that waxes and wanes for unexplained reasons is a counsel of despair that offers no guidance on how to reawaken that spirit once it has lagged. If stimulating and sustaining this "spirit" is the task assigned to policymakers, they are destitute: they have no means of knowing how to carry it out. But if what is required is the adjustment of the rules of the game to induce a more felicitous allocation of entrepreneurial resources, then the policymaker's task is less formidable, and certainly not hopeless. In this chapter, I will illustrate how the prevailing rules that affect the allocation of entrepreneurial activity can be observed, described, and, with luck, modified.

ON THE HISTORICAL CHARACTER OF THE EVIDENCE

Since the rules of the game that are fundamental for my central hypothesis usually change very slowly, a case study approach to investigation of the hypothesis drives me to continue to focus, as in chapter 8, on examples spanning considerable periods of history. The historical illustrations I will provide encompass the main economic periods and locations—ancient Rome, medieval China, and the European Middle Ages—that economic historians usually single out when examining the process of innovation and its diffusion. The case studies I present here will demonstrate that the relative rewards for different types of entrepreneurial activity, in fact, have varied dramatically from one time and place to another, which, in turn, seems to have had profound effects on patterns of entrepreneurial behavior.

Of course, arguments rooted in the analysis of historical case studies cannot be considered conclusive. Still, it is a tenet of scientific method that tentative confirmation of a hypothesis is provided by observation of phenomena that a hypothesis helps to explain, and that could not be accounted for if that hypothesis were invalid. Historians have long been puzzled, for example, by the failure of ancient Roman society to disseminate and put into widespread practical use some of the sophisticated technological developments that are known to have been in its possession. Similarly, scholars have struggled to explain modern China's failure to capitalize on the breakthrough discoveries attributed to ancient and medieval Chinese inventors.[2] My hypothesis about the allocation of entrepreneurial effort between productive and unproductive activity will help to account for this phenomenon—although I certainly do *not* claim that it is a complete explanation.[3]

THE SCHUMPETERIAN MODEL EXTENDED: ALLOCATION OF ENTREPRENEURSHIP

Schumpeter tells us that innovation, which he refers to as "the carrying out of new combinations," takes various forms, aside from mere improvements in technology:

> This concept covers the following five cases: (1) the introduction of a new good—that is one with which consumers are not yet familiar—or of a new quality of a good. (2) The introduction of a new method of production, that is one not yet tested by experience in the branch of manufacture concerned, which need by no means be founded upon a discovery scientifically new, and can also exist in a new way of handling a commodity commercially. (3) The opening of a new market, that is a market into which the particular branch of

manufacture of the country in question has not previously entered, whether or not this market has existed before. (4) The conquest of a new source of supply of raw materials or half-manufactured goods, again irrespective of whether this source already exists or whether it has first to be created. (5) The carrying out of the new organization of any industry, like the creation of a monopoly position (for example through trustification) or the breaking up of a monopoly position. (1936, 66)

The fact that entrepreneurs undertake such a variety of tasks suggests that theory should consider what determines the *allocation* of entrepreneurial inputs among those tasks. Just as the literature traditionally studies the allocation of other inputs—for example, capital resources—among the various industries that compete for them, it seems natural to ask what influences the flow of entrepreneurial talent among the various activities in Schumpeter's list.

Presumably no such line of inquiry was pursued by Schumpeter or his successors because analysis of the allocation of entrepreneurial resources among the five items in his list, for example, would not promise to yield any profound conclusions, particularly for policy.[4] For example, there is no obvious reason to make much of a shift of entrepreneurial activity away from, say, improvement of the production process and toward the introduction of new products. The general implications of such a change for the public welfare, productivity growth, and other related matters hardly seem startling.

To derive more substantive results from an analysis of the allocation of entrepreneurial resources, it is necessary to expand Schumpeter's list so that, for example, it encompasses innovative acts of technology transfer that take advantage of opportunities to introduce already-available technology (usually with some modification to adapt it to local conditions) to geographic locales whose suitability for the purpose had previously gone unrecognized or unused. Most important for the discussion here, Schumpeter's list of entrepreneurial activities can be expanded to include innovations in rent-seeking procedures—for example, discovery of a previously unused legal gambit that diverts rents to those who are first in exploiting it. It may seem strange to propose inclusion of activities of such questionable value to society in the list of Schumpeterian innovations,[5] but, as I will demonstrate here, this is a crucial step for the analysis that follows. If innovative entrepreneurs are defined as people who excel at finding creative ways to add to their own wealth, power, and prestige, then it must be expected that not all of them will be overly concerned with whether or not an activity that achieves these goals adds to the social product or, for that matter, actually impedes production.[6] In addition, suppose that, at any time and place, the magnitude of the benefit the economy derives from its entrepreneurial talents depends *substantially*, among other variables, on the allocation of this resource between productive and unproductive entrepreneurial activities of the sorts just described. If this is the case, the reasons for including such activities in an expanded version of Schumpeter's list become clear—chief among them, the need to emphasize that entrepreneurship is not a synonym for virtue, but rather, a means of pursuing wealth, power, and prestige that adapts to a society's legal and economic circumstances.

In this chapter, I will not attempt to provide an exhaustive analysis of the process of allocating entrepreneurial activity among the set of available options. Rather, I will argue only that *one* of the prime determinants of entrepreneurial behavior at any particular time and place is the prevailing set of rules that govern the payoff of one entrepreneurial activity, relative to another. If the rules impede the earning of much wealth via activity A, or impose social disgrace on those who engage in A, then the efforts of entrepreneurs will tend to be channeled to other activities, call them B. However, if B contributes less to production or to the general welfare than A, the social consequences of such incentives, which attract entrepreneurs to B rather than A, may be considerable.[7]

As a last preliminary note, it should be emphasized that the set of active entrepreneurs may be subject to change. Thus, if the rules of the game begin to favor activity B over A, those entrepreneurs who engaged in A will not necessarily switch their activities to B. Rather, some people with talents suited for activity A may simply drop out of the picture, while individuals with abilities adapted to B become entrepreneurs for the first time. Joan Robinson's analysis of the allocation of heterogeneous land resources (1969, chap. 8), following Shove's suggestion,[8] provides perhaps the best description of the way entrepreneurship is allocated among different activities, likening this allocation to the solution of a jigsaw puzzle, in which each piece is fitted into the place selected for it by the concatenation of pertinent circumstances.

PRODUCTIVE AND UNPRODUCTIVE ENTREPRENEURSHIP: THE RULES DO CHANGE

Let us now turn to this chapter's central hypothesis, which contends that the exercise of entrepreneurship can sometimes be unproductive or even destructive, and that whether it takes one of these directions, or another that is more benign, depends heavily on the structure of payoffs in the economy—the rules of the game. Later in this chapter, I will present dramatic illustrations from world history that confirm emphatically the following:

PROPOSITION 9.1: The rules of the game that determine the relative payoffs to different entrepreneurial activities change dramatically from one time and place to another.

Moreover, the examples I will cite suggest the following proposition strongly, though they may not prove it outright:

PROPOSITION 9.2: Entrepreneurial behavior changes direction between productive and unproductive activity from one economy to another, in a manner that corresponds to the variations in the rules of the game, the institutional arrangements that determine the relative payoffs offered by the various activities available to entrepreneurs.

CASE STUDY 1: ANCIENT ROME

The avenues open to those seeking power, prestige, and wealth in ancient Rome are instructive. First, it may be noted that Romans of this era had no reservations about the desirability of wealth or its pursuit (Finley 1985, 53–57). *As long as it did not involve participation in industry or commerce*, there was nothing degrading about acquiring wealth in ancient Rome. Accordingly, in addition to warfare, people of honorable status could choose among three primary and acceptable sources of income: landholding, money lending, and what Finley describes as "political moneymaking":

> Money poured in from booty, indemnities, provincial taxes, loans and miscellaneous extractions in quantities without precedent in Graeco-Roman history, and at an accelerating rate. The public treasury benefited, but probably more remained in private hands, among the nobles in the first instance; then, in appropriately decreasing proportions, among the *equites,* the soldiers and even the plebs of the city of Rome. . . . Nevertheless, the whole phenomenon is misunderstood when it is classified under the headings of "corruption" and "malpractice," as historians still persist in doing. Cicero was an honest governor of Cilicia in 51 and 50 B.C., so that at the end of his term he had earned only the legitimate profits of office. They amounted to 2,200,000 sesterces, more than treble the figure of 600,000 he himself once mentioned (*Stoic Paradoxes* 49) to illustrate an annual income that could permit a life of luxury. We are faced with something structural in the society. (1985, 55)

Who, then, operated commerce and industry in ancient Rome? According to Veyne (1961), it was an occupation heavily undertaken by former slaves who had been granted freedom. Indeed, Veyne argues that slavery may have represented the one avenue for advancement for lower-class Romans. A clever (and handsome) member of the lower orders, for instance, might arrange to be sold into slavery to a wealthy and powerful master.[9] Then, through luck, skill, and hard work, he would grow close to his owner, perhaps managing his financial affairs (and sometimes engaging in some homosexual activity with him). The master then gained cachet by granting freedom to the slave and setting him up with a fortune of his own. The freedmen, apparently not atypically, invested their financial stakes in commerce, hoping to multiply their wealth sufficiently to enable them to retire in style to the countryside.

There is a final point regarding the Romans' attitude toward the promotion of technology and productivity. Finley makes much of the "clear, almost total, divorce between science and practice" (1965, 32) in ancient Rome. To illustrate, Finley reports the following tale:

> There is a story, repeated by a number of Roman writers, that a man—characteristically unnamed—invented unbreakable glass and demonstrated it to Tiberius in anticipation of a great reward. The emperor asked the inventor whether anyone shared his secret and was assured that there was no one else; whereupon his head was promptly removed, lest, said Tiberius, gold be reduced to the value of mud. I have no opinion about the truth of this story, and it is only a story. But is it not interesting that neither the elder Pliny nor Petronius nor the historian Dio Cassius was troubled by the point that the inventor turned to the emperor for a reward, instead of turning to an investor for capital with which to put his invention into production?[10] . . . We must remind ourselves time and again that the European experience since the late Middle Ages in technology, in the economy, and in the value systems that accompanied them, was unique in human history until the recent export trend commenced. Technical progress, economic growth, productivity, even efficiency have not been significant goals since the beginning of time. So long as an acceptable life-style could be maintained, however that was defined, other values held the stage. (1965, 147)

Thus, although the Roman reward system offered wealth to those who engaged in commerce and industry, it offset this gain through the attendant loss in prestige. In this structure, economic effort "was neither the way to wealth nor its purpose" (Finley 1965, 39). Instead, ancient Romans were expected to rely on methods of wealth acquisition that Finley describes as "political and parasitical": the treasures of conquest and "usury" (39), for instance. Labor was certainly not among these methods, Finley notes, "not even the labour of the entrepreneur" (39).

CASE STUDY 2: MEDIEVAL CHINA

In China, as in Europe before the existence of the kinds of guarantees exemplified by England's Magna Carta, the monarch commonly claimed possession of all property in his territories.[11] As a result, when the sovereign was in financial straits, confiscation of the property of wealthy subjects was entirely in order—particularly in China. This arguably led those with resources to avoid investing them in any sort of visible capital stocks, which, in turn, impeded economic expansion.[12]

Imperial China reserved its most substantial rewards in wealth and prestige for those who passed the imperial examinations, which were devoted to subjects such as Confucian philosophy and calligraphy. Successful examination candidates were eligible for high-ranking positions within the bureaucracy, which carried with them high social standing. Such superior status was denied to anyone engaged in commerce or industry, including those who gained great wealth in the process.[13] In other words, the rules of the game in medieval China seem to have been heavily biased against the acquisition of wealth *and position* through productive entrepreneurial behavior. The avenue to success lay elsewhere.

Because of the difficulty of the examinations, the mandarins (scholar-officials) rarely succeeded in keeping bureaucratic positions in their own families for more than two or three generations (Marsh 1961, 159; Ho 1962, chap. 4 and appendix). The scholar families devoted enormous effort and considerable resources to preparing their children, through years of laborious study, for the imperial examinations, which, during the Sung dynasty, for instance, were held only once every three years. Typically, only several hundred people in all of China passed the examinations each time (Kracke, cited in Liu and Goias 1969, 14). Still, it was not uncommon for people *not* from mandarin families to attain success through this avenue.[14]

For those who passed the examination and were appointed to government positions, the opportunity to accumulate wealth became a likely prospect. Like the ancient Romans, the sources of these earnings usually were not associated with productive economic activity:

Corruption, which is widespread in all impoverished and backward countries (or, more exactly, throughout the pre-industrial world), was endemic in a country where the servants of the state often had nothing to live on but their very meager salaries. The required attitude of obedience to superiors made it impossible for officials to demand higher salaries, and in the absence of any control over their activities from below it was inevitable that they should purloin from society what the state failed to provide. According to the usual pattern, a Chinese official entered upon his duties only after spending long years in study and passing many examinations; he then established relations with protectors, incurred debts to get himself appointed, and then proceeded to extract the amount he had spent on preparing himself for his career from the people he administered—and extracted both principal and interest. The degree of his rapacity would be dictated not only by the length of time he had had to wait for his appointment and the number of relations he had to support and of kin to satisfy or repay, but also by the precariousness of his position. (Balazs 1964, 10)

On the other hand, enterprise in medieval China was not only frowned on, but may have been subjected to impediments deliberately imposed by officials during the fourteenth century, if not much earlier. Balazs describes

the state's tendency to clamp down immediately on any form of private enterprise (and this in the long run kills not only initiative but even the slightest attempts at innovation), or, if it did not succeed in putting a stop to it in time, to take over and nationalize it. Did it not frequently happen during the course of Chinese history that the scholar-officials, although hostile to all inventions, nevertheless gathered in the fruits of other people's ingenuity? I need mention only three examples of inventions that met this fate: paper, invented by a eunuch; printing, used by the Buddhists as a medium for religious propaganda; and the bill of exchange, an expedient of private businessmen. (1964, 18)

As a result of the low status of mercantile activity and recurrent intervention by the state to curtail personal liberty and seize any accumulated innovative advantages, members of the medieval Chinese merchant class focused their ambitions not on innovation, but rather on the more respectable activity of investing in land and on preparing their descendents for entry into the bureaucracy, via the imperial examinations (Balazs 1964, 32).

CASE STUDY 3: EUROPE IN THE EARLY MIDDLE AGES

Before the rise of European cities and before monarchs were able to subdue the bellicose activities of the nobility, military activity provided the prime means of achieving wealth and power. Since land and castles were the most highly valued forms of wealth in medieval Europe, it seems reasonable to interpret the warring of the barons, in good part, as the pursuit of economic objectives. For example, during the reign of William the Conqueror, barons in Normandy and neighboring portions of France frequently attempted to take over each other's lands and castles (Douglas 1964). Indeed, a prime incentive for William's supporters in his conquest of England was their aspiration for land.[15] Violent conquest also provided more liquid forms of income—captured treasure, for instance—that the nobility used to support both private consumption and investment in military equipment. Moreover, in England, where primogeniture held that the eldest son had the exclusive right to inherit his father's estate, younger sons who chose not to enter the clergy often had no socially acceptable means—other than warfare—of making their fortunes. William Marshal, fourth son of a minor noble, exemplifies the spectacular success achieved by some of these younger sons (Painter 1933). Through his military accomplishments, Marshal became one of the wealthiest men in England and, eventually, a leading advisor to Henry II and Richard I.

Just as no modern capitalist is motivated purely by economic objectives, Europe's medieval nobles were not purely economic men. Many of the rebellious barons undoubtedly enjoyed fighting for its own sake, and success in combat was an important avenue to prestige in their society. Thus, warfare—pursued for a variety of reasons—*also* was undertaken as a primary source of economic gain. This was especially true of the mercenary armies of fourteenth-century France and Italy.

Although medieval warfare, in itself, was a form of entrepreneurial activity, it is also important to note that such violent economic activity inspired frequent and profound *innovation* on the battlefield. The introduction of the stirrup, for instance, was a requisite for effective cavalry tactics. Meanwhile, castle building evolved from wooden to stone structures, with once-rectangular towers redesigned as rounded structures that could not be made to collapse by undermining their corners. With the introduction of the crossbow, the longbow, and, ultimately, artillery based on gunpowder, armor and weaponry grew steadily more sophisticated, as did military tactics and strategy.

These entrepreneurial activities obviously differ from the introduction of a cost-saving industrial process or a valuable new consumer product. Indeed, individuals who pursue wealth through the forcible appropriation of others' possessions surely do not add to the national product. Moreover, the net effect of such activity may not be merely a transfer of wealth, but an overall reduction in a society's economic wealth.[16]

CASE STUDY 4: EUROPE IN THE LATE MIDDLE AGES

By the end of the eleventh century the rules of the game that had prevailed during the Dark Ages had changed. The revival of towns was well under way, and with the towns came a number of new privileges—among them, protection from arbitrary taxation and confiscation. Many towns also granted freedom to runaway serfs, after a relatively brief residence (a year and a day), thereby creating a labor force. Amid these changes, a number of activities that were neither agricultural nor military began to yield handsome returns. The small group of architect-engineers who were in charge of building cathedrals, palaces, bridges, and fortresses, for instance, lived in great luxury in the service of their kings. Water-driven mills, a technological innovation common in France and southern England by the eleventh century, were a far more common source of earnings, however. The prospect of holding monopoly rights to such technical advances—rather than any resulting improvements in efficiency—provided the prime incentive for the development of such new innovations (Bloch 1935, 554–57; Brooke 1964, 84).

Not all innovation during the late Middle Ages followed the model of entrepreneurship described here. Take, for example, the Cistercian monks, who played a critical role in the adoption of water mills for grinding flour, sawing lumber, hammering metal, and preparing cloth, among other productive purposes. In the twelfth century, the Cistercians constructed thousands of such mills (Gimpel 1976, 46–47 and 229–30), but historians have no ready explanation for the entrepreneurial propensities of this monastic order. One hypothesis, offered by Constance Berman Ovitt,[17] a leading authority on the subject, proposes that the monks undertook such entrepreneurial activities in an effort to reduce manual labor and, thus, maximize the time available for more satisfying activities, such as preparation of manuscripts.

The Cistercians' story differs from that of ordinary entrepreneurs in yet another notable way: despite their dedicated pursuit of wealth, the monks adhered to a simple, austere lifestyle. Accordingly, they were not typical entrepreneurs, intent on pursuing the usual goals—wealth, power, and prestige. Instead, ironically, they perhaps represent an early manifestation of the Protestant ethic.

CASE STUDY 5: FOURTEENTH-CENTURY EUROPE

The fourteenth century brought with it a considerable increase in military activity—notably, the Hundred Years' War between France and England. Accordingly, payoffs must have tilted to favor inventions designed for military purposes. Cannons appeared as siege devices, and armor was made heavier. The remarkable monk Roger Bacon proposed especially imaginative, new war devices—among them, a windmill-propelled war wagon, a multibarreled machine gun, and a diving suit for use in underwater attacks on ships. This unhappy century of war also brought with it mercenary troops—the condottiere—who roamed Europe, supported by the side that could offer the most attractive terms. When the fighting reached a lull, threatening unemployment for the condotierre, these soldiers-for-hire created military enterprises of their own, at the expense of the general public (Gimpel 1976, chap. 9).[18] Clearly, the rules of the game—the system of entrepreneurial rewards—had changed again, to the disadvantage of productive, welfare-enhancing entrepreneurship.

ON THE HISTORY OF RENT-SEEKING ENTREPRENEURSHIP

Unproductive entrepreneurship—a slight generalization of chapter 8's redistributive entrepreneurship concept—may take less violent forms, usually involving various types of rent seeking. This form of (possibly) unproductive entrepreneurship seems most relevant today, but enterprising use of the legal system for rent-seeking purposes has a long history. There are, for example, records of the use of litigation in the twelfth century in which the proprietor of a water-driven mill sought and won prohibition of the use of mills driven by animal or human power in the vicinity (Gimpel 1976, 25–26). In another case, the operators of two dams—one upstream of the other—sued one another repeatedly from the second half of the thirteenth century until the beginning of the fifteenth century, when the upstream dam ran out of money to pay the court fees and went out of business (Gimpel 1976, 17–20).

Beginning in about the fifteenth century, in the upper strata of society, rent seeking gradually replaced military activity as a prime source of wealth and power. This transition perhaps can be ascribed to the imposition of law and order that accompanied the establishment of stable European monarchies, after centuries of ongoing warfare. Rent-seeking entrepreneurship then took a variety of forms, notably, the quest for grants of land and patents of monopoly from monarchs. Such activities sometimes contribute to production, as when the recipient of land given by a monarch uses it more efficiently than the previous owner. However, there seems to have been nothing in the structure of the land-granting process that ensured even a tendency toward transfer to more productive proprietors, nor was the individual who sought such grants likely to use, as an argument in favor of his suit, the claim that he was apt to be the more productive user (in terms of, say, the expected net value of the land's agricultural output).

By the time the eighteenth-century industrial revolution arrived, matters had changed once again. According to Ashton, grants of monopoly, by the monarchs, for the manufacture or sale of certain products were, in good part, "swept away" by the Monopolies Act of 1624 (1948, 9–10). Indeed, Adam Smith (1937) wrote that, by the end of the eighteenth century, monopolies were rarer in England than in any other country.

Meanwhile, despite its obvious financial rewards, productive activity continued to be considered somewhat degrading. In England, where primogeniture forced the younger sons of noble families to resort to commerce and industry—rather than inherited wealth—these activities gradually came to be seen as respectable. Still, ambivalent skepticism of such professions lingered well into the Industrial Revolution. Thus, "The [French] nobility . . . were envious of the English lords who enriched themselves in bourgeois ways" (Lefebvre 1947, 14). At the same time, however, French nobles continued to look down on industrial activity—for, in France, "the noble 'derogated' or fell into the common mass if he followed a business or profession" (Lefebvre 1947, 11).[19] It is unsurprising, therefore, that the Industrial Revolution in England substantially preceded similar developments in France.

CONCLUDING COMMENT

If entrepreneurship is the imaginative pursuit of position, with limited concern about the means used to achieve the purpose, we can expect changes in the structure of entrepreneurial rewards to modify the nature of the entrepreneur's activities, sometimes drastically. Consequently, legal, social, and economic incentives for entrepreneurial activity—the rules of the game—play a critical role in helping to determine whether or not a society's supply of entrepreneurship will be allocated predominantly to activities that are productive or to those that are unproductive.

The Allocation of Entrepreneurship
Does Matter

Nor was the mere knowledge of these matters sufficient; for that knowledge might possibly have lain dormant in the memory of one or two persons, or in the pages of literature. It was further requisite that [an entrepreneur] should have been found, possessed of the means of reducing the knowledge into practice.

—J. B. Say, *A Treatise on Political Economy* (1827, 22)

This chapter goes on from the point where chapter 9 left off. There we argued, with the aid of a profusion of historical examples, that the tasks to which entrepreneurs choose to devote their efforts are not haphazardly selected, but are determined by the prevailing institutions and the relative payoffs they promise for the different activities available to the entrepreneur. In this chapter, we will use additional historical evidence to support the contention that the allocation of entrepreneurial activity directly affects the growth of an economy, as well as the general welfare of that society. Thus, this chapter focuses on our concluding proposition:

> **PROPOSITION 10.1:** The allocation of entrepreneurship between productive and unproductive activities—though not the only pertinent influence—can have a profound effect on an economy's innovativeness and the degree of dissemination of its technological discoveries.

It is hard to believe that a system of payoffs that moves entrepreneurship in *unproductive* directions is not a substantial impediment to industrial innovation and growth in productivity. Still, history permits no test of this proposition through anything resembling a set of controlled experiments, as other influences undoubtedly help to shape innovation in any economy, as Proposition 10.1 implicitly recognizes. One can only note the remarkable correlation between the degree to which an economy rewards *productive* entrepreneurship and the vigor shown in that economy's innovation record.

Historians tell us of several industrial "near revolutions" and their attendant technological progress and relative prosperity, which occurred before *the* Industrial Revolution of the eighteenth century (Braudel 1979–86, 3:542–56; for a more skeptical view, see Coleman 1956). Although some of these incipient revolutions never went anywhere, others were rather successful in their fashion. In the discussion that follows, we will consider some of the consequences of these situations, which we discussed in chapter 9.[1]

CASE STUDY 1: ANCIENT ROME

Chapter 9's discussion cited ancient Rome and its empire as a case in which the "rules" did not favor productive entrepreneurship. Let us compare this structure of rewards with the evidence on the vigor of innovative activity in that society.

Alexandria was the center of technological innovation in the Roman Empire. By the first century BC, that city knew of virtually every form of machine gearing that is used today, including a working steam engine. However, these breakthroughs seem to have been used only to make what amounted to elaborate toys. The steam engine, for instance, is reported to have been used only to open and close the doors of a temple, as if by magic.

The Romans also had the water mill. This may well have been the most critical pre-eighteenth-century industrial invention because, aside from the use of sails in transportation by water, such mills provided the first significant source of power other than human and animal labor (Forbes 1955, 2:90). Water mills could have served as the basis for a leap in productivity in the Roman economy, as they did during the eleventh, twelfth, and thirteenth centuries in Europe. However, as Finley reports, the Romans failed to seize the opportunity:

> Though [the water mill] was invented in the first century B.C., it was not until the third century A.D. that we find evidence of much use, and not until the fifth and sixth of general use. It is also a fact that we have no evidence at all of its application to other industries [i.e., other than grinding of grain] until the very end of the fourth century, and then no more than one solitary and possibly suspect reference . . . to a marble-slicing machine near Trier. (1965, 35–36, citing White 1962)

Such evidence of Roman technical stagnation is only spotty, at best. Some historians suggest that such historical reports give inadequate weight to the Roman preoccupation with agricultural improvement, relative to improvement in commerce or manufacture.[2] Still, it is curious, as Brooke (1964) notes, that "landlords of the Middle Ages proved so much more enterprising than the landlords of the Roman Empire, although the latter, by and large, were much better educated, had much better opportunities for making technical and scientific discoveries if they had wished to do so" (88). It seems at least plausible that some part of the explanation can be found in the ancient world's "rules of the game," which, as we saw in chapter 9, encouraged the pursuit of wealth but severely discouraged the exercise of productive entrepreneurship.

CASE STUDY 2: MEDIEVAL CHINA

The spate of inventions that occurred in medieval China before it was conquered by the barbarian Yuan dynasty in 1280 constituted one of the earliest potential industrial revolutions. Among the many Chinese technological contributions are paper, waterwheels, printing, sophisticated water clocks, the umbrella, playing cards, the spinning wheel, and, of course, gunpowder. However, some historians suggest that these inventions failed to spur a flowering of industry[3] and, with that, some degree of general prosperity.

In China at that time, as noted in chapter 9, the rules did not favor productive entrepreneurship. Indeed, as Balazs concludes,

> What was chiefly lacking in China for the further development of capitalism was not mechanical skill or scientific aptitude, nor a sufficient accumulation of wealth, but scope for individual enterprise. There was no individual freedom and no security for private enterprise, no legal foundation for rights other than those of the state, no alternative investment other than landed property, no guarantee against being penalized by arbitrary exactions from officials or against intervention by the state. But perhaps the supreme inhibiting factor was the overwhelming prestige of the state bureaucracy, which maimed from the start any attempt of the bourgeoisie to be different, to become aware of themselves as a class and fight for an autonomous position in society. Free enterprise, ready and proud to take risks, is therefore quite exceptional and abnormal in Chinese economic history. (1964, 53)

Of course, we cannot claim certainty for such pronouncements, but the observations of scholars surely provide us with a significant part of this story.

CASE STUDY 3: SLOW GROWTH IN EUROPE IN
THE EARLY MIDDLE AGES

The era between the death of Charlemagne, in 814, and the end of the tenth century is often noted for its slow economic growth. However, even this period was not without technological advances, such as the agricultural improvements that attended the introduction of the horseshoe, harness, and stirrup, the heavy plow, and the substitution of horsepower for oxen. Indeed, these innovations may have played a role in enabling peasants to move to more populous villages located farther from their fields (White 1962, 39ff.). Still, growth during this period occurred at a significantly slower pace than it did during the European industrial revolution of the eleventh, twelfth, and thirteenth centuries (Gimpel 1976). Military violence, which was a prime outlet for entrepreneurial activity during the Dark Ages, may help to explain the dearth of productive entrepreneurship. This can hardly be the sole explanation for the era's relative stagnation, but it is hard to believe that this factor had no effect.

CASE STUDY 4: LATE MIDDLE AGES EUROPE

The successful industrial revolution of the late Middle Ages and its ac-companying commercial revolution, sparked by inventions such as double-entry bookkeeping and bills of exchange (De Roover 1953), lasted two centuries—as long as our own industrial revolution, which began in the eighteenth century and continues today (Carus-Wilson 1941; White 1962; Gimpel 1976).

Perhaps the hallmark of this industrial revolution was that remarkable source of productive power, water mills, which covered the countryside in the south of England and crowded the banks of the Seine in Paris (Gimpel 1976, 3–6; Berman 1986, 81–89). The mills were not only simple grain-grinding devices, but accomplished an astonishing variety of tasks, such as crushing olives, grinding mash for beer production, crushing cloth for papermaking, sawing lumber, hammering metal and woolens, milling coins, polishing armor, and operating the bellows of blast furnaces. Moreover, they involved an impressive variety of mechanical devices and sophisticated gear arrangements, which entailed many forms of ingenuity. Indeed, the mechanical skill and knowledge associated with increasingly sophisticated water mills resulted in the invention of the mechanical clock at the end of the thirteenth century.

In a period in which agriculture probably occupied some 90 percent of the population, the expansion of industry, by itself, could not have created a major upheaval in living standards.[4] Still, the industrial activity of the twelfth and thirteenth centuries was substantial. By the beginning of the fourteenth century, for instance, 68 water mills were in operation on less than one mile of the banks of the Seine in Paris, and they were supplemented by floating mills anchored to the Grand Pont (Gimpel 1976). Activity in metallurgy was also considerable—sufficient to denude much of Europe of its forests and to produce an increase in the price of wood that forced recourse to coal (Nef 1934).[5] In sum, the European industrial revolution of the twelfth and thirteenth centuries was a surprisingly robust affair, and it is surely plausible that improved rewards to industrial activity had something to do with its vigor.

CASE STUDY 5: THE FOURTEENTH-CENTURY RETREAT

The period of buoyant economic activity, described in the previous section, ended in the fourteenth century.[6] Historians and economists offer a variety of explanations for this economic slowdown—many of them unrelated to entrepreneurship. For one thing, it has been deduced by study of the glaciers that average temperatures dropped, possibly reducing crop yields and creating other hardships.[7] The plague also returned, decimating much of the population.

In addition to these natural disasters, there were at least two pertinent developments of human origin. First, the church clamped down on new ideas and personal rights. Roger Bacon, perhaps the most notable scientific thinker of his time, was even put under constraint.[8] The fourteenth century also included the first half of the devastating Hundred Years' War. With the rewards for military enterprise renewed by the arrival of war, it is plausible that entrepreneurs of this era were lured away from productive activity to better-compensated military endeavors.

ON "OUR" INDUSTRIAL REVOLUTION

The Industrial Revolution that began in the eighteenth century and continues today generally has brought to the industrialist and the businessperson a degree of wealth and a respect unprecedented in human history. Moreover, this period has yielded an equally unparalleled explosion of output.

It is highly implausible that such remarkable growth in output and innovation is not intimately connected with the extraordinarily high financial and respectability rewards for productive entrepreneurship that induce entrepreneurs to devote themselves to the necessary tasks. As indicated in Proposition 10.1, the allocation of entrepreneurship *does* influence an

169

economy's promotion of innovative vigor via the attraction of entrepreneurial activity to this task.

ON UNPRODUCTIVE AVENUES FOR
TODAY'S ENTREPRENEUR

Unproductive entrepreneurship takes many forms. Rent seeking—often via litigation, corporate takeovers, or tax evasion—arguably constitutes the prime current threat to productive entrepreneurship. The spectacular fortunes amassed by "arbitrageurs" and others associated with the scandals that have emerged almost continuously since the mid-1980s, for instance, surely were—at least *sometimes*—the reward for unproductive and even illegal entrepreneurial acts.

Other, less sensational examples of rent-seeking behavior are also plentiful. Corporate executives devote much of their time and energy to legal suits and countersuits, using litigation to blunt or prevent excessive vigor in competition by rivals. Huge awards by the courts bring prosperity to the victor and threaten the loser with insolvency. Entrepreneurial firms spend hundreds of millions of dollars for a single legal battle and rush to sue other firms before they, in turn, can be sued. Given this reality, it must be tempting for entrepreneurs to select their closest advisers from among lawyers—rather than engineers.[9]

Similarly, taxes can influence the allocation of entrepreneurial effort. As Lindbeck has observed, "The problem with high-tax societies is not that it is impossible to become rich there, but that it is difficult to do so by way of productive effort in the ordinary production system" (1988, 15). Examples of resulting unproductive entrepreneurship can include anything from " 'smart' speculative financial transactions without much (if any) contribution to the productive capacity of the economy" to "illegal 'business areas' such as drug dealing" (Lindbeck 1988, 15, 25).

It is true that threats of corporate takeovers are sometimes used as a means to extract "greenmail"—a somewhat more polite form of economic blackmail—while recourse to the courts has become a means of preserving rents through legally imposed impediments to competition. Such activities attract entrepreneurial talent and channel their efforts in unproductive directions. But because takeovers do discipline inefficient corporate management, and legitimate antitrust intervention can contribute to productivity, it is important to preserve these legal institutions. Some promising proposals for institutional reforms have been offered, but it will be difficult to change the rules in a way that discourages allocation of entrepreneurial effort into such unproductive activities without, at the same time, undermining the legitimate role of these institutions.

CONCLUDING COMMENT

The material presented in this chapter is intended to constitute a minor expansion of Schumpeter's theoretical model of the determinants of the *allocation* of entrepreneurship. Although the material here does not constitute a formal test of these hypotheses—much less a rigorous proof, the discussion here is substantive and, moreover, yields clear policy implications.

The key change in theory proposed here is the reinterpretation of changes in the number and magnitude of *productive* entrepreneurs' activities—from the old story, which attributes the sudden outburst or disappearance of this population of entrepreneurs to somewhat mysterious exogenous influences, to a new one, in which their efforts are understood to be simply reallocated between productive and unproductive activities. Since resource allocation is the bread and butter of microtheorists, this observation should facilitate further investigation and expansion of the theory of entrepreneurship.

This view of the matter also offers much clearer guidance for policy. If, as asserted by Propositions 9.1, 9.2, and 10.1, the rules of the game that specify the relative payoffs to different entrepreneurial activities also play a key role in determining whether entrepreneurship will be allocated in productive or unproductive directions, we have clearer guidance toward means that can significantly affect the vigor of the economy's productivity growth. After all, the prevailing laws and legal procedures of an economy are prime determinants of the profitability of entrepreneurial activities.

The overall moral, then, is that we do not have to wait patiently and passively for slow cultural change to redirect the flow of entrepreneurial activity toward more productive goals. On the contrary, it should be possible to change the rules in ways that help to offset undesired institutional influences or that establish payoffs that reward productive entrepreneurial activities over those that generate less beneficial results.

Mega-enterprising Redesign of Governing Institutions: Keystone of Dynamic Microtheory

God helps those who help themselves.

—Early American proverb

The spirit of the age is the very thing that a great man changes.

—Benjamin Disraeli, *Coningsby* (1904, 158)

As we have seen in the preceding chapters, this book follows the literature that ascribes determination of the activities and rewards of entrepreneurs to prevailing institutions. Rather than being carefully planned and implemented, many of these institutions were created and shaped by historical accident—for example, the financial pressures that led the combat-prone English monarchy to introduce measures protecting the economic positions of the nobility and yeomen.

But it is not credible that entrepreneurs would be content to leave such matters altogether to chance. The "rules of the game"—an economy's entrepreneurial reward structure—can be modified intentionally, and who more than the entrepreneur can be expected to undertake this task? Here, Kirzner's (1973) key observation that an entrepreneur's primary qualification is alertness to unexhausted opportunities is especially relevant. *Among the opportunities that surely would attract capable entrepreneurs is the search for ways to modify the institutions and attendant rules of the game that determine the compensation for their activities.* Entrepreneurs may do this exploration in order to increase their own direct earnings. But more than that, *they also can be expected to seek to sell this service to others.* As a result, these "mega-entrepreneurs" commercialize the service of redesigning institutions in ways that further the interests of their customers.

In societies in which the rule of law does not prevail, entrepreneurs may be drawn to stand for political office, or may even take on the role of warlord. In doing so, they hope to be able to change institutions and the rules of the game by influence or fiat. But in a generally law-abiding society, such as the United States, entrepreneurs generally do not want to undermine the rule of law, which protects their earnings and property. Instead, they operate within the rules, seeking to preserve or modify the pertinent features of current institutions, as their interests dictate. In this role, they become "lobbyists"—that is, professional influencers of the law.[1]

Contrary to Schumpeter, entrepreneurs must be prepared to accept risk and live with uncertainty. However, we can be confident that entrepreneurs will seek to reduce the risks their activities entail, while enhancing their rewards. The obvious way to achieve both of these goals is to modify the rules of the game—that is, to shape the institutions that govern an entrepreneur's payoffs. Accordingly, entrepreneurs and institutions have a two-way relationship: the institutions are primary determinants of entrepreneurial activity and its reward, while the entrepreneurs return the favor, doing what they can to mold the relevant institutions in ways that best serve their own interests.[2] Indeed, this relationship has evolved into a markedly prosperous and rapidly expanding industry.

Here it is helpful to adopt an impressionistic distinction between "mega-institutional innovations," which influence the very existence of the society to which they pertain, and "routine institutional innovations," whose influence is limited, but not insignificant. The former evidently entail such upheavals as the religious revolutions launched by Mohammed and Luther or the cessation of interference in monarchical activities that followed the conclusion of the Wars of the Roses and the establishment of the Tudors. Indeed, one such major development served as the focus of Weber's *Religion and the Rise of Capitalism*.

The entrepreneurs who are the focus of this book, however, generally undertake less radical changes. That is, they focus on the more modest institutions that define the specific rules of the game that affect their activities. Changes in antitrust laws, the constraints on interstate banking activities, or the rules of bankruptcy, for instance, are hardly revolutionary, but together they exert powerful influence on the business environment. Indeed, a substantial change in these rules can materially modify general business behavior and rewards—especially those of entrepreneurs.

Among the influences that lead to changes in the prevailing institutions are the deliberate actions of entrepreneurs who seek, as their professional activity, to modify these relatively minor institutions in order to benefit themselves or their clients by increasing the rewards offered by certain entrepreneurial activities. These entrepreneurs generally do not seek to influence

the current institutional structure by attacking its mega-institutions—
an approach that is recognized to be overambitious, and which may subject
those who undertake such a course to the killing of their golden goose, if
the effort fails. Instead, such entrepreneurs generally direct their attention
to the modification of routine institutions, using routine methods for the
purpose.

HISTORICAL MALLEABILITY OF INSTITUTIONS

Until perhaps the sixteenth century, businesspeople were in no position
to do anything about the institutions that constrained their existence and
activities. Instead, we must look beyond the business sector—the source of
so much modern entrepreneurial activity—to find the prime entrepreneurs
of earlier eras.

If Julius Caesar, surely one of the most dramatically successful redistributive entrepreneurs in recorded history, is not a prime example, his
successor certainly was. Shakespeare implies that despite Marc Antony's
denial—"You all did see that on the Lupercal / I thrice presented him
[Caesar] a kingly crown, / Which he did thrice refuse" (act 3, scene 2, ll.
94–96)—Caesar was most ambitious. Indeed, when he crossed the Rubicon,
he dramatically initiated the crucial step in the process of undermining the
Roman republic—a striking change in institutions that was calculated to
enhance Caesar's wealth, power, and prestige.[3] In the end, it was left to
Augustus, Caesar's nephew, to terminate the republic and introduce the
rule of the emperors. This institutional upheaval is so patently self-serving
that it seems almost ridiculous to cite it here as an illustration of enterprising institution changing. However, I argue that there is little fundamental
difference between this upheaval and that entailed in the corporate take-
over of an undeveloped country, which transforms a society of hunter-
gatherers into an island of slave-worked sugar plantations. Were not those
who undertook such imperialistic ventures true entrepreneurs—even *innovative* entrepreneurs—no matter how distasteful their activities? Moreover,
was not the changing of institutions a critical part of their activities?

Aside from the example of Caesar, history is replete with cases of enterprising usurpation. There are also many instances—a number of them
described in preceding chapters of this book—in which influential citizens
rose up against their kings to demand radical revision of the rules of the
game. (Such changes, no doubt, also entailed economic advantages for the
brave revolutionaries.) This demonstrates the characteristic precariousness
of monarchical power—a fact that must have provided additional incentive for institution-attacking entrepreneurs.

IMPERIAL INSTITUTIONS IN SUNG CHINA

Not all kings and emperors disdained enterprising activity. Throughout history, monarchs seeking to promote their vital interests have played key roles in the game of institution-molding. The imperial examination system of Sung Dynasty China (AD 960–1279) provides a fascinating example.

Awareness of China's imperial examinations is widespread, but there are many misconceptions about the nature of the examination system. First, the examinations focused on verbatim memorization of ancient Confucian texts, emphasizing ability to recognize instantly the most obscure passage and to report accurately its officially approved interpretation.[4] Second, despite the adoption of painstaking measures to impede favoritism, the examinations were beset by cheating.[5] Most important, the examinations were not intended to open the civil service to the population as a whole, as part of a move toward democracy. They did bring personnel from outside the aristocracy and the entrenched bureaucracy into government service, but the number of such neophyte members of the bureaucracy was minuscule in comparison with the portion of the population at issue.[6] Moreover, many groups, such as merchants and Buddhist priests, were excluded from the examinations.

Instead, as some historians argue, the central purpose of the examinations may have been to reduce the role of the old aristocracy in the government. In chapter 8, we discussed the conflicts that characterized the sometimes turbulent relationship between medieval kings and their nobles, noting that more than one British king was deposed and replaced by a member of the nobility. Chinese emperors, too, suffered this fate, as well as other less extreme problems with aristocrats. As Lee notes, "The history of the civil service examination system since its inception in the late sixth century shows that the system was designed with a specifically defined purpose: it was to be used to curtail the influence of the hereditary aristocratic families" (1985, 201).[7] Thus, the Chinese imperial examinations arguably provide another example of the enterprising use of influence to ensure that the rules of the game served an enterprising goal—that of the Sung emperor.

DELIBERATE REDESIGN OF INSTITUTIONS UNDER CAPITALISM

With the advent of the Renaissance, the powers of entrepreneurial business people grew. Members of the commerce-financed Medici family, for instance, were propelled by their wealth and status into the papacy and the French royal family. From these positions, they effectively became the (temporary) rulers of Florence and, in the process, influenced—sometimes profoundly—the institutions under which the economy operated.

A number of critical institutions—banks, limited corporate liability, and the patent system, for instance—surely were introduced, at least in part, to encourage entrepreneurship and to serve the interests of the entrepreneurs. It is remarkable, for instance, that an institution as economically motivated as the patent system—which has little in common with political ideals such as individual freedom—should have been incorporated so directly into the Constitution of the United States. I do not intend to go as far as the thesis ascribed to the noted historian Charles Beard, who is often taken to have asserted that the constitutional convention was a gathering of self-interested businessmen intent on drafting an instrument whose primary purpose was to promote their economic interests. However, the opposite interpretation seems equally untenable. I propose that, although many of the members of the constitutional convention were, no doubt, deeply idealistic, they evidently saw no harm in making sure that their financial interests would be undamaged by their new country's laws—probably believing that doing so would benefit other Americans, as well as themselves.

Such institutional changes, deliberately designed and adopted, did make a substantial difference for the workings of the economy and the opportunities it offered entrepreneurs. A prime example is constituted by the banks, including those of the Medici family in fifteenth-century Italy, the Bank of Amsterdam (1609), the Bank of England (1694), and Alexander Hamilton's eighteenth-century Bank of the United States. These institutions, undertaken by businesspersons or with the support of the business community, affected their economies substantially.

Obviously, throughout history, banks have provided many services to the economies in which they operate. I will discuss only one such service, international money transfers, which seems particularly pertinent here—especially as it still seems to be missing in many of the world's poorest economies and even in rapidly growing China. This service is critical in permitting a firm to deliver products to customers in distant markets who are not known and trusted by the seller. In practice, such sales once required that a member of the family own the firm, or that a trusted friend be the recipient of the shipment. For if the distance involved a travel time of days or even weeks, the customer who paid in advance had no assurance that the shipment would ever be sent out, much less received. Similarly, if the payment were to be made after receipt of the product, the seller had no assurance of reimbursement by the customer. This condemned firms to deal in small markets, or in a very few more distant markets in which a fully trusted representative, often a family relative, was located. Thereby, economies of scale were inhibited or precluded.

The solution to this problem was the presence of a bank with many branches. For that bank's profitability and, indeed, survival, a reputation of integrity and reliability was essential. Thus, parties located at great distances from one another who did not know one another could carry on business with confidence, if the bank at the seller's location could guarantee that a shipment had been sent, while a branch at the customer's location could offer assurance that the payment had been made. For enterprising sellers, the advantages of such an institution are clear, and it is not surprising that they would undertake the effort to facilitate its creation and promote its acceptance and use by other businesspeople.

Still, in much of the world, such institutions are hardly ubiquitous. Indeed, as Parker and Basu (2001) note, it is still common for international transactions to be carried out only between family members or trusted friends. For a variety of reasons, entrepreneurs in such places have not yet attempted or succeeded in establishing the banking institutions that open the way to expansion of firms, their markets, and profits.

One can easily think of other such institutions whose establishment has drawn the support of entrepreneurs. The patent system has already been mentioned. The corporation, with its limited liability, is another example. Entrepreneurs are apt to leave as little as possible to chance for their operations, and they are well aware that protection of their interests requires a number of critical institutions. Accordingly, they can be expected to support the creation and operation of those institutions.

LOBBYISTS: ENTREPRENEURIAL INSTITUTION-MOLDERS

We have just seen cases in which individuals influenced or, by themselves, made profound changes in the rules of the game, with the aim of modifying the economy or promoting what they took to be the interests of their society. Alexander Hamilton, who laid out his goals for the newly created United States and the means by which he believed they could be accomplished in his *Report on Manufactures*,[8] is a prime example. The Napoleonic Code, introduced in France during the reign of Napoleon Bonaparte, is another illustration.

In more recent times, entrepreneurs have continued to influence the institutions that affect their concerns. More than that, they have routinized the process of making institutional changes, making its procedures commonplace. Political contributions are the most obvious instruments for this purpose. In an American election campaign, it has become common for interested parties—notably, wealthy business firms—to pour contributions into the coffers of *several* of the main opposing candidates. In return, those candidates may or may not make explicit (if concealed) commitments to their most generous supporters, thereby recognizing the existence of a debt that ultimately must be repaid.

The prime modern instrument for influencing the redesign of institutions, however, is the lobbyist, whose sole job is to influence the actions of legislators and other government personnel by inducing them to support measures that serve their interests or the interests of the business firms that employ them.[9] Moreover, the organizers of such profitable lobbying firms are themselves entrepreneurs, whose services are for hire by others.

Under U.S. law, lobbyists must register themselves, in order to prevent concealed and underhanded activities. The reports based on the information this provides indicate that, since World War II, the number of registered lobbyists in Washington, D.C., has increased dramatically. At least in part, this surely can be ascribed to the value of lobbyists' achievements in modifying institutions that affect the welfare of their customers' firms. Thus, one class of entrepreneurs does well by doing good for other entrepreneurs, who are engaged in different activities.

ENTERPRISING METHODS OF MOLDING INSTITUTIONS

Institution changing can sometimes serve as a competitive instrument, in which firms with divergent interests battle over the shape of institutional modifications. This can entail recourse to the courts, the regulatory agencies, or Congress—institutions where those seeking favorable changes in the rules that directly affect their firms can hope to achieve their goals. A striking illustration is the recent history of AT&T—once the world's largest corporation, but now effectively dead (its name survives, having been adopted by another entity as a marketing device). The story begins at the end of the 1950s, when AT&T held an effective monopoly of the United States' telecommunications network. The firm had been granted this monopoly in return for its provision of "universal service," including service at attractive prices to distant and isolated communities that were costly to serve. Eventually, complaints about the firm's resulting discriminatory price pattern, which included relatively high prices for some customers, led government regulators to legalize the entry of new firms that specialized in serving only the most profitable customers, driving down those prices. However, these new entrants were handicapped by AT&T's possession of "last mile" facilities—the final telephone connection with individual homes and offices that would have been impractical, financially, for AT&T's competitors to replicate. In 1981, the issue was resolved when AT&T agreed to divest itself of its local operating subsidiaries. As newly separate companies, these subsidiaries received possession of the last-mile facilities—each with a monopoly in a different region of the United

States. As part of the agreement, the subsidiaries were required to give both AT&T—now solely a provider of long-distance phone service—and its competitors equal access to last-mile facilities.

These children of AT&T—known as the "Baby Bells"—soon realized that their possession of the last-mile facilities was a critical advantage that allowed them to determine the prices companies providing long-distance phone service paid for access to customers, and AT&T quickly discovered that it could expect no favors from its offspring. Battles over the rules governing the prices the divested firms could charge AT&T and long-distance companies for access to last-mile infrastructure ensued in Congress and the courts. Finally, the Supreme Court undercut such institutional interference and, not long after, the vestigial AT&T, unprotected from high access prices, among other problems, was acquired by SBC Communications, one of its "offspring" firms.

Throughout this story, enterprising modification of regulatory institutions played a pivotal role—from the first attack on AT&T's legal monopoly by new entrants, to the ensuing battle over the instituted regime of last-mile access pricing. This entailed endless and costly hearings before state and national regulatory agencies and the courts, extending over decades. In other words, the battle over new pricing institutions, which settled the matter, was waged *outside* the marketplace, in those agencies and courts that determine regulatory institutions.

This brief history demonstrates some of the less obvious entrepreneurial means of modifying constraining institutions—specifically, government regulations. Other such rules, which govern modes of manufacture, product quality, and safety, are also institutions of enormous interest to business firms. As can be expected, enterprising efforts to modify these institutions often call for weakened constraints—for example, standards of product quality and methods of enforcement—as such constraints can be very costly to those engaged in producing and supplying the products in question.

Matters are not always so straightforward, however. In 2007, a number of imported products were found to be contaminated by lead paint or other dangerous substances. The resulting threat to customers' health and survival led to a substantial public outcry. As a result, the suppliers of these items and related products realized that their interests would be promoted by *tougher* rules and *more vigorous* enforcement, as a means of restoring customer confidence in their products. At this point, according to newspaper reports, affected firms, at least temporarily, switched their stances toward the rules and began pressing for more effective constraints.

In this instance, even those firms whose products had not raised any such safety issues could be expected to favor more constraining rules. This is a prime example of Ackerloff's lemons analysis, which holds that because customers generally have little ability to test such products for dangerous components—and may even possess little knowledge of what ingredients are dangerous—the unacceptable performance of *some* suppliers must unavoidably raise customer suspicions about products of other suppliers that do satisfy reasonable standards of safety. Thus, even firms that already provide acceptable products can be driven to favor more constraining regulations.[10]

LOBBYISTS AND MEGA-LOBBYISTS: DIFFERING SCALES OF INSTITUTION-MOLDING EFFORTS

There is no obvious way to quantify most of the activities carried out by innovative entrepreneurs, for their inherent and fundamentally inescapable heterogeneity means that few numerical data are available. As a consequence, abstract theories of entrepreneurship are apt to have little substance. They may offer us the platitude of the "rational" entrepreneur who brings her expenditures on any pertinent activity to the point where the marginal cost equals marginal revenue, but this truism offers little illumination, since the mere instincts of entrepreneurs are difficult to translate into observable magnitudes.

Still, there are some illuminating indicators of entrepreneurial activity, and the scale of the efforts they report are impressive. For one, there are data on lobbying expenditures by individual sponsoring firms and industries, compiled by the U.S. Congress.[11] Recent data indicate that there are approximately 35,000 lobbyists at work in the federal government alone. Moreover, as the *Washington Post* reported, between 2000 and 2005 the amount these lobbyists charged new clients doubled:

> To the great growth industries of America . . . add one more: influence peddling . . . Only a few other businesses have enjoyed greater prosperity in an otherwise fitful economy. . . . Lobbying firms can't hire people fast enough. Starting salaries have risen to about $300,000 a year for the best-connected aides eager to "move downtown" from Capitol Hill or the Bush administration. . . . The fees that lobbyists charge clients have also risen substantially. Retainers that had been $10,000 to $15,000 a month for new corporate clients before President Bush took office now are $20,000 to $25,000 a month or more, lobbyists say. Such fee inflation is widespread, even by newcomers. (Birnbaum 2005, A1)

Indeed, total spending on lobbying increased steadily between 1998 and 2009, as shown in table 11.1.

Moreover, among lobbyists' many clients, those that devote the largest sums of money to the activity are some of the best-established and most

Table 11.1

Total Spending on Lobbying Activities, 1998–2009 ($ billions)

1998	1999	2000	2001	2002	2003	2004	2005	2006	2007	2008	2009
$1.44	1.44	1.56	1.62	1.82	2.04	2.19	2.47	2.61	2.85	3.28	1.62

respected American firms and organizations. A list of the top spenders on lobbying during the decade between 1998 and 2009, as reported by the Center for Responsive Politics, is provided in table 11.2.

We can conclude, then, that lobbying is not conducted haphazardly. Rather, it is a well-organized industry, with at least one professional association, the American League of Lobbyists. The industry also has at least one public interest "watchdog" group, the Center for Responsive Politics, monitoring its activities. The number of clients to which professional lobbyists devote themselves ranges from one or two clients to as many as 50. Few, if any, of the economy's giant enterprises (including nonprofit organizations) eschew lobbying activities, but it is important to note that even small enterprises, which can only afford to purchase limited amounts of a busy lobbyist's time, are not excluded from this arena. In other words, lobbying is a prime example of a well-organized industry, with a widespread customer base, founded and maintained by entrepreneurs.

A huge amount of information on this very active industry is readily available. The Center for Responsive Politics, for instance, publishes periodic reports on lobbying expenditures, which provide spending totals by client name, lobbying firm, individual lobbyist, industry, government agency, or even specific political issue. This information reveals that the industry goes well beyond merely lobbying for others. As might be expected of the entrepreneurs who organized these activities into a formal industry, the institution-modification efforts that lobbyists specialize in carrying out often help not only their clients, *but also themselves*. Such mega-lobbying, which is composed of specialized entrepreneurs, who serve entrepreneurs, more generally, but also strive to facilitate further lobbying, can be interpreted as an effort to change the rules of the game in ways that enhance and protect lobbyists' own earning opportunities. Indeed, on its website, the American League of Lobbyists openly describes its mega-entrepreneurial activities:

> The American League of Lobbyists strongly supports a strong code of ethics for lobbyists, as evidenced by passage of our own code 20 years ago. We expect *all* lobbyists to comply with LDA reporting requirements, as well as House and Senate rules governing the conduct of legislators and lobbyists. However, we are concerned about some of the recent proposals for limiting lobbying activities,

Table 11.2
Top 20 Spenders on Lobbying, 1998–2009

Lobbying Client	Total Lobbying Expenditures (1998–2009)
U.S. Chamber of Commerce	$487,645,680
American Medical Association	$208,472,500
General Electric	$194,885,000
American Hospital Association	$172,900,431
AARP	$164,072,064
Pharmaceutical Research & Manufacturers of America	$154,533,400
Northrop Grumman	$133,515,253
Edison Electric Institute	$128,645,999
Business Roundtable	$127,980,000
National Association of Realtors	$127,977,380
Exxon Mobil	$124,626,942
Blue Cross/Blue Shield	$121,081,385
Verizon Communications	$116,423,908
Lockheed Martin	$115,067,888
Boeing Co.	$108,728,310
General Motors	$104,774,483
Southern Co.	$97,570,694
Freddie Mac	$96,164,048
Altria Group	$88,380,000
Ford Motor Co.	$86,069,808

feeling that once again we have become the scapegoats for all perceived abuses in the system. ALL [i.e., American League of Lobbyists] leadership will continue to be involved in the issue as Congress considers changes, seeking input from our membership but hopefully representing the profession as a whole.[12]

LOBBYING FOR THE PROMOTION OF PRODUCTIVE ENTREPRENEURSHIP

As Adam Smith emphasized, a central feature of the market mechanism is its ability, under certain circumstances, to harness greed and direct it for the promotion of the general welfare. That, after all, is what the invisible hand doctrine is about. However, that doctrine also emphasizes that greed unconstrained can materially damage the general welfare.

Lobbying is no exception. While it patently can have results that are exceedingly harmful to society, not all lobbying pursues self-interest and wealth. For example, universities, hospitals, and other nonprofit organizations engage in lobbying. Moreover, the rules that lobbying produces, even while in pursuit of self-interest, can work both ways. One expects, for example, that lobbying will be directed to creation of opportunities for the escape of taxation by those in the best position to bear taxes. But even this tendency can sometimes work the other way. Particularly relevant here is the manner in which this effort can lead to the promotion of innovative entrepreneurship.

In a simulating book, Zoltan Acs (forthcoming) draws our attention to the extraordinary record of philanthropic giving by entrepreneurs in the United States, a record apparently not matched, nor even remotely approximated, elsewhere. Moreover, he points out, higher education in the United States is, to an amazing extent, the creation of this philanthropy. Thus, for example, the University of Chicago and Rockefeller University are patently the creation of Rockefeller funding, Stanford University rests on the founding grant of Leland Stanford, Duke and Carnegie Mellon have a similar base, and the finances of most other private universities in the country continue to rely, to a substantial extent, on giving from the great American fortunes, which, in turn, derive from success in entrepreneurial (frequently, innovative entrepreneurial) activities. That U.S. tax policy has long provided strong incentives for such philanthropy is arguably part of the explanation for this special feature of the behavior of America's successful entrepreneurs.

But if entrepreneurs-turned-philanthropists are important to higher education, the reverse is also true. Although the education of a number of noted inventors and entrepreneurs—most obviously Edison and the Wright brothers—was limited, the evidence is that successful entrepreneurs, and especially inventors, are better educated than the general population (Baumol, Schilling, and Wolff 2009).[13] More than that, as the complexity of technology and other arenas of invention has steadily increased, the education of these groups similarly has improved (Baumol, Schilling, and Wolff 2009). Rather than abandoning their educations after elementary school, they now drop out of college—as did Bill Gates and a number of other leading figures in America's high-tech sector. Indeed, the prosperous performance of the American economy after World War II is arguably attributable, in significant part, to the federal financing of higher education for former members of the military forces, which led to a noteworthy surge in university attendance.

In other countries, however, entrepreneurial philanthropy plays a very small role in the financing of higher education—both because such giving is not traditional and also because other countries offer no special institutionalized incentives for such donations. Rather, the funding of higher education outside the United States almost exclusively comes from government, although that is beginning to change.

This distinction is important not because private funding is more (or less) virtuous than governmental support. Rather, the significance stems from the consequences of single-source funding as compared to financing derived from a multiplicity of sources. The general consequence of the former, no matter how well intended, is a tendency toward uniformity in approaches and education. This is hardly surprising, as government agencies are driven to enforce uniform rules in order to preserve the appearance and substance of impartiality. The homogenization that results from this approach also can be illustrated by the process of government funding of the arts in Europe, where, in one country, the funds may be channeled overwhelmingly to classical drama and ballet, while, in another country, experimental drama and modern dance are favored.

In contrast, in the United States, if an innovative arts organization's application for funding is rejected by a conservative grantor, the applicant can turn to an alternative source for funding, and creativity and diversity are thereby facilitated. Similarly, it can be argued that higher education in the United States has benefited significantly from the diversity of sources of funding and the consequent flexibility and opportunity for experimentation in teaching approaches. Perhaps this is why, in so many universities in other countries, the best and brightest faculty members have received their higher educations in the United States.

The point of this discussion is that the American approach, arguably, is exceptionally beneficial for the education of prospective inventors and entrepreneurs—for whom rigid educational approaches and drumming in of the methods and conclusions of the past can undermine imagination and creativity. In terms of practical policy, this implies that deliberate design of governments' tax policies, with the aim of encouraging the sort of philanthropy that has characterized the U.S. experience, can be one very helpful means to encourage innovative entrepreneurs and, thus, economic growth. It is true that such incentives will also encourage giving for worthy purposes other than education, as well as for purposes that many will consider questionable. However, one can be reasonably confident from experience that successful entrepreneurs will consider entrepreneurship to be a particularly meritorious object of support. It follows, then, that if stimulation of innovative entrepreneurship is a source of productivity and growth, as I have argued, it is important for the general welfare that the incentive structure of the tax system be considered from this viewpoint.

CONCLUDING COMMENT

This chapter describes a dynamic process in which the future of the economy is influenced heavily, or even guided, by its institutions. However, my discussion here departs from the general descriptive approach, which treats the emergence and development of existing institutions as a fortuitous accident of history. Nothing said here is intended to deny the important role of exogenous influences and accidental occurrences in shaping institutions. However, at least in the American economy, such developments rarely are left to chance—whether in the past, the present, or the foreseeable future. But surely this pattern is only to be expected of entrepreneurial individuals, who thrive on searching for and creating the opportunities that serve their interests.

Understanding this reality allows us to study and analyze the underlying mechanism in the relationship between institutions and entrepreneurs, its results, and its implications for the intertemporal trajectory of the economy. From the viewpoint of the larger social welfare, however, the virtues and vices of this process are not clear, despite the unpopularity that besets lobbying activity. First, it is not obvious whether entrepreneurially induced institutional change ultimately can be expected to enhance or hold back growth. As repeatedly emphasized in this book, unparalleled growth is surely the main accomplishment of the capitalist mechanism, of which lobbying is apt to be a significant part.

Moreover, the net benefit of economic expansion is not as clear-cut as many observers are prone to conclude. On this side, there is the argument in favor of growth as the indispensable source of the resources required to combat poverty, a position that I accept. Without growth, huge segments of the world's population—at least 1.4 billion people, as of 2008 (Chen and Ravallion 2008)—will continue to be condemned to lives that are, in Hobbes's much-cited phrase, "nasty, brutish, and short," without resources for improvement of health, provision of education, and availability of even rudimentary creature comforts. In response, however, environmentalists and others are apt to argue that economic growth, like the Trojan horse, carries with it hidden threats to our quality of life, or worse, even to human existence and other life on the planet.

There is still more to consider in this matter. A little thought suggests that entrepreneurial control of, or even substantial influence over, the institutions that ultimately govern society does not always lead to the best result in this best of all possible worlds. There is good reason, for example, why lobbyists are forbidden to conceal their occupation and their activities, as those activities are designed to promote lobbyists' own interests and those of their clients—sometimes even at the expense of society. Indeed,

185

that much-cited comment by Charles Wilson, former president of General Motors, on the parallel between benefits to his corporation and to the country as a whole, surely cannot be valid. Instead, a more accurate statement might be, "What is good for General Motors *may be* good for the country (but it ain't necessarily so)."

The analysis in this book supports the notion that, under market-driven, democratic capitalism, the incentives for productive entrepreneurship are likely to be enduring and can be expected to promote continuation of the flood of innovation and growth in per capita income for the foreseeable future. Certainly, there are threats to this process—indeed, the process itself is capable of creating its own obstacles. However, I hope that my analysis here will help us to recognize those threats, understand their workings, and design effective countermeasures.

APPENDIX

TOWARD A FORMAL MODEL OF MEGA-ENTREPRENEURSHIP

As already noted, formal modeling seems to contribute little to the discussion of mega-entrepreneurship. However, the intertemporal trajectory of the entrepreneurial activities discussed in this chapter can be summarized and explored, to a degree, using the most elementary of formal dynamic models. What has been described here can be represented by a pair of (multivariate) relationships: one represents the influence of the economy's institutions on the activities of entrepreneurs, while the other reports the inverse relationship, the purposeful enterprising influence that affects the shape of these institutions. As the earlier discussion of lobbying demonstrates, institution-molding activities entail entrepreneurship of a high order, as lobbyists seek to shape institutions in order to enhance both their clients' and their own financial rewards.

Thus, this story can be represented by a two-relationship dynamic model built on differential equations. These activities lend themselves to easy representation in a two-dimensional graph (though it is not shown here because it is so elementary). In that graph, institutionally determined entrepreneurial earnings appear on one axis and expenditures devoted to the redesign of institutions on the other. The curves representing the two relationships are both upward sloping and entail trajectories that clearly increase monotonically.

The first function indicates that the prospect of creating more rewarding institutions is, in itself, an incentive for the enhanced expenditure of entrepreneurial effort and resources directed at making those institutions even more rewarding than they initially were (or, if the institutions are under attack, more rewarding than they otherwise might have been). The other function deals with the inverse relationship, which tells us that devoting more resources (both funds and effort) to institution building ultimately leads to greater returns from entrepreneurship.

This simple formalization contributes one key insight, indicating that there may be limits to such mega-entrepreneurial activities. Although the intertemporal trajectory may entail a rapid rise in lobbying and other activities devoted to the purpose, the mathematics easily show—particularly if the two relationships in the graph are nonlinear—that the process can slow down and ultimately reach an equilibrium, at which no further self-generated or self-directed movement will occur.[14]

Evidently, this formalization offers a very small direct return. It is offered here in the hope that it will stimulate the work of other investigators who will be able to add significant substance to this line of analysis, which, despite offering only limited illumination at this stage, may very well turn out to have important implications.

Summing Up: Yes, the Theory
of Entrepreneurship Is on Its Way

. . . To hear the replication of your sounds.

—William Shakespeare, *Julius Caesar*
(act 1, scene 1, l. 51)

This book started off by drawing attention, yet again, to the virtual expulsion of the entrepreneur from the contemporary mainstream literature of economics. In doing so, it joins the growing call for the restoration of entrepreneurs' place in the theory, given their importance for the future prosperity of the free-market economy, in general, and for its growth and innovation performance, in particular.

But this highlighting of their absence was only a prologue to the central purpose of the book: to show *how* one can begin the process of restoring inventors and their entrepreneur associates to their proper place in basic production and distribution theory and, moreover, to take the first steps toward realization of that objective. To that end, the discussion in this book offers theory that undertakes to explain inventors' and entrepreneurs' activities, analyzes their remuneration, and shows the pricing patterns that market forces impose on this group. In short, this book seeks to expand the classical tripartite division of factors of production—land, labor, and capital (with the fourth group, entrepreneurs, only lurking in the background)—into a genuine four-group subdivision of the economy's inputs.

Let it be clear that this constitutes no claim to origination of the theory of entrepreneurship and innovation. There is already a substantial body of sophisticated and illuminating writings on the subject, starting at least as early as Schumpeter and most recently including the work of Aghion and Howitt and many other analysts. However, little of this work provides the simplicity and easy insights that permit ready incorporation into mainstream value theory, which, in turn, can obtain for this subject its own chapter in the basic textbooks, as a matter of course. Although growth is recognized universally as the key to the general economic welfare in the future—with entrepreneurs cited as major determinants of economic growth, little or no formal analysis of the nature of entrepreneurs' activities and decision processes is included in the basic economics texts.

This book seeks to remedy the situation, providing models for this purpose. Their very simple and elementary character, though an evident limitation, is, at the same time, something of a virtue because they easily can be conjoined to the mainstream theory of distribution, pricing, and production and thereby incorporated into teaching material.

DOES A COHERENT THEORY OF ENTREPRENEURSHIP ALREADY EXIST? DISTRIBUTION THEORY AS A STANDARD

The question is whether we already have a moderately systematic and encompassing theory of entrepreneurship. I argue that such a theory does now exist and that it is as systematic and comprehensive as can be expected at this stage of the game. I base this conclusion on comparison with the standard theory of distribution and production, which centers on the marginal productivity model.

Granted, this theory clearly does not concern itself with the details of the activities of any of the economy's inputs. For instance, it does not distinguish the day's activities of a computer programmer from those of a plumber—and this is perfectly appropriate, given the objectives of theoretical analysis. Indeed, this type of abstraction is arguably all but unavoidable for an illuminating theory of an arena in which heterogeneity is the name of the game and where little common activity is carried out in a common way. Indeed, perhaps all we can say about universal elements in the day-to-day activities of innovative entrepreneurs is that, as Cantillon and Knight noted, risk is an unavoidable feature of those activities and that, as Say and Schumpeter emphasized, innovation can, but need not be, the entrepreneur's focus and the product she promotes.

However, such observations alone surely cannot contribute much to the construction of an illuminating body of theory. Instead, we must refer to the standard distribution theory, as it relates to all the factors of production. This theory focuses on a simple supply-demand model, in which the demand analysis starts off from the marginal productivity structure and is applied identically to all of the factors of production. Only on the supply side do we find substantive distinctions among the different factors—for instance, land is, for all practical purposes, fixed in supply, while the supply of labor is determined, in part, by a society's marriage customs, reproductive practices, and retirement provisions.

For these inputs, as already noted in chapter 1, distribution and production theory primarily seeks to provide results pertinent to the following subjects:

1. The price that the input will command
2. The price of the output in whose production the input is used
3. The quantity of the input that will be supplied
4. The quantity of the input that will be demanded
5. The allocation of that input among its different possible uses and the distance of that allocation from the requirements of economic efficiency.

In addition, distribution theory addresses the implications of these arrangements for economic welfare. In this chapter, I will argue that the existing theory of entrepreneurship already offers insights on each of these matters.[1] The material in this book is designed to supplement those insights.

The obvious question, then, is whether or not the existing theory already deals with, or can be extended to address, the remaining issues that are at the center of the theory of distribution and production, as it pertains to the entrepreneur. I will argue next that this can be done and, indeed, that considerable progress already has been made toward this goal—with the material offered in this book contributing to that progress to some degree. Let us consider each of the constituent elements of the general theory of distribution and production, in turn.

REMUNERATION OF THE ENTREPRENEUR

The Schumpeterian scenario is constructed with the pattern of entrepreneurial earnings as its foundation. The story, as we know, is that when successful innovative entrepreneurs first introduce their novel product, process, or mode of organization, they are faced with no effective rivals who can prevent them from earning profits above the competitive level. This is the innovator's reward, which is fated to be eroded by the appearance of imitators who are eager to share in the booty. The entry of the imitators eliminates the supercompetitive profits and forces the innovative entrepreneurs back to the drawing board in order to qualify for another round of above-normal earnings.

More recent theory, in conjunction with empirical evidence, generally takes off in the same direction as Schumpeter, but reaches the conclusion that far from offering expectable returns that exceed the monopoly level, the market tends to drive long-run earnings to the "normal" profit level or even below it.[2] In this book, I argue that what, in Schumpeter, appears to be a (temporary) monopoly profit is actually a "down payment"—one of a set of intertemporal discriminatory prices that enables the innovative entrepreneur to recover his sunk innovation costs. Ease of entry will preclude earnings above that level over the life of the innovation, but will not preclude prices above marginal costs sufficient for the recoupment of sunk investments. Thus, here too, we have a theoretical construct that is entirely consistent with received theory, but which tells us about as much about the expected earnings of innovative entrepreneurs as we learn in other portions of the theory of distribution about the wages of labor or the rent of land.

PRICING THE ENTREPRENEUR'S PRODUCTS

I have argued here that the central feature of the pricing of products provided under the leadership of innovative entrepreneurs is price discrimination and, moreover, that discriminatory pricing is a normal state of affairs in this arena—even in the classic Schumpeterian model. The price discrimination model, on which the earlier portions of this book's analysis focus, is not just applicable to entrepreneurs—rather, it deals with a considerably broader arena in pricing and distribution theory. In its particular application here, however, it deals with the pricing and remuneration of entrepreneurs as directed by the market mechanism. The logic of the argument is simple: ease of entry into at least some substantial portion of the occupation of innovative entrepreneurship drives final product pricing so that the representative entrepreneur can expect to earn zero economic profits. She can expect no more because entry will wipe out profits higher than that and she can hope for no less because, unless entrants can expect to recoup their investments along with the normal rate of return on equally risky outlays, entry will not occur. However, this means that any prices other than those that yield maximal profits must result in losses. Since, in general, discriminatory prices yield profits higher than uniform prices, the result follows.

Thus, in a wide range of cases, competitive market forces make those who conduct innovative activities into discriminatory price *takers*—that is, they are forced to seek that vector of discriminatory prices which maximizes profits. But for the innovative entrepreneur, this discrimination will not take the form usually discussed: charging two customers different prices for the same product. Rather, the difference in prices, in accord with both Schumpeter's scenario and with intertemporal variation in competitive pressures, results in high prices (which appear to be monopoly prices) soon after an innovation reaches the market, followed by reduced prices as competing innovators appear.

Here it is critical to observe that the common formal analysis of price discrimination among different buyers at a given point in time and the analysis of the entrepreneur's intertemporal discriminatory prices are exactly the same, in terms of differences in competitive pressures on the demand function of the firm. The conclusion, then, is that we have a theory of the pricing of the products of innovation, which the entrepreneur promotes. This analysis fits right in with the mainstream analysis of discriminatory pricing.

SUPPLY AND ALLOCATION OF ENTREPRENEURIAL ACTIVITY

The historical analysis offered here provides no formal theory concerning the supply and allocation of entrepreneurship. There is, however, a simple underlying model that fits in with the most elementary comparative statics conclusions of conventional theory. This model holds that if a resource can be employed in two different occupations and the price it commands rises in one of the occupations, relative to that in the other, the supply of the resource will shift away from the occupation whose relative remuneration has fallen and will move toward the one whose comparative rate of pay has risen. This story, of course, is already found in Adam Smith's *The Wealth of Nations* and earlier, but in this book, we are dealing with a particular application of this general principle: the choice entrepreneurs must make between devoting their efforts to redistributive or productive activities.

Again, the same conclusion emerges. When the rules of the game have favored earnings in productive entrepreneurship, many of society's enterprising individuals have shifted their efforts from organizing private armies or pursuing grants of monopoly from the monarch to constructing canals and railroads and promoting improved technology, more generally. A superficial look at this phenomenon makes it appear that innovative entrepreneurs have suddenly appeared from nowhere. In reality, all that has happened is that evolving institutions have changed the structure of payoffs, and entrepreneurs have merely chosen to change jobs. Thus, the heart of the story of the supply of productive entrepreneurship rests entirely on the allocation of that critical resource—the economy's entrepreneurs. Such reallocation is crucial for the economy's achievement in the arena of innovation and growth, but it entails a theoretical structure so simple and straightforward that it has been all but overlooked in the literature.

Of course, as with all elementary models, this is a drastic oversimplification that deliberately neglects such powerful influences as custom and culture. However, they are neglected because they are largely exogenous to the workings of the economy and, perhaps more importantly, are hardly subject to easy modification via economic or even political actions. Models that focus on the role of culture and influences such as religion are not wrong, but they are prone to neglect the other critical determinant, the structure of payoffs, which is subject to economic pressures and changes and which can be improved by suitable policies.

RELEVANT WELFARE THEORY

The theory grows somewhat more sophisticated when we turn to the relevant welfare economics. This book has offered three pertinent welfare-theoretic propositions, as well as several related propositions that are less formal in derivation and accuracy. These can be summarized as follows:

1. If a unique discriminatory price vector, to which the innovators' products are driven by market forces, yields maximal economic profits (equal to zero), then it will satisfy the requirements for (second-best) Ramsey optimality.
2. An expansion in the number of Cournot-behavioral firms that make up the membership of a technology-sharing consortium will tend to lower the costs of innovative activities and increase the outlays devoted to them.
3. The ECPR (efficient component-pricing rule) formula provides prices of licenses for the use of intellectual property that yield compensation to the proprietors that is at least equal to what they could have earned if no such license had been provided, thereby allowing entrants who are at least as efficient as the licensor at supplying the final product to compete profitably with the licensor, no matter how discriminatory any of the prices may be.[3]

In addition to these relatively formal theoretical results, a number of far less rigorous observations with theoretical implications have emerged from historical evidence, general observation, and recently collected and analyzed data, as well as from heuristic consideration of the issues:

1. The psychic rewards of innovative activity must lead to a market equilibrium in which independent inventors and entrepreneurs earn less than persons of comparable education and experience who are employed in innovative activities by others (notably by large firms).
2. Where the markets for innovation are characterized by substantial competition and mobility of labor, the Ricardian rent theory implies that employees of business firms engaged in innovative activity will, in equilibrium, receive financial rewards equal to the differential value of their innovative output (among independent inventors and

entrepreneurs, competition may ensure a differential structure of remuneration, corresponding to the differences among the market values of their outputs).

3. From the point of view of the general welfare, the substantial spillovers generated by innovative activity entail a significant trade-off between the resulting disincentive for further expenditure of resources on the innovation processes and the resulting rise in living standards for the preponderant share of the population that has made no contribution to innovation; consequently, the magnitude of these spillovers varies widely, and any value of the spillover ratio (the share of the total benefits received by persons who have not engaged in innovative activity) is Pareto optimal, in the sense that any improvement in the circumstances of one of the two groups (innovators and noninnovators) must come at the expense of the other.

4. Easier dissemination of innovations reduces incentives for innovative activity, but speeds elimination of obsolete substitutes; the market mechanism, together with institutions such as the patent system, have reduced the magnitude of this trade-off by enabling the owners of the intellectual property to charge an appropriate price for its use, thereby providing an incentive for these proprietors not only to acquiesce to such transfers, but actually to facilitate and promote them, as a profitable activity.

5. The institutions that have led entrepreneurial talent to shift into productive channels have played a crucial role in the unprecedented appearance of innovations and the rate of economic growth experienced by a number of nations in recent centuries.

CONCLUDING COMMENT: YES, THERE IS A MAINSTREAM THEORY OF ENTREPRENEURSHIP, BUT SIGNIFICANT OBSTACLES REMAIN

The preceding discussion shows that there already exists a theory of entrepreneurship far more substantial than frequently supposed—so long as we do not demand of this theory more than the theory of distribution offers for inputs of other types. Drawing directly upon the theory of rent, the theory of capital, or even the theory of exchange in multiple currencies, entrepreneurship theory tells us about the supply function of productive entrepreneurship, reminds us that the theory should contain no demand function (in the usual sense), explains the pricing of the product of this input, and accounts for the rewards to its supplier—the profits of the entrepreneur.

Surely this is more than enough to justify inclusion of the theory of entrepreneurship, which plays a leading role in the future of the economy, in elementary economics textbooks. Still, substantial obstacles endure—some of which we may not be able to overcome. For instance, product heterogeneity makes it difficult to construct any formal and operational theory that yields categorical implications, yet inventions are, by their very definition, the ultimate heterogeneous products. Moreover, an entrepreneur's activities entail relationships beset with uncertainty and discontinuity, which, therefore, cannot be described in neat, simple mathematical forms. For that reason, there is little room for formal optimization analysis of entrepreneurs' decisions. In this arena, "satisficing"[4]—rather than maximizing—may be all that can be done. Finally, unlike more routinized activities, entrepreneurship requires psychological traits such as exuberance, optimism, and an affinity for research and the process of discovery. None of these qualities, however, lends itself to translation into the form of mathematical functions or other, more sophisticated formal relationships.

For analysts, there are two inherent sources of pleasure: what has already been discovered and what remains to be investigated. Fortunately, the theory of entrepreneurship offers an abundance of both. It is true that, within this arena, there is still a good deal of substance that has not been analyzed. However, this book demonstrates that there is also much that we *do* know—and, indeed, that what we know is not much less than what we know in the theories of labor, land, and capital, a triad whose analysis economists have long considered to be sufficiently advanced to merit full and unimpeded entrée into the domain of mainstream microtheory. Moreover, the theory of *innovative* entrepreneurship, unlike other factors of production, marries microanalysis with the analysis of economic growth, a subject that is surely *primus inter pares* from the point of view of the general welfare. It is because of the implications for the well-being of society that this book, although it focuses on the theory, does not refrain altogether from comments relevant to policy.

This ends my story, which I trust has suggested the way to formalize the work and accomplishments of the innovative entrepreneur. However, this is surely not the end of the discussion. My hope, of course, is that this book will stimulate abundant contributions from others who will add to the ideas offered here.

NOTES

Preface
The Innovative Entrepreneur in Dynamic Microtheory

1. I should like to thank the Accademia Nazionale de Lincei for providing this paragraph.

Introduction
Bringing Entrepreneurship and Innovation into the Theory of Value

1. Of course, there are some excellent works on the microtheory of replicative entrepreneurial activity—that is, the theory of the activity of the creator of firms who undertakes little or no innovation—notably in the writings of Mark Casson (1982, 2000) and Kihlstrom and Laffont (1979). Crucial and illuminating contributions via growth theory also have been made by Nelson and Winter (1982). Most recently, Daniel Spulber's (2009) discussion of endogenous entrepreneurs within the larger context of the theory of the firm is a notable contribution to the field. For additional, related references, see Spulber (184–85 and 198–99).

2. See, for example, Astebro (2003) and Nordhaus (2004) for fine examples of such studies. For excellent surveys, see Bianchi and Henrekson (2005), van Praag and Versloot (2007), and Parker (forthcoming).

3. For a detailed discussion of these issues, see Simon Parker's *The Economics of Self-Employment and Entrepreneurship* (2004).

4. As further indication of the extraordinary magnitude of recent growth, we see how little ahead Italy was during the Renaissance, when its economy was reputed to have led the Western world.

5. Unfortunately, I have not found any estimates of per capita income in China at any earlier date. I am aware, however, of the period of prosperity during the Tang and Sung dynasties (roughly 600–1300) that preceded the data presented here, which begins in 1500, by more than two centuries. Nevertheless, very rapid growth between the Tang-Sung period and the onset of the sixteenth century is

hardly plausible, as that would have required that per capita income in China during the earlier period be much *lower* than the very low figure estimated here for 1500. That possibility hardly is consistent with the notion of Sung prosperity and is perhaps not even consistent with survival of much of China's population.

6. China's GDP per capita grew by an astonishing average of 9.2 percent each year between 1990 and 2006 (OECD/Korea Policy Centre 2009).

Chapter 1
Entrepreneurship in Economic Theory: Reasons for Its Absence and Goals for Its Restoration

1. For illuminating data on this subject, see van Praag and Versloot (2007).

2. The two cited exceptions are, of course, Knight and Schumpeter. A return to the subject was recently injected by the neo-Austrian school, under Israel Kirzner.

3. Aside from the fact Viner emphasized—that one can never be sure of having found the very first contributor of anything, Cantillon's writing is beset by special obscurities. The book was written in English, but all copies were destroyed in 1734 in the fire set by his murderer, apparently a larcenous servant. Fortunately, the book had been translated into French, according to internal evidence, by Cantillon himself (he was an Englishman of Irish extraction, with homes throughout Europe and much business in France), where it came into the hands of Mirabeau and the physiocrats. Much of the English version survives thanks to extensive quasi-plagiarism (another author was acknowledged by the plagiarist, but not named) by Postlethwayt. Incidentally, there must have been much to steal in Cantillon's London home, since he had been sufficiently foresighted to bail out of John Law's schemes, taking with him enormous profits, before the famed bubble collapsed.

4. This is precisely the explanation I have proposed for the failure of medieval China and the Soviet Union to translate abundance of nonmilitary inventions into viable consumer products (see chapter 9 in this book for a fuller discussion).

5. However, Marshall (1923, 172) briefly digresses to mention Matthew Boulton's significant role as entrepreneur dealing with Watt's inventions.

6. There is one residual and rather curious role sometimes left to entrepreneurs in the neoclassical model. They become the indivisible and nonreplicable input that accounts for the U-shaped cost curve of a firm whose production function is linear and homogeneous. How the mighty have fallen!

7. This problem was recognized long ago by Thorstein Veblen. One may recall the characteristic passage in which he describes the economic man as "a lightning calculator of pleasures and pains, who oscillates like a homogeneous globule of desire of happiness under the impulse of stimuli that shift him about the area, but leave him intact. He has neither antecedent nor consequent. He is an isolated, definitive human datum, in stable equilibrium except for the buffets of impinging forces that displace him in one direction or another. Self-imposed in elemental space, he spins symmetrically about his own spiritual axis until the parallelogram of forces bears down upon him, whereupon he follows the line of the resultant. When the force of the impact is spent, he comes to rest, a self-contained globule of desire as before. . . . [He] is not a prime mover. He is not the seat of a process

of living, except in the sense that he is subject to a series of permutations enforced upon him by circumstances external and alien to him" (1919, 73–74).

Some readers may suspect that this argument is subtly putting forward alternative models of the firm with which this author has already been associated. That is certainly not the intention—rather, it seems clear that these past models of mine are no better for the purpose than the most hidebound of conventional constructs. For example, consider what Oliver Williamson has described as the "managerial discretion models," in which the businessman is taken to maximize the number of persons he employs, the number of sales he makes, or some other objective distinct from profits. True, this businessman has (somewhere outside the confines of the model) made a choice that was no mere matter of calculation. He has decided to assign priority, in at least some sense, to some goal other than profit. But having made this choice, he becomes the profit maximizer, a calculating robot—a programmed mechanical component in the automatic system that constitutes the firm. He makes and enforces the maximizing decision and, in this, the choice of maximand makes no difference.

8. Such inefficiencies are, presumably, a matter of management's limited knowledge and ability—not of a static efficiency failure in the overall economic arrangements, like those stemming from widespread monopoly, as discussed in the introduction.

9. Professor Magnus Henrekson, Stockholm School of Economics, offers the helpful suggestion that it is useful to think of the innovative entrepreneur as one who shifts the economy's production possibility frontier upward, while a replicative entrepreneur pushes the economy upward toward the current frontier.

10. These will be discussed more fully in chapters 8 and 9.

11. See, for example, McClelland (1961) and the work of eminent historians, such as Landes (1998) and North and Thomas (1973).

Chapter 2
Toward Characterization of the Innovation Industry: The David-Goliath Symbiosis

Portions of this chapter are based on my article "Entrepreneurship, Innovation and Growth: The David-Goliath Symbiosis," *Journal of Entrepreneurial Finance and Business Ventures* 7, no. 2 (2002): 1–10. © The Journal of Entrepreneurial Finance: The Official Publication of the Academy of Entrepreneurial Finance.

1. For more on this, see Norbäck and Persson's forthcoming article in the *Journal of the European Economic Association*, which formalizes the David-Goliath symbiosis beautifully.

2. In a recent paper, Naomi Lamoreaux and Kenneth Sokoloff (2005) seem to have found evidence of a tendency to disappearance among *independent* inventors and entrepreneurs, but not among entrepreneurs per se: "Joseph Schumpeter argued in *Capitalism, Socialism and Democracy* that the rise of large firms' investments in in-house R&D spelled the doom of the entrepreneurial innovator. We explore this idea by analyzing the career patterns of successive cohorts of highly productive inventors from the late nineteenth and early twentieth centuries. We find that over time highly productive inventors were increasingly likely to form

long-term attachments with firms. . . . Entrepreneurship, therefore, was by no means dead, but the increasing capital requirements—both financial and human—for effective invention and the need for inventors to establish a reputation before they could attract support made it more difficult for creative people to pursue careers as inventors. The relative numbers of highly productive inventors in the population correspondingly decreased, as did rates of patenting per capita." Here it is important to bear in mind that Lamoreaux and Sokoloff classify an entrepreneur who creates a firm to promote a particular invention as "attached to a firm." This is, of course, an appropriate way to proceed, but for my purposes, I consider this entrepreneur to be independent. Thus, there is not necessarily conflict between my conclusions and those of Lamoreaux and Sokoloff.

3. For an illuminating review of the evidence on the innovative entrepreneur's contribution to this process, see van Praag and Versloot (2007).

4. For a related view of the role of the large firm in the innovation process, see Romer (1990). In Romer's model, diminishing returns to the firm set in at some level of firm size, so that, as in my model, a number of these large enterprises can coexist in an industry. The explanation of my model will be found in chapter 4, notably in the discussion of the diagrams.

5. This story is consistent with a recent Booz Allen Hamilton study of "1,000 publicly held companies around the world that spent the most on R&D in 2004," which reported that the odds of success "increase when senior management makes sure that there is clear customer demand [for the innovation to be worked upon] and a profitable way to bring the innovation to market before any project gets the go-ahead" (Brown 2005, C5). For more, see Jarulzelski, Dehoff, and Bordia (2005).

6. Consider the comments of A. G. Lafley, CEO of Proctor and Gamble: "P&G was always really good at branding and commercializing products, but we weren't better than anyone else at that fragile front end, where the idea is created. So in 2000 we decided to stop being fortress P&G, and move to an open innovation system that could attract innovations of all stripes from the outside. . ." (www.PG.com, accessed 15 April 2009). This occurred after a period when, according to Lafley, "new product introductions [based on in-house innovations] had slowed to a trickle, and no more than 15 percent of those had wound up making money. . . . These days more than half of Proctor's new products are commercially successful" (Deutsch 2008). Still, on its website, P&G reports that its "research and development organization . . . includes 1,250 Ph.D. scientists. For perspective, this is larger than the combined science faculties at Harvard, Stanford and MIT" (www.PG.com, accessed 15 April 2009).

7. It should be made clear that there remains considerable disagreement in the empirical studies on matters related to entrepreneurship. For example, Chandy and Tellis conclude, on the basis of their empirical data on 64 "radical innovations," that "contrary to conventional wisdom . . . today's incumbents and large firms account for many radical innovations, especially since World War II" (2000, 12). They conclude that "large firms account for a substantially larger proportion of radical innovations relative to their number in the economy" (11).

8. As part of the SBA's study, according to the accompanying press release, "[A] total of 1,071 firms with 15 or more patents issued between 1996 and 2000 were examined. A total of 193,976 patents were analyzed. CHI [the firm that

carried out the study] created a data-base of these firms and their patents. This list excluded foreign-owned firms, universities, government laboratories, and nonprofit institutions."

9. The SBA study defines small firms as "businesses with fewer than 500 employees."

10. Indeed, a May 2009 *New York Times* article reports that big companies play an increasingly important role in the innovation process. Unlike small start-ups, large companies, like General Electric and IBM, have the resources to affect sweeping change: "The lone inventor will never be extinct, but W. Brian Arthur, an economist at the Palo Alto Research Center, says that as digital technology evolves, step-by-step innovations are less important than linking all the sensors, software and data centers in systems. . . . 'It's not individual inventions that matter so much, but when large bodies of technology come together and have an impact across the economy,' he said. 'That's what we're seeing now'" (Lohr 2009).

11. My description of the role of the large firm in the process of innovation invites the hypothesis that all routinized R&D activity in an industry will tend to be captured by a single firm that has a slight efficiency advantage. However, routine improvement is not a homogeneous activity, and even firms that provide improvements that are "second best," in terms of attracting consumer demand, may be able to survive by accepting lower prices for their outputs, in a manner analogous to the Ricardian rent model. I will expand this discussion in chapter 4.

12. The U.S. patent system undoubtedly has contributed enormously to the country's innovative performance, though it has recently been subject to substantial criticism of its delays and the inadequacy of its enforcement of the novel idea requirement, among other issues. For excellent material on the superiority of the early U.S. approach to patenting, see the superb book by Zorina Khan (2005) and the pathbreaking writings of Lamoreaux and Sokoloff. For some of the telling recent criticisms of the U.S. patent system, see Jaffe and Lerner (2004) and Bessen and Meurer (2008).

13. For more on this, see also "A Futurist's View: An Interview with Richard M. Satava, M.D." in *Yale Medicine*, Winter 2003, accessed 10 October 2009 at http://yalemedicine.yale.edu/ym_wi03/future.html.

Chapter 3
Entrepreneurship, Invention, and Pricing: Toward Static Microtheory

Portions of this chapter are based on a paper that I prepared for the AEI-Brookings Joint Center for Regulatory Studies, "Entrepreneurship and Invention: Toward Their Microeconomic Value Theory" (December 2005).

1. A set of prices is called "Ramsey optimal" if there is no alternative price that makes everyone who is affected either better off—or at least no worse off. In addition, a Ramsey optimal set of prices must yield some preselected target amount of revenue to the sellers.

2. One reader of this manuscript asked why it is not natural for total market demand to be covered by a single firm, eliminating the competitive forces that underlie the model. That issue will be dealt with at various points throughout the book, but, at this point, it may be helpful to list some of the reasons that this is so.

These include diminishing returns and rising costs for firms whose size surpasses a given point, product heterogeneity in accordance with differing consumer tastes, and a Ricardian rent structure in which firms with less valuable variants of a new product survive by offering lower prices.

3. Within the innovative sector, intertemporal price discrimination can be illustrated by the relatively recent introduction of the iPhone. The phone was prohibitively expensive when it first appeared, but soon after its appearance, its price dropped. The 2G, 3G, and 3GS iPhones exhibited the same pricing dynamics, though their initial price spikes were much less significant. Thus, the ability to impose price discrimination is proportionate to the marginal improvement an innovation represents.

4. Of course, there also are innovative firms that do possess market or monopoly power, which may not earn zero profits. These cases clearly require further investigation. But even an industry in which entry into the *production process* is difficult may not be safe from relatively easy entry by inventors and entrepreneurs—even Microsoft, for instance, appears to be concerned about such entry. Where entry effectively is impeded, firms, of course, still may charge discriminatory prices in order to enhance their profits.

5. Such segmentation is virtually automatic in the case of intertemporal discrimination, in which high prices are succeeded by price reductions, because there is no way for someone who buys at the subsequent high prices to resell the purchase in the earlier period—bygones are bygones. Of course, in other cases, such segmentation of customers incurs costs that are substantial, although sometimes recognition of the price category into which each particular falls is easy and almost automatic (e.g., it is easy to recognize elderly customers who are, therefore, eligible for senior citizen discounts for theater admission). Where the cost of segmentation is significant, a model can be used to determine the profit-maximizing level of such expenditures by the firm.

6. It is important to emphasize that the equilibrium considered here is not part of a static depiction of the behavior of the firm and the market. First, there is no guarantee that the equilibrium ever will be attained, even approximately, though even those we can describe as "mainstream Austrians" speak of "those important tendencies which markets display toward continual discovery and exploitation of pure profit opportunities thus tending to nudge the market in the equilibrium direction" (Kirzner 1979, 73). Moreover, the equilibrium entails a choice of R&D expenditure levels by the firm, an outlay whose purpose surely is to *prevent* stationarity.

7. In figure 3.1, the *AC* curve represents a fixed total cost and, therefore, provides an absolutely limited capacity to the firm. However, it should be clear that our discussion here does not depend on that premise.

8. Such a heightening of the *TR* curve also will occur under uniform pricing, when the firm begins to serve Submarket 2. However, the heightened curve will begin at a level of *y* greater than that under discriminatory pricing, while the uniform-price-heightened curve segment generally will lie below the level under discriminatory pricing. The second assertion follows from the superior profitability of discriminatory pricing, when the cost function is given. In the linear case, the earlier rise in the total revenue curve under discrimination also is shown easily.

Using the equations given in this section, we see that the equations of the marginal revenue curves are of the form, $MR = a - 2by$, that the vertical axis intercept of Submarket 2's AR curve is a_2, and its slope at that axis is also b_2. Therefore, with a uniform price, the firm will begin to serve Submarket 2 when the price in Submarket 1 reaches a_2, which will occur when $a_2 = a_1 - b_1y_1$ or $y_1 = a_1 - a_2/b_1$. However, under discriminatory pricing, Submarket 2 will begin to be served when Submarket 1's MR falls to that of Submarket 2 at the vertical axis, requiring $a_2 = a_1 - 2b_1y_1$ or $y_1 = a_1 - a_2/2b_1$.

9. So far, only the price-taker side of the firm's activities has been discussed, leaving little room for insights from game theory. However, we will see presently that there is more to the story because the market's equilibria are vulnerable to constant disturbance.

10. On this point, I have my only disagreement with Hausman and Mackie-Mason's excellent and illuminating article when they speak of "the necessary monopoly power for price discrimination to take place" (1988, 245n). For the origin of the argument that discriminatory pricing need not require monopoly power, see Levine (2002). This analysis has been expanded and its conclusions explored in Baumol and Swanson (2003). Incidentally, the analysis I have laid out in this section was accepted explicitly by the U.S. Supreme Court, which cited the latter article in *Illinois Tool Works Inc. et al. v Independent Ink, Inc.*, 547 U.S. 28, 45 (2006).

11. Of course, some innovations are contributed by firms that possess monopoly power, for whom the zero-profit constraint patently does not hold. For such firms, if all of Proposition 1's assumptions—except the easy-entry premise—are satisfied, their economic profits will generally be positive. Consequently, discriminatory prices still serve their interests, and profit-maximizing discriminatory prices still meet the requirements of Ramsey second-best welfare optimality, as shown by the argument with $k > 0$ earlier in this text.

12. Here, I follow Schumpeter in not distinguishing between inventors and innovating entrepreneurs. We can think of inventors who, like Thomas Edison, are also their own entrepreneurs, marketing their intellectual property on their own. Alternatively, we can think of the inventor as a partner to the entrepreneur, as James Watt was associated with Matthew Boulton.

13. None of this is meant to imply that the activities of replicative entrepreneurs are unimportant and offer little benefit to society. It surely is clear that the creation of small, replicative firms is one of the significant ways for impecunious individuals to make their way out of poverty. Second, the new firms may well be more efficient than their predecessors and, as other writers have argued convincingly, growth largely stems from reallocation within an industry—from less efficient to more efficient firms.

14. However, this is not the whole story. For another side to the matter, see van der Sluis, van Praag, and van Witteloostuijn (2006), where returns to education are shown to be higher for entrepreneurs than for employees.

15. Using a cruder and more intuitive approach, I also have estimated a very low figure for the returns to innovation that are not dissipated in spillovers (see Baumol 2002b, 134–35).

16. For more on open sourcing, see Lerner and Tirole (2004).

17. Van Praag (1999) reached a similar conclusion: "Apart from the level of expected earnings, there are other factors that affect the decision to start in business. Difficulty and strain of the work and the variance of earnings will usually have a negative effect on the decision, 'though a few extremely high prices have a disproportionately great attractive force' (Marshall 1890, 1930, 554). The latter phenomenon occurs because (young) risk lovers are more attracted by the prospect of a great success than they are deterred by the fear of failure. These rarely experienced high incomes make entrepreneurship stand out as a position of high esteem, which also serves as a major attraction" (319).

For a new take on the theory of firm taxation, see Henrekson and Sanandaji (2008), who propose that the tax system should tax successful entrepreneurs more heavily. This, in turn, may affect the supply of would-be innovative entrepreneurs.

18. Indeed, there is strong evidence that overoptimism is characteristic of entrepreneurs. Parker (2006) writes: "The available evidence certainly supports the notion that entrepreneurs are unrealistically optimistic. 68% of respondents to Cooper et al's (1988) survey of American entrepreneurs thought the odds of their business succeeding were better than for others in the same sector, while only 5% thought that they were worse. Pinfold (2001) chronicles confirmatory evidence from New Zealand entrepreneurs. Arabsheibani et al (2000) compare expectations of future prosperity with actual outcomes using British panel data and find that while employees and self-employed Britons both held systematically overoptimistic expectations about future incomes, the self-employed are consistently and substantially the most over-optimistic. Optimism involves strong commitments to loss-making ventures in the context of innovation, as well. . . . Most recently, Puri and Robinson (2005) have measured optimism as the difference between self-reported life expectancy and survey respondents' statistical life expectancy based on smoking-, age-, education-, race- and gender-corrected mortality tables. They find all respondents over-optimistically expect to live longer than the life tables suggest, but that entrepreneurs are substantially more likely to think they will live longer. Puri and Robinson also establish that optimism is significantly positively associated with the propensity to be an entrepreneur" (Parker 2006, 2). On the other hand, Xu and Ruef (2004) report that although "entrepreneurs have long been assumed to be more risk-tolerant than the general population . . . our empirical results consistently show that nascent entrepreneurs are more risk-averse than non-entrepreneurs. To reconcile the financial risk aversion of entrepreneurs with the high risk of financial loss among startups, we suggest that many of the motivations that individuals have for founding business ventures are non-pecuniary in nature" (2004, 331).

19. This suggests one way in which it sometimes may be possible to place a monetary value on psychological enjoyment and even aesthetic pleasure. A similar situation has been noted in other arenas. For example, there are data showing that the average financial return on investment in works of art usually is significantly lower than the return on investment in bonds. This difference is interpreted as the financial valuation of the aesthetic yield of painting ownership (see Frey and Pommerehne 1989).

20. Innovators might be more willing to work in large firms if they were offered high-powered incentives, such as abundant stock options and large performance

bonuses. However, large firms typically find it difficult to offer such cost-efficient contracts.

21. Other areas where some element of nonpecuniary income is likely to exist include scientific research, academic occupations, and, more generally, professional work. Nonpecuniary rewards also may be present among the self-employed, who perhaps enjoy freedom from control by superiors (see Hamilton 2000; and Benz and Frey 2004). This phenomenon and its relation to the work of innovators has long been recognized: "The knowledge of the man of science, indispensable as it is to the development of industry, circulates with ease and rapidity from one nation to all the rest. And men of science have themselves an interest in its diffusion; for upon that diffusion they rest their hopes of fortune, and, what is more prized by them, of reputation too" (Say 1827, 23).

22. Adam Smith: "The wages of labour vary with the ease or hardship, the cleanliness or dirtiness, the honourableness or dishonourableness of the employment. . . . A journeyman weaver earns less than a journeyman blacksmith. His work is not always easier, but it is much cleaner. . . . The exorbitant rewards of players, opera-singers and opera-dances, &c. are founded upon these two principles: the rarity and beauty of the talents, and the discredit of employing them in this manner. It seems absurd at first that we should despise their person, and yet reward their talents with the most profuse liberality. While we do the one, however, we must of necessity do the other" (1937, book 1, chap. 10, part 1).

23. The role institutions play in influencing the supply of entrepreneurs has been emphasized by a number of authors, notably North and Thomas (1973). However, Proposition 3.3 adds a new aspect to the discussion—the assertion that institutional changes do not induce the creation of new entrepreneurs, where there were few before, but, rather, entice enterprising individuals away from their previous unproductive activities and lead them to transfer their efforts to productive undertakings.

Chapter 4
Oligopolistic "Red Queen" Innovation Games, Mandatory Price Discrimination, and Markets in Innovation

Portions of this chapter are based on a paper that I prepared for the AEI-Brookings Joint Center for Regulatory Studies, "Entrepreneurship and Invention: Toward Their Microeconomic Value Theory" (December 2005).

1. In Baumol (2002b, 40) I cite evidence that, on average and taking account of both the spectacular successes and spectacular failures, the earnings of all computer-related activities together seem to have yielded something close to the normal (competitive) rate of profit. Professor Bronwyn Hall—University of California, Berkeley—who is as well informed on the subject as any of our colleagues, reports (in correspondence with me), on the basis of work underlying a forthcoming article, that "the return to R&D in large corporations has been driven towards normal returns over the past 20 years."

2. Of course, some such firms possess market power that can be substantial. Clearly, this power can open the way to positive profits. These firms, too, however, will be enabled to enhance their profits if they can adopt discriminatory pricing,

and, as shown in chapter 3, if those prices maximize profits, they still will be Ramsey optimal. Now, however, they will be subject to the constraint that they yield the available monopoly profits. In addition, it is important to note that the empirical evidence raises doubts about the overall profitability of the innovation process, as we saw in the previous chapter's section on returns to entrepreneurs and inventors. Of course, there are some big winners, but on average, the opposite outcome is very likely to be true.

3. Williams and Kreitzman (2008) report that these firms' "average and median economic returns equal 0.82% and 0.56%, respectively" (33), as shown in figure 4.1. The authors note that "these rates likely exceed zero because the sample is of large firms, which on average have been more successful than their rivals over time" (33).

4. These properties are oversimplifications because the firm's total production cost will vary with its sales volume, which must vary in accordance with its own and its competitor's R&D outlays. Moreover, oligopoly profits surely are not always zero. However, this does not affect the structure of the analysis or its conclusions, and we can avoid such problems by assuming (1) that all costs other than those of research and development are zero and (2) that the state of competition imposes a given level of maximum profit. In any event, there is evidence suggesting that, in a number of industries—including those that are computer related, oligopolistic firms, on average, earn profits that are not far from the competitive level.

5. This scenario is consistent with Booz Allen Hamilton's 2005 study of the 1,000 biggest R&D spender firms in the world, which reported that "while spending more does not necessarily help, spending too little will hurt."

6. Professor Bronwyn Hall comments (in our correspondence), "The ratchet effect . . . certainly seems to be there. . . . I looked at the median and aggregate R&D intensity in a few quasi-2-digit industries for the past 30 years. . . . I have not studied them carefully (in particular, the pharmaceutical sector seems to be sensitive to the presence of a lot of biotech firms that have little sales, so the median fluctuates a lot). . . . Another support of the ratchet model that you did not mention: many firms seem to choose their R&D budget by looking at industry R&D to sales ratios and matching. That is, the relevant variable is R&D intensity rather than level." Note that I agree fully with the required correction of my text called for by Professor Hall's last observation. Unfortunately, the available evidence on the profitability of investment in innovation by large firms is hardly definitive. Impressions seem to indicate that, as a group, such investments return no more than competitive profits. However, these oligopoly firms certainly can lose money, as the airline industry unquestionably demonstrates. For more sources on this topic, see Baumol (2002b, 40 n. 6).

7. This statement somewhat exaggerates the effectiveness of the ratchets in preventing the economy from *ever* sliding backward in its R&D expenditures. After all, in machinery, ratchets sometimes slip. Firms may be forced to cut back their R&D expenditure, for example, if business is extremely bad. Alternatively, they simply can make mistakes in planning how much to spend on R&D investment, or they may be discouraged by repeated failures of their research division to come up with salable products. The economy's ratchets are, indeed, imperfect, but their presence is important. They cannot completely prevent backsliding in

R&D expenditure, but they can be a powerful influence that is effective in resisting such retreats.

8. There is evidence that a period of substantial deterioration in business conditions can be favorable to R&D. Thus, there are clear indications that the Great Depression was a high point in innovative research, perhaps because scientists and engineers were available and willing to work for lower pay. For more on this, see Fano (1987) and Field (2003).

9. It is also possible that those independent entrepreneurs who care only about monetary payout will choose to purchase intellectual property for the low price demanded by the inventor. Such transactions probably do occur, perhaps not infrequently. However, this does not exclude large, high-tech firms from this activity.

10. Professor Bronwyn Hall comments (in correspondence), "It is a long-standing stylized fact in innovation that radical change usually comes from small firms/individuals and incremental change from large firms. There does not seem to be a single explanation. The idea that this is because inventors are willing to accept a lower average rate of return makes sense, but I tend to think there are other reasons. An important one is the nature of technology trajectories and sunk R&D costs—large firms are good at what they currently do (that is how they got large) and face much lower costs than new entrants when improving existing products because they don't have to sink the learning costs to develop their current level of capability again. New entrants can imitate (*pace* patents), but a pretty substantial investment is necessary to reach the same capability. That explains why large firms are the experts at incremental improvement. On the other side (radical invention), I had some conversations with biotech/pharmaceutical-financial types, which suggested to me that large established firms find it more difficult to shut off risky R&D projects, even when they are not viewed as successful. This leads to a preference for alliances with bio-techs, rather than bringing them in house. The reasons have to do with the demoralizing effect on the scientists involved, which is contagious, and the inertia built into a larger organization. Terminating a particular alliance contract seemed easier. I do not know how widespread this type of problem is. I do agree that in the case of really radical innovations, the motivator is not expected return—there is some other utility component that is not financial. Or there is over-optimism. Or both." One of the key implications of Professor Hall's remarks is that entry is not always achieved as quickly and easily as we may assume.

11. See chapter 3 in this book for more evidence on inventors' and entrepreneurs' propensity to overoptimism.

12. Speaking in Tilburg, the Netherlands, at a conference held in September 2003, Dr. Ad Huijser, executive vice president and chief technology officer, Royal Phillips Electronics noted, "In established businesses, innovation is mostly shaped through small, incremental steps of additional features to augment basic functionalities. With short product lifecycles, time to recoup R&D investments is limited. . . . Success is relatively predictable through the execution of well-defined innovation processes and in-depth knowledge of their markets in the respective business units."

13. For more on institutional incentives that spur innovative entrepreneurship, see Henrekson (2007) and Henrekson and Johansson (2009).

14. For more on creative destruction, see chapter 7 in this book.

15. This appendix is intended to suggest some possible directions for further research to my fellow economists. Nonspecialist readers may prefer to ignore it.

Chapter 5
Optimal Innovation Spillovers: The Growth-Distribution Trade-off

This chapter is based on chapter 8 of my book *The Free-Market Innovation Machine: Analyzing the Growth Miracle of Capitalism* (Princeton, N.J.: Princeton University Press, 2002).

1. See chapter 3, particularly the reference to the Nordhaus (2004) study.

2. I fully agree with George Akerlof's observation that applied economists generally are well aware that lump-sum transfers are simply not possible. I would venture that, at heart, most pure theorists know this to be true. However, that does not stop them from using this mythical device to focus exclusively on allocative efficiency and ignore the implications for distribution.

3. Throughout this chapter, I use the term "efficiency" in the standard sense, in order to exclude any consideration of distribution. Obviously, if an allocation has reprehensible distributive consequences but does meet standard efficiency requirements, my use of the term should not be taken to mean that I approve of the result.

4. For more about historical changes in income ratios of top managers versus workers, see Atkinson and Salverda (2005).

5. Some writers on innovation use the term "spillovers" in a more restricted sense than the connotation here—to refer, for example, to direct gains in knowledge by customers of the industry that supplies the R&D in question (see Grilliches 1979). Such use of the term is entirely legitimate. Here, however, the term is synonymous with *total* external effects. Thus, it represents *all* of the social benefits of innovation that do not accrue as private benefits to the inventor or to those who invested in or otherwise contributed to it. This connotation clearly is required by the issue under discussion—the disincentive to innovation activity that results from the difference between that activity's social and private reward.

6. It is true that innovation raises the marginal productivity of the labor force, in general. Competition then forces wages appropriately upward. This is part of the mechanism by which the spillovers of innovation are distributed. Nothing about the process implies that such wage gains are undeserved—clearly, that is not the issue here. Rather, the point is that this process cuts into innovators' direct monetary rewards. However, this is offset to some degree by the increased purchases induced by spillover recipients' enhanced purchasing power. This, in turn, increases the demand for and the market value of innovations. I am indebted to Professor Magnus Henrekson, Stockholm School of Economics, for this observation.

7. A reader of this chapter has argued that this conclusion is unrealistic because innovations *do* benefit workers. That is correct, but by definition, zero externalities mean that no such benefits go to workers who are not engaged in innovative activity. This implies that zero externalities cannot occur in the world of reality because this is an unattainable goal. However, the question under discussion here

is whether or not that imaginary goal, if it could somehow be achieved, could be accepted as optimal. Contrary to what might be inferred from the literature, in this chapter I answer emphatically that an economy with zero spillovers would not be optimal. Although a reduction in externalities would increase the number of beneficial innovations by ensuring that more of the benefits would accrue to the inventors, tautologically this would preclude any of the benefits from going to persons other than the innovators. Romer (1994) explains the matter very clearly: "This pattern of industrialization without wage gains is what it would take to ensure that the industrialist captures all of the benefits he creates when he introduces machinery. . . . [This] cannot be a historically accurate description of the process of development in industrial countries, for if it were, unskilled labor would still earn what it earned prior to the Industrial Revolution" (29).

8. In effect, this assumes that utility is transferable so that efficient behavior is independent of the distribution of benefits. This may be a heroic assumption, but it does no real damage in this context. I adopt it only to facilitate a simple graphical exposition.

9. If the functions are twice differentiable, the situation is straightforward. For the *Group I* curve, ZY, the first derivative (with respect to Z) equals $ZY' + Y$, which clearly is positive at $Y' = 0$. ZY has the second derivative, $ZY'' + 2Y'$, which certainly is negative in the region $Y' \leq 0$ if $Y'' < 0$.

10. The intuitive explanation of this expression and its implications are straightforward. We can think of Y as the total size of the pie that is to be distributed between the two groups, Z, as the share of the pie that goes to *Group I* and Y', or dY/dZ, as the decline in the size of the pie resulting from an increase in the (excessive) share going to that group. Hence it will not pay *Group I* to obtain a larger share, as the gain from an increase in its *share* is more than offset by the reduction in total size of the pie. This interpretation also explains why an increase in the absolute value of Y' will reduce the range of Pareto optima.

11. However, this is not intended to deny the important role of marginal considerations in the theory of innovation. For example, in deciding how much to increase or decrease the budget for R&D to improve a particular invention—or how much longer to work on that invention before releasing it to the market, the usual sorts of marginal calculations evidently apply.

12. Professor Jean Gadrey, Université Lille, has noted (in personal correspondence) that, in reality, C is unlikely to be horizontal, as more beneficial innovations are apt to incur a higher sunk cost, so that this line (curve) may well have a negative slope. This change leads to no fundamental modification of this analysis.

13. Associating point N with optimality in the set of innovations that are carried out forces me to use the broad definition of spillovers employed in this chapter, rather than a more restricted concept, such as one including only unpaid-for benefits obtained by an innovator's competitors. Clearly, in itself, an innovation is beneficial to society if its costs are exceeded by the sum of the benefits to *anyone*, including consumers in other countries, unrelated producers, and members of future generations.

14. More generally, it is easy to prove that, with C fixed, so long as there is no shift in B, $di/dS < 0$ at the least remunerative invention, I, whose production causes no loss at the given S value. Note that zero profit requires $(1 - S)B(i) - C = 0$,

so that $(1 - S)B'di = BdS$—or, since $B' = dB/di < 0$ by construction, $di/dS = B/(1 - S) dB/di) < 0$.

15. Incidentally, this is not a problem of private enterprise alone. The public sector will fare no better, unless it provides financing to cover the deficit between the revenues and costs that result when part of the benefits accrue to others who have not contributed to the innovation at issue—with the benefits going to the latter in the form of spillovers. Of course, private innovators can do just as well if they are subsidized or can use some other source of revenue to offset the share of total benefit that escapes them as spillovers.

16. I owe the observations in this paragraph to Richard Nelson, Henry R. Luce Professor of International Political Economy at Columbia University. Indeed, most of this paragraph is a lightly edited quotation from a letter he sent to me.

17. It is easy to show that where B^* is concave and twice differentiable, the same will be true near the maxima of B^*_w and B^*_i. Thus, since $B^*_i = SB^*$, we have $B^*_w = B^* + SB^*$, and the second derivative will be $B^*_w = 2B^*' + SB^*''$, which clearly must be negative, if $B^*' = 0$ and $B^*'' < 0$.

18. Conceivably, this can be a corner maximum at $S = 0$. This will occur if, at this point, $B^* > B^*' > 0$ so that at $S = 0$, the slope of the innovators' benefit curve, $(1 - S)B^*' - B^*$, is negative.

19. The issue here and my related conclusion have close analogies in the literature on optimal patent life—notably, in the work of Nordhaus (1969) and Scherer (1965). There, the issue is the trade-off between rewarding the inventor before the time of patent expiration and transferring subsequent benefits to the general public.

20. This arguably is a very conservative figure.

21. Holcombe (2007) emphasizes the debt of current innovative entrepreneurs to previous innovative entrepreneurs, creating a sort of internal spillover within that activity.

22. British prime minister Margaret Thatcher's effort to reintroduce the "poll tax" in the late 1980s—in order to replace income-related local taxation—is an interesting example of a failed attempt to put a lump-sum tax into practice. Of course, progressive taxes can be and have been used to reduce income inequalities, but surely they are not without consequences for incentives.

23. An exception to this is the exceedingly unlikely case where the productive optimum also happens to yield a desirable distribution—or, as mathematicians call it, a set of measure zero.

24. Even a transfer unconnected with wealth or income cannot easily be made lump-sum. A clearly silly example will bring out this point. Suppose a fixed and substantial tax payment is imposed upon the birth of a child to any family whose surname begins with a letter in the first half of the alphabet. The tax payment is then transferred upon each birth to families with names later in the alphabet (with name changes prohibited by law). Surely this would entail an incentive affecting family sizes in the two groups. More important, such a scheme could not be used to correct any perceived maldistribution of income resulting from the requirements of economic efficiency or from the behavior of the market, precisely because it would be designed to have no connection with any choices of economic behavior. There is, however, no reason for the members of the lexicographically

disadvantaged group to be the same as those who have acquired what is deemed to be excessive wealth.

25. The concept seems unfamiliar, so an example may be useful in bringing out this point. Let individual A be the generator of, say, a beneficial externality worth D dollars to both individual A and individual B. Then, assume that B receives that externality. Let the resulting distribution of benefits be desirable, but the efficiency effects be detrimental. Accordingly, if we take step 1 and eliminate the externality, then in step 2, we must use a tax to get back to the previous income distribution. This involves requiring A to pay a tax in the amount of D dollars and then giving the D dollars to B. If A and B recognize what has happened and why, are we not back at the previous inefficiency incentives?

Chapter 6
Enterprising Technology Dissemination: Toward Optimal Transfer Pricing
and the Invaluable Contribution of "Mere Imitation"

Portions of this chapter are based on materials in chapter 13 of my book *The Free-Market Innovation Machine: Analyzing the Growth Miracle of Capitalism* (Princeton, N.J.: Princeton University Press, 2002).

1. For examination of the legal issues that arise in the design and execution of optimal terms for technology transfer, see Swanson and Baumol (2005).

2. For a definitive and extremely illuminating descriptive summary and analysis of such alliances in the United States, see Schilling (forthcoming).

3. Economists call a product a "public good" if any increase in its output or the number of its users does not add to its cost. For example, if a road is cleared of snow, the removal costs are the same whether five or fifty cars use that road in the next hour. R&D cost is evidently of this variety—once this effort is completed, even if a flood of customers appear, no more must be expended on the R&D.

4. For more, see Lamoreaux and Sokoloff (2007).

5. This data was provided by Arora in a personal communication.

6. Indeed, Schilling (forthcoming) has demonstrated that such alliances have become commonplace.

7. It is important to note that the social benefits of patents, which will be discussed in the following section and elsewhere in this book, do not render the details of the system beyond criticism. Indeed, the current workings of the U.S. patent system recently have been subjected to criticism on a number of reasonable grounds. In particular, Jaffee and Lerner (2004) have raised the concern that patenting has become too easy in recent decades, thereby creating unjustifiable barriers to entry into the marketplace by other inventions that infringe any patent that was inappropriately granted.

8. The term "patent" comes from "letters patent"—that is, letters issued by the monarch meant to be visible (patent) to all, as distinguished from confidential "letters close."

9. For more on the history of the American patent system, see Lamoreaux and Sokoloff's forthcoming book, *Beyond Monopoly: Patents, Inventors, and the Market for Technology in the United States during the Second Industrial Revolution*.

10. For a fuller discussion of these problems, see Shapiro (2001).

11. The model I present here assumes that the firm's behavior is of the type described by Cournot (1897), but it is not difficult to show that the result is more general. Schilling (forthcoming) provides powerful empirical evidence that expansion in the number and size of networks increases the volume of innovation, as indicated by the magnitude of patenting. Levin's (1988) earlier evidence provides an empirical underpinning to this result. Thus, note Levin's comments on the predictions made by Spence's model: "Spillovers discourage R&D investment but may be conducive to rapid technical progress" (1988, 427). Moreover, Levin indicates that his results, "though only suggestive, give some support for the latter hypothesis [the incentive for technical progress], but none for the former" (427).

12. The proof of Proposition 6.1 is provided in the appendix to this chapter.

13. The proof of Proposition 6.2 also is provided in the appendix to this chapter.

14. The assumption that each member of the consortium expects the other members' decisions to be identical to its own can be interpreted to mean either that the outcomes are symmetrical or that the choices are made jointly. In this instance, I refer to the former—because the firms are all similarly situated, their profit-maximizing decisions on outputs and investment in R&D will be the same, and that experience will have led each firm to recognize the identity of its own behavior and that of the other members of the network.

15. For a similar result for the case of cooperation in R&D activity—in contradistinction to the sharing of the results of independent R&D activity—see the excellent paper by D'Asprement and Jacquemin (1988).

16. This formula originally was contributed by Robert Willig (1979).

17. In particular, if the license price is not sufficient to enable the innovator to cover its continuing sunk outlays, that price clearly will constitute a subsidy from the innovator to the licensee.

18. As before, the proof of this proposition is provided in the appendix to this chapter.

19. In other words, the license price = I's final-product price $-$ I's incremental cost of remaining inputs.

20. The relevant opportunity cost given here is *average* profit forgone—the total profit forgone by the IP holder as a result of the transaction per unit of final product sold. Note that this is not the *marginal* opportunity cost, which is likely to be zero because a profit-maximizing IP holder that produces the final product in which the innovation in question is used will produce the quantity of final product at which marginal profit falls to zero.

21. However, as I will discuss later in this chapter, the opportunity cost element of this result is the focus of current debate over the use of ECPR in the regulation of firms deemed to possess monopoly power.

22. It follows from (6.1) that if final product J is the recipient of a cross-subsidy and, therefore, is priced below incremental cost (i.e., its profit yield to the bottleneck owner is negative), then the competitively neutral license fee for IP used in the production of J *must also be less than the incremental cost* of supplying the bottleneck service for the purpose. That is, the license also must offer a subsidy—this time, to the licensee. Although this result may be surprising, its logic is straightforward. If the IP owner sells J to consumers at a price that is below cost,

then she must provide rivals with IP access at a price that also does not cover cost. In other words, if final product J is the recipient of a cross-subsidy when sold by the IP proprietor, then competitive neutrality requires that the same cross-subsidy be made available to rival suppliers of J through the license fee.

23. Earlier, with identical products, I demonstrated that equations (6.1) and (6.2) are equivalent. Here, however, I take the position that (6.2) provides more appropriate guidance. Royalties under this approach literally will be discriminatory, but nonetheless, they still will be competitively neutral. In the case of imperfect-substitute final products, however, it is not so easy to provide a level-playing-field theorem, since it is difficult in that state of affairs to define a "level playing field."

24. Armstrong (2002) proposed a similar generalization of the ECPR rule, showing that it is necessary for preserving the efficiency properties of the approach.

25. An analogy demonstrates why this is so. Consider a piece of real estate that a prospective shopkeeper, A, wants to rent from landlord B in order to create an establishment that will compete with a nearby shop that is also owned by landlord B. It is evident that a landlord in this position will decline to rent her property to tenant A, unless the rental fee covers the direct cost entailed, plus the opportunity cost that landlord B will forego in her own shop as a result of the entry of new shop operator, A. Competition would, however, prevent landlord B from charging significantly more than this price.

26. The only difference is the substitution in ECPR of incremental cost, the cost of the pertinent increment of output—whatever its magnitude, for marginal cost, the cost of an "infinitesimal" increase in output.

27. Of course, as in our formalized Schumpeterian model in chapter 3, imitators do increase the competitiveness of the relevant market, thus reducing its prices and profits.

28. Rey and Tirole (1997) questioned the effectiveness of ECPR and concluded that it "may not preclude or impose any constraint on foreclosure" (26). In Rey and Tirole's game-theoretic model, the owner of the bottleneck input seeks to avoid the loss of monopoly power that may result when prospective purchasers of access who are quoted high license fees fear that later purchasers will be offered lower license fees, and so, reject the owner's price offer. In the model, the IP-owning firm preserves its monopoly power by forward integration—in effect, becoming its own IP customer. This is supposed to solve the assumed price commitment problem posed by the IP owner's opportunistic later reductions in input prices and thereby "restore" the bottleneck input owner's market power. Rey and Tirole conclude that ECPR does not prevent the input owner from achieving this restorative solution, noting that ECPR does not prevent the exclusion of efficient entrants (for full details, see Rey and Tirole 1997, 26). However, as I show here, Rey and Tirole's argument is incorrect. To prove explicitly that ECPR *does* prevent foreclosure, we first simplify the notation of formula (6.13). The ECPR price is given by $E = P_f - IC_{r,i}$ per unit of final product, where P_f is the final product price, and $IC_{r,i}$ is the incremental cost of the remaining (non-IP) portion of the IP owner's final-product input. Note that E is given by an equality—not an inequality, as Rey and Tirole mistakenly report. Thus, a rival, C, is equally efficient if its $IC_{r,c} = IC_{r,i}$—that is, if its IC for non-IP inputs is the same as the IP owner's. A rival who is exactly as efficient as the IP owner will always earn exactly zero economic profit (i.e.,

competitive profit) if it is charged the ECPR license fee, and if its final-product price is the same for all suppliers. As proof, note that C's (supracompetitive) profit per unit of final output $= P_f - IC_{r,i} - E = P_f - IC_{r,i} - (P_f - IC_{r,i}) = 0$ exactly. Thus, C earns competitive profits, so that entry is always possible for it and is even easier for a more efficient rival. In sum, ECPR does prevent foreclosure of efficient entry—contrary to what Rey and Tirole suggest.

Chapter 7
The Entrepreneur and the Beneficial Externalities of Creative Destruction

1. Innovation spillovers are discussed in detail in chapters 3 and 5 of this book.

2. For more detailed discussion of these arguments, see chapters 5 and 6 in this book.

3. For a more detailed discussion of this, see Nordhaus (1969), 39.

4. In his Ph.D. dissertation at New York University, Chung Yi Tse (1996) introduced heterogeneous innovation races very similar to those just described and analyzed their welfare properties systematically and far more deeply than in the brief discussion here. His results also indicate that these races need not conflict with economic efficiency.

5. Recall that the term "non-lump-sum Pareto optimal," introduced in chapter 5 of this book, refers to optimality that takes account of the trade-off between efficiency and distributive equity in a scenario in which lump-sum redistribution is not feasible.

Chapter 8
Economic Warfare as a "Red Queen" Game: The Emergence of Productive Entrepreneurship

Portions of this chapter are based on chapter 5 of my book *The Free-Market Innovation Machine: Analyzing the Growth Miracle of Capitalism* (Princeton, N.J.: Princeton University Press, 2002).

1. For more on this, see Holcombe (2007).

2. For a more detailed discussion of "Red Queen" innovation games, see chapter 4 in this book.

3. Perhaps I, more than others, have emphasized the unproductive activities of some entrepreneurs, but the observation is hardly new. Schumpeter (1936, 66) includes "the creation of a monopoly position (for example through trustification)" in his list of "new combinations," which defines the role of the entrepreneur. The creation of a monopoly is not generally an act that contributes to the economy's productivity. Moreover, Cantillon (1755), in what is perhaps the earliest use of the term "entrepreneur" in the economic literature, remarks that "les Gueux meme & les Voleurs sont des Entrepreneurs de cette classe" ("the Beggars and the Robbers even are entrepreneurs of this class"). That is, even beggars and criminals are entrepreneurs, as they are self-employed and operate in accord with their own aspirations and strategic plans. Here it may be appropriate to remind the reader

that, although Cantillon's work was originally written in English, no complete copy survived the fire set by his murderer, although some pages were stolen by an English contemporary and published without attribution. Fortunately, there was a French translation. Note that the word "entrepreneur" appears only in the French text. As late as the end of the nineteenth century, the English translation of the word was "adventurer" or "undertaker."

4. For more on entrepreneurship in ancient Rome, see the following chapter.

5. The Renaissance papacy, as we know, was a traded commodity whose price was enormous. For example, Alexander II, the Borgia pope, paid vast sums to the cardinals who voted for his election. Cardinal Sforza, the pope's future vice chancellor, is reported to have received four mule-loads of sacks of silver, in addition to the lucrative bishoprics of Eriau in Hungary, Seville, and Cadiz and the legations of Bologna, the Romagna, and the exarchate of Ravenna. Cardinal Orsini received bishoprics and other positions valued at 7,000 ducats, plus a direct payment of 20,000 ducats in an era when a person who possessed a total of 20,000 ducats was considered extremely wealthy (Cloulas 1993, 71–72).

6. The business of ransom collection has sometimes been rationalized, systematized, and carried out with businesslike efficiency. In some societies, prisoners of clearly low economic status were subject to summary execution because they were not worth the cost required to keep them alive. There were periods when ransom was charged by military rank of the prisoner in accord with a fixed schedule of prices: so much for a colonel, somewhat less for a captain, and much more for a general.

7. For additional examples of the redistributive activities, in the legal and regulatory arenas, of firms operating in the United States, see Holmes and Schmitz (2001).

8. Murphy, Shleifer, and Vishny (1991) argue persuasively that the significant positive correlation between economic growth and the proportion of engineering college majors (a socially productive occupation) and the significant negative correlation between the proportion of law majors (a socially unproductive, rent-seeking occupation) demonstrates that occupational choices affect economic growth.

9. This included French financing of the American Revolution, an act undertaken to restore the international standing of France after its defeat in the Seven Years War. Pierre Beaumarchais, author of the drama (not the opera) *The Marriage of Figaro*, was the prime French promoter of this aid. It was vigorously opposed by Anne-Robert-Jacques Turgot, the high government official and very capable economist, who was sympathetic to the American cause, but felt, with good justification, that his country's finances could not stand up to the requirements of such support.

10. Aside from the limitations of our conclusions stemming from the very imperfect information available to us, the story of the Battle of Hastings, from the viewpoint of the issue under discussion here, is complex. Duke William of Normandy had a reputation as a very effective military leader, having twice defeated the king of France. However, as Dunbabin (2000) notes, William's "victory [at Hastings] was also the fruit of wealth; mercenaries were an essential constituent of William's armies; paid soldiers, both mounted and on foot, provided crucial reinforcements

to the Norman military endeavors. Their presence was accounted for by the well-developed money economy, a striking feature of Normandy since the mid-tenth century; and also by the duke's ability to tap the duchy's resources" (202).

11. Howard (1976) notes: "To the Bank of England and the Treasury . . . must go at least as much responsibility for ultimate British success in that war [the War of the Spanish Succession]—as indeed in all subsequent wars—as is due to the generalship of Marlborough and to the professionalism of armed forces" (48–49).

12. There was substantial warfare in virtually every one of the 18 English reigns of the medieval period, starting with William the Conqueror and ending with Henry VII, the first Tudor king.

13. One of this book's reviewers, Simon Parker of the University of Western Ontario, rightly points out that another consequence of such royal Red Queen games—in particular, the one involving England and Holland—was England's adoption of an important financial innovation: the government bond.

14. "The King will be no merchant," Sir Francis Bacon told the House of Commons in 1614 (Jardine and Stewart 1998, 332). In that statement, Bacon, speaking on behalf of James I, asserted that the king would not offer concessions in exchange for the funds he so desperately needed. In the end, however, the king was forced to make the concessions.

15. It also may be argued that, in the long run, warfare contributed to prosperity by sweeping away obsolete infrastructure and outmoded ways of thinking—one step beyond the concept of "creative destruction" introduced by Schumpeter. Dunbabin offers evidence in support of this hypothesis: "Surprisingly it seems that those areas [of France] which suffered the most from raids and disruption in the early tenth century . . . were just the places which, by the end of the tenth century, were prospering" (2000, 141).

16. In desperation, John literally *gave* proprietorship of England to the pope, reducing himself to the status of the pope's vassal. This did not work, however, as the pope was unable to protect John from his nobility.

17. It is important to note that this was not a parliament in the modern sense but, rather, an assemblage of nobles and upper clergy convened at the summons of the king.

18. That violence—notably, that of the nobility—was persistent, pervasive, and served to undermine effective government is suggested by the fate of the 18 monarchs of the late medieval period. Two of these kings died in battle involving quarrels with the nobility (Richard I, Richard III), five were murdered in questionable circumstances in which nobles were the prime suspects (William Rufus, John, Edward II, Richard II, and Edward V), four were deposed (Edward II, Richard II, Henry VI, and Richard III), and five were held captive (Matilda, Richard I, Henry III, Edward I—*before* becoming king, and Edward IV). Only six of the 18 died peacefully of natural causes, having never been a prisoner of domestic foes. As Shakespeare's Richard II famously declares, "some have been depos'd; some slain in war / some poison'd by their wives; some sleeping killed; / all murdered: for within the hollow crown / that rounds the mortal temples of a king / keeps death his court" (*Richard II*, act 3, scene 2, ll. 157–62).

NOTES TO CHAPTER 9

Chapter 9
On the Origins of Widespread Productive Entrepreneurship

This chapter is based on my article "Entrepreneurship: Productive, Unproductive, and Destructive," *Journal of Political Economy* 98 (1990): 893–921. © 1990 by The University of Chicago.

1. For an excellent analysis of the basic hypothesis, independently derived, see Murphy, Shleifer, and Vishny (1991). For an illuminating examination of the supply of productive entrepreneurship in a welfare state, see Henrekson (2005). Henrekson concludes that the tax and welfare arrangements in such states tend to reduce economic incentives for entrepreneurship.

2. In the introduction to Robert Temple's *The Genius of China* (1987), Joseph Needham, the noted historian of Chinese science, writes: "The extraordinary inventiveness, and insight into nature, of ancient and Medieval China raises two fundamental questions. First, why should they have been so far in advance of other civilizations; and second, why aren't they now centuries ahead of the rest of the world? We think it was a matter of the very different social and economic systems between China and the West. . . . Modern science arose only in Europe in the seventeenth century when the best method of discovery was itself discovered; but the discoveries and inventions made then and thereafter depended in so many cases on centuries of previous Chinese progress in science, technology and medicine" (6).

Of course, as James Schwartz, adjunct professor of history at Eastern Illinois University, rightly reminded me, China does not provide the only historical examples of such failures to make productive use of important inventions. For instance, archaeologists believe that pre-Columbian Mesoamerican civilizations developed the wheel, but used it only in small toys and ritual objects and never put it to practical use as a means of transportation (Diehl and Mandeville 1987).

3. The discussion here is not meant to imply either that China's limited utilization of its inventions can be ascribed only to a single influence or that these inventions remained crude and fundamentally underutilized. There is a growing literature that ascribes such problems to climate, geography (Pomeranz 2000, chap. 5), demographic patterns (Clark 2007, chap. 13), and other influences, while other writings deny the existence of such a problem at least until well into the nineteenth century. Here I focus on entrepreneurship not in the belief that it is the only influence, but because it is the one that appears to be most readily amenable to the influence of policy. For example, the patent laws clearly can be changed more easily than the location of the Gobi Desert.

To illustrate my basic contention, consider the claim that the Chinese discovered America in 1421, nearly three-quarters of a century before Columbus (Menzies 2002). The evidence here is certainly suggestive and even persuasive. But my argument focuses on the sequel—or rather, the lack of sequel. For nothing followed for the Chinese economy from the discovery of America: no colonization, no importation of new products, no capture of gold and silver. The contrast with the history subsequent to the Spanish discovery of the New World is striking indeed. The hypothesis about China that is discussed here is a generalization of this example. The Chinese may have been the first to discover printing, the compass, and other innovations, but it was left to the West, post–Industrial Revolution, to exploit these inventions with unprecedented effectiveness.

Gunpowder provides another telling illustration of this idea. The use of gunpowder by the Chinese clearly went well beyond the oft-cited fireworks: "By the beginning of the 10th century [gunpowder] was applied in Chinese flamethrowers and by 969 it was used to fire arrows. By 1231 it was used in bombs, grenades, and rockets (which took the form of a mortar made in an iron tube)" (Hobson 2004, 59). However, even with such sophisticated weapons, the Chinese were unable to defend themselves against conquest by comparatively primitive Mongol armies in 1279. (Perhaps this is because the Mongols engaged in effective Schumpeterian entrepreneurship in the form of transfer of military technology from China. According to Elvin [1973, chap. 7], the Mongols succeeded in using effectively—and even improving—Chinese military inventions, including those based on gunpowder.) In all of this, my position follows that of Needham (1954–2004) and Landes (1998, chap. 6).

4. This is true for all of the items on Schumpeter's list, *except* for the last concerning the creation or destruction of a monopoly.

5. However, the creation of a monopoly, which Schumpeter does include as an innovation, is surely as questionable, as just implied.

6. This notion goes back, at least, to Veblen (1904).

7. There is a substantial literature, following the work of Jacob Schmookler, which provides strong empirical evidence for the proposition that even the allocation of inventive effort is, itself, heavily influenced by relative payoff prospects. However, it is now agreed that some of these authors go too far when they appear to imply that almost nothing except the demand for the product of invention influences which inventions will occur, to any great extent. For a good summary of this issue, with references, see Abramovitz (1989, 33).

8. For more on Shove's suggestion, see Robinson (1969, 106–7).

9. Stefano Fenoaltea of the Università degli Studi di Roma "Tor Vergata," commented (in conversation) that he knows no documented cases in which this self-selling occurred and notes that it was undoubtedly more common to seek advancement in ancient Roman society through adoption into an upper-class family.

10. North and Thomas (1973, 3) make a similar point about John Harrison's eighteenth-century invention of the ship's chronometer, an instrument indispensable for the determination of longitude. The authors point out that the incentive for this invention was a large prize offered by the British government, rather than the prospect of commercial profit—presumably because of the absence of effective patent protection.

11. It is amazing that so much information about early Chinese history survives, despite the repeated and deliberate destruction of manuscripts and printed items from previous reigns, which was ordered by Chinese emperors—from the first unifier of China, Qui Shi Huang (221–210 BC), to the early Ming emperor, Quianlong (AD 1756–1795). This is in contrast with the huge gaps in Western history—for instance, there is no contemporary documentation of the existence of kings of Israel named Solomon or David, and there exist only a handful of contemporary mentions of Eleanor of Aquitaine, not all of them clearly reliable.

NOTES TO CHAPTER 9

We can conjecture that the early Chinese invention of printing and the possibly resulting multiplicity of copies aided in the preservation of so many documents. The story of their discovery parallels the finding of the Dead Sea Scrolls. In 1907, the eminent Hungarian-Jewish-British explorer Mark Aurel Stein discovered, for the Western world, a set of caves at the Dunhuang Oasis on the Silk Road. The caves contained many treasures, including the Diamond Sutra, the oldest surviving printed volume, which proved Gutenberg to be a latecomer to printing. Near Dunhuang, at Mogao, there was a small cave, later labeled Cave 17. According to Winchester (2008), Stein found within that cave, which had been concealed by a camouflaged doorway, a mass of manuscripts, "close on 500 cubic feet" in volume. Stein persuaded his guide to accept 220 British pounds as payment for the entire collection, "one of the richest finds in all of archeological history," and it was then bundled up for shipment to England.

12. For more on this history, see Balazs (1964, 53), Landes (1969, 46–47), Rosenberg and Birdzell (1986, 119–20), and Jones (1987, chap. 5).

13. However, wealthy merchants often used their resources to prepare their descendants to contend, via the all-important imperial examinations, for a position in the scholar bureaucracy.

14. For evidence on social mobility in imperial China, see Marsh (1961) and Ho (1962).

15. The conquest has at least two noteworthy entrepreneurial aspects. First, as noted in the previous chapter, it involved an innovation—the use of the stirrup by the Normans at Hastings—that enabled William's warriors to use the same spear to impale a series of victims with the force of the horse's charge, rather than just tossing the spear at the enemy, as an infantryman would. Second, the invasion was an impressive act of organization, in which William convinced his untrustworthy allies that they had more to gain by joining him in England than by staying behind to profit from his absence by trying to grab away his lands, as they had tried to do many times before.

16. It is important to note that I do not mean to take the conventional view that warfare is an unmitigated source of impoverishment that never contributes to an economy's prosperity. Careful recent studies have indicated that matters are more complicated (see, for example, Milward 1970 and Olson 1982). Certainly the unprecedented prosperity enjoyed afterward by the countries on the losing side of World War II suggests that warfare need not always preclude economic expansion. Moreover, the three great economic leaders of the pre–United States, Western world—Italy (thirteenth–sixteenth centuries), the Dutch Republic (seventeenth–eighteenth centuries), and Great Britain (eighteenth–nineteenth centuries)—each attained the height of their prosperity after periods of enormously costly and sometimes destructive warfare. Still, the wealth gained by a medieval baron from the adoption of a novel warfare technique hardly could have contributed to economic growth in the way that adopting a new steelmaking process or introducing a new product, like the motor vehicle, did in the nineteenth and twentieth centuries, respectively.

17. Personal communication.

18. For more on the entrepreneurial activities of the condotierre, see also McNeill (1969, 33–39).

19. However, Schama (1989) tells us that "even a cursory examination of the eighteenth-century French economy . . . reveals the nobility deeply involved in finance, business and industry—certainly as much as their British counterparts. . . . In 1765 a royal edict officially removed the last formal obstacles to their participation in trade and industry" (118).

Chapter 10
The Allocation of Entrepreneurship Does Matter

This chapter is based on my article "Entrepreneurship: Productive, Unproductive, and Destructive," *Journal of Political Economy* 98 (1990): 893–921. © 1990 by The University of Chicago.

1. I shall report conclusions of some leading historians on these episodes, but it should be recognized by the reader that many of the views summarized here have been disputed in the historical literature, at least to some degree.

2. It has been suggested by historians (see, for example, Bloch 1935, 547) that an abundance of slaves played a key role in the Romans' failure to use the water mill widely. However, this implies that the Romans were not efficient wealth-seekers. As the cliometric literature has made clear, the cost of maintaining a slave is not low and certainly is not zero, and slaves are not apt to be efficient and dedicated workers. Thus, if it had been efficient to replace human or animal power by the inanimate power of the waterways, failure to do so would have cut into slaveholders' wealth, in effect saddling them with the feeding of unproductive persons or keeping those slaves who turned the mills from other, more lucrative occupations. Perhaps Roman landowners were fairly unsophisticated in the management of their estates, as Finley (1985, 108–16) suggests. If so, there may be some substance to the hypothesis that slavery goes far to account for the failure of water mills to spread in the Roman economy.

3. As in Rome, none of these Chinese inventions were associated with the inauguration of any organized science involving coherent theoretical structure and the systematic testing of hypotheses on the basis of experiment or empirical observation. The thirteenth-century work of Bishop Grosseteste, William of Henley, and Roger Bacon was an early step toward that unique historical phenomenon: the emergence, in the sixteenth century, of a systematic body of science (Needham 1956).

4. The same was true of the first half-century of "our" industrial revolution, which, until the coming of the railways, was centered on the production of cotton that constituted only 7 or 8 percent of national output (Hobsbawm 1969, 68). Initially, the eighteenth-century industrial revolution was a very minor affair, at least in terms of investment levels, output, and growth in productivity (Landes 1969, 64–65; Feinstein 1978, 40–41; Williamson 1984).

5. Other historians assert that this increase did not occur to any substantial degree until the fifteenth or sixteenth century, with some question even about those dates (Coleman 1975, 42–43).

6. For more on this, see the classic revisionist piece by Lopez (1969), as well as Gimpel (1976, chap. 9).

7. However, recent studies indicate that the historical relation between climate changes and crop yields is ambiguous, at best.

8. The restraints imposed by the church had another curious effect: they apparently made bathing unfashionable for centuries. Until then, bathhouses had been popular as centers for social and, perhaps, sexual activity. But by requiring constant separation of the sexes and limiting other pleasures associated with nude bathing, the church undermined the inducements for such sanitary activities (Gimpel 1976, 87–92).

9. For an illuminating quantification of some of the social costs of one widely publicized legal battle between two firms, see Summers and Cutler (1988).

Chapter 11
Mega-enterprising Redesign of Governing Institutions: Keystone of Dynamic Microtheory

The idea of this chapter was suggested by a very valuable paper by Douhan and Henrekson (2007). See also the illuminating paper by Desai and Acs (2007).

1. In Europe, where there is no organized lobbying industry, this American service industry is regarded as something of a puzzle. However, I am inclined to take this as yet another indication that the U.S. economy continues to lead the world in entrepreneurial activity.

It is important to note that lobbying is not only a means of furthering greed and unrestrained pursuit of profit. Indeed, as we will see, some of the largest lobbying expenditures are incurred by nonprofit organizations working in what they conceive to be the public interest.

2. Li, Feng, and Jiang (2006) take this point a step further, arguing that entrepreneurs can help to deregulate centralized economies by demonstrating the success that can be achieved by evading—or formally changing—restrictive laws. The authors provide several examples of institutional entrepreneurs who have stimulated economically valuable reforms in China.

3. For more on this, see Holland (2005).

4. This memorization-based examination system was exactly the wrong way to train mathematicians, for instance, as Professor Chang Hsiu-Jung of National Taiwan University has asserted. Anthony Tang reports Professor Chang's observation, noting that, in China, "the few noted mathematicians . . . tended to be rejects of the Imperial Examination System" (Tang 1979, 10 fn. 30). Similarly, in the modern United States, rote learning apparently has not been the most effective way to educate entrepreneurs like Thomas Edison and Bill Gates, who succeeded after dropping out of the mainstream education system.

5. For example, copyists were employed to rewrite all of the answers before submission for grading so that the graders could not recognize the handwriting of friends or favored students (Lee 1985, 155).

6. In approximately AD 1100 China's population is estimated to have been about 100 million, while the size of the bureaucracy, including military personnel, was about 50,000. In comparison, "At any time during the Sung, there were about 8,038 degree-holders serving in the government or waiting for appointment. Of them, about 4,606 . . . were of common background" (Lee 1985, 215 n. 43).

7. See Lee's (1985) notes on p. 201 for further references and disputing interpretations.

8. For a very illuminating discussion of Hamilton's *Report on Manufactures*, see Wright (2008).

9. Lobbying is hardly a new invention. After 1688, with the accession of William and Mary and the adoption of annual parliaments, such practices became common in Britain. Colley (2005) writes: "The papers of virtually every Member of Parliament and peer from this time show just how large initiatives to do with trade—petitions for new bridges, new roads, new market places or better street lighting, plans for improvements to ports and lighthouses, requests for new duties on imports, or demands for an end to old monopolies—loomed in the political business of the day. Lesser tradesmen would band together to petition their local magnate or MP for what they wanted. More powerful men lobbied directly, or employed agents to do so for them. In 1739, for example, the prosperous merchants who ran the Convention of the Royal Burghs in Edinburgh paid a London-based solicitor called Thomas White the sum of 100 pounds to lobby in support of legislation for Scotland's linen industry. Over the next dozen years, this same body petitioned Parliament on the state of the coinage, on the problem of smuggling, in support of convoy protection for merchantmen in time of war, in favour of a standardisation of weights and measures, and on behalf of legislation changing the bankruptcy laws" (68).

10. In some instances, however, as Parker (2007) notes, large firms seek regulations to impose large fixed costs on smaller rivals that lack the economies of scale to absorb them.

11. All active lobbyists are required to register with the U.S. Congress: "(1) General rule: No later than 45 days after a lobbyist first makes a lobbying contact or is employed or retained to make a lobbying contact, whichever is earlier, such lobbyist (or, as provided under paragraph (2), the organization employing such lobbyist), shall register with the Secretary of the Senate and the Clerk of the House of Representatives. . . . (2) Employer filing: Any organization that has 1 or more employees who are lobbyists shall file a single registration under this section on behalf of such employees for each client on whose behalf the employees act as lobbyists" (U.S. Code, Title 2, chap. 26, sec. 1603).

12. Further information can be obtained from the American League of Lobbyists (2007).

13. This is true, despite the fact that the current author, among others, has questioned the value—for inventors and entrepreneurs—of educational approaches that focus on retention of received knowledge, rather than creativity.

14. For further formalization of the process discussed here, see Murphy, Shleifer, and Vishny (1993).

Chapter 12
Summing Up: Yes, the Theory of Entrepreneurship Is on Its Way

1. It is important to note one exception for the case of the entrepreneur. By the very nature of their activity, entrepreneurs are generally self-employed. As a result, there is no standard demand function for them. Indeed, it is the entrepreneur, herself, who decides whether to devote her time and effort to one activity, rather than another—a reality that clearly breaks down the distinction between demand

and supply. The clear exception is the "necessity entrepreneur," who is driven to start a (small) firm because even marginally acceptable employment opportunities are unavailable. In principle, the demand for his services surely is observable and just as surely governs his remuneration prospects from entrepreneurial activity.

2. According to evidence cited in chapter 3, the average monetary earnings of innovative entrepreneurs are below those of employed personnel with similar education and experience and may even fall below average competitive levels. Instead, as I suggested in that chapter, part of the reward of the independent and innovative entrepreneur takes the form of psychic compensation. Add to this the attraction of the occasional enormous prizes, which induce overoptimistic gamblers (entrepreneurs) to accept actuarially expected returns that are negative. If these types of rewards were substantial and widely valued, market forces would reliably and automatically drive the pecuniary remuneration below the earnings of those who received no reward other than money. This is a simple idea, but one that clearly is implied by the generally recognized theory of market pricing.

3. It can also be argued that both licensors and licensees possess incentives to agree to the ECPR license fee voluntarily and that the ECPR fee is the license price that would emerge in an effectively competitive market for such licenses.

4. The term "satisficing," it will be remembered, was contributed by the Carnegie-Mellon school of economists under the leadership of the late Professor Herbert Simon, who held that economic decisions normally are not reached through any optimization process because of the unavailability of the necessary data, as well as other obstacles. Rather, decision-makers are content to accept any choice for which there is reason to believe that the results will be good enough to be considered "satisfactory" by the decision-maker.

REFERENCES

Abramovitz, M. 1989. *Thinking about Growth and Other Essays of Economic Growth and Welfare*. New York: Cambridge University Press.

Acs, Z. Forthcoming. *American Money, American Opportunity: Making It, Giving It Away, and Why It Will Continue to Shape the World*.

Acs, Z. J., and D. B. Audretsch. 1988. Innovation in Large and Small Firms: An Empirical Analysis. *American Economic Review* 78:678–90.

———. 1990. *Innovation and Small Firms*. Cambridge: MIT Press.

Aghion, P., and P. Howitt. 1998. *Endogenous Growth Theory*. Cambridge: MIT Press.

Allmand, C. 1989. *The Hundred Years War*. Cambridge: Cambridge University Press.

American League of Lobbyists. 2007. Lobby Reform Activities 1 October. Accessed 17 July 2009 at http://www.alldc.org/publicresources/lobbyreformactivities.cfm.

American Philosophical Society. 2003. *Proceedings of the American Philosophical Society* 147, no. 3.

Arabsheibani, G., D. de Meza, J. Maloney, and B. Pearson. 2000. And a Vision Appeared unto Them of a Great Profit: Evidence of Self-Deception among the Self-Employed. *Economics Letters* 67:35–41.

Armstrong, M. 2002. The Theory of Access Pricing and Interconnection. In *Handbook of Telecommunications Economics*, ed. Martin E. Cave, Sumit K. Majumdar, and Ingo Vogelsang. Amsterdam: Elsevier.

Arora, A., Fosfuri, A., and A. Gambardella. 2001. *Markets for Technology: The Economics of Innovation and Corporate Strategy*. Cambridge: MIT Press.

Ashton, T. S. 1948. *The Industrial Revolution, 1760–1830*. London: Oxford University Press.

Astebro, T. 2003. The Return to Independent Invention: Evidence of Unrealistic Optimism, Risk Seeking or Skewness Loving. *Economic Journal* 113:226–39.

Atkinson, A., and W. Salverda. 2005. Top Incomes in the Netherlands and the United Kingdom over the 20th Century. *Journal of the European Economic Association* 3:883–913.

Baker, G. 2002. Distortion and Risk in Optimal Incentive Contracts. *Journal of Human Resources* 37:728–51.

Balazs, E. 1964. *Chinese Civilization and Bureaucracy: Variations on a Theme.* New Haven: Yale University Press.

Baumol, W. J. 1990. Entrepreneurship: Productive, Unproductive, and Destructive, *Journal of Political Economy* 98:893–921.

———. 1993. *Entrepreneurship, Management, and the Structure of Payoffs.* Cambridge: MIT Press.

———. 2002a. Entrepreneurship, Innovation and Growth: The David-Goliath Symbiosis. *Journal of Entrepreneurial Finance and Business Ventures* 7, no. 2: 1–10.

———. 2002b. *The Free-Market Innovation Machine: Analyzing the Growth Miracle of Capitalism.* Princeton, N.J.: Princeton University Press.

———. 2005. Entrepreneurship and Invention: Toward Their Microeconomic Value Theory. AEI-Brookings Joint Center for Regulatory Studies. December. http://aei-brookings.org/admin/authorpdfs/redirect-safely.php?fname=../pdffiles/Baumol_mainbodyv3_12282005.pdf.

Baumol, W. J., and D. G. Swanson. 2003. The New Economy and Ubiquitous Competitive Price Discrimination. *Antitrust Law Journal* 70:661–85.

Baumol, W. J., J. C. Panzar, and R. D. Willig. 1988. *Contestable Markets and the Theory of Industry Structure.* Rev. ed. San Diego: Harcourt Brace Jovanovich.

Baumol, W. J., M. Schilling, and E. Wolff. 2009. The Superstar Inventors and Entrepreneurs: How Were They Educated? *Journal of Economics & Management Strategy* 18, no. 3: 711–28.

Benz, M., and B. S. Frey. 2004. Being Independent Raises Happiness at Work. *Swedish Economic Policy Review* 11:95–134.

Berman, C. H. 1986. *Medieval Agriculture, the Southern French Countryside, and the Early Cistercians,* Philadelphia: American Philosophical Society.

Berthollet, C. 1791. *Elements of the Art of Dyeing.* Trans. William Hamilton. London: Stephen Couchman.

Bessen, J., and M. J. Meurer. 2008. *Patent Failure: How Judges, Bureaucrats, and Lawyers Put Innovators at Risk.* Princeton, N.J.: Princeton University Press.

Bianchi, M., and M. Henrekson. 2005. Is Neoclassical Economics Still Entrepreneurless? *Kyklos* 58, no. 3: 353–77.

Birnbaum, J. H. 2005. The Road to Riches Is Called K Street: Lobbying Firms Hire More, Pay More, Charge More to Influence Government. *Washington Post*, 22 June, A1.

Bloch, M. 1935. Avenement et conquetes du moulin a eau. *Annales d'Histoire Economique et Sociale* 7:538–63.

Braudel, F. 1979–86. *Civilization and Capitalism, 15th to 18th Century.* 3 vols. New York: Harper and Row.

Brooke, C.N.L. 1964. *Europe in the Central Middle Ages, 962–1154*. London: Longman.

Brown, P. B. 2005. R&D under the Microscope. *New York Times*, 24 December, C5.

Cantillon, R. 1755. *Essai sur la nature de commerce en general*. Paris: Chez Fletcher Gyles.

Carroll, L. 1902. *Through the Looking Glass*. New York: Harper & Brothers.

Carus-Wilson, E. M. 1941. An Industrial Revolution of the Thirteenth Century. *Economic History Review* 11:39–60.

Casson, M. 1982. *The Entrepreneur: An Economic Theory*. Oxford: Martin Robertson.

———. 2000. *Enterprise and Leadership*. Cheltenham: Edward Elgar.

Center for Responsive Politics. N.d. Total Lobbying Spending, 1998–2009. Accessed 30 July 2009 at http://www.opensecrets.org/lobby/index.php.

———. N.d. Top Spenders, 1998–2009. Accessed 30 July 2009 at http://www.opensecrets.org/lobby/top.php?indexType=s.

Chandy, R. K., and G. J. Tellis. 2000. The Incumbent's Curse? Incumbency, Size, and Radical Product Innovation. *Journal of Marketing* 64, no. 3: 1–17.

Chen, S., and M. Ravallion. 2008. *The Developing World Is Poorer than We Thought, but No Less Successful*. Washington, D.C.: World Bank.

Clark, G. 2007. *A Farewell to Alms: A Brief Economic History of the World*. Princeton, N.J.: Princeton University Press.

Cloulas, I. 1993. *The Borgias*. New York: Barnes and Noble.

Coleman, D. C. 1956. Industrial Growth and Industrial Revolutions. *Economica* 23, no. 3: 1–20.

———. 1975. *Industry in Tudor and Stuart England*. London: Macmillan.

Colley, L. 2005. *Britons: Forging the Nation, 1707–1837*. New Haven: Yale University Press.

Cooper, A. C., C. Y. Woo, and W. C. Dunkelberg. 1988. Entrepreneurs' Perceived Chances for Success. *Journal of Business Venturing* 3, no. 2: 97–108.

Cournot, A. 1897. *Researches into the Mathematical Principles of the Theory of Wealth*. Trans. Nathaniel T. Bacon. New York: Macmillan.

D'Asprement, C., and A. Jacquemin. 1988. Cooperative and Non-cooperative R&D in Duopoly with Spillover. *American Economic Review* 78:1133–37.

Dana, J. D., Jr. 1998. Advance-Purchase Discounts and Price Discrimination in Competitive Markets. *Journal of Political Economy* 106:395–422.

De Camp, L. S. 1990. *The Ancient Engineers: Technology and Invention from the Earliest Times to the Renaissance*. New York: Barnes and Noble.

DeLong, J. B. 2000. Cornucopia: The Pace of Economic Growth in the Twentieth Century. NBER Working Paper no. 7602. Cambridge: National Bureau of Economic Research.

de Mees, A. 1962. *History of the Belgians*. New York: Frederick A. Praeger.

De Roover, R. 1953. The Commercial Revolution of the 13th Century. In *Enterprise and Secular Change*, ed. F. Lane and S. Riemersa. London: Allen and Unwin.

Desai, S. and Z. J. Acs. 2007. A Theory of Destructive Entrepreneurship. Jena Economic Research Paper no. 2007-085.

Deutsch, C. H. 2008. Changing the Game with Innovations. *New York Times*, 24 May, C2.

Diehl, R. A., and M. D. Mandeville. 1987. Tula, and Wheeled Animal Effigies in Mesoamerica. *Antiquity* 61, no. 232: 239–46.

Disraeli, B. 1904. *Coningsby, or The New Generation.* In *The Works of Benjamin Disraeli Earl of Beaconsfield*, vol. 12. New York: M. Walter Dunne.

Douglas, D. C. 1964. *William the Conqueror: The Norman Impact upon England.* Berkeley: University of California Press.

Douhan, R., and M. Henrekson. 2007. The Political Economy of Entrepreneurship. IFN Working Paper no. 716.

Dunbabin, J. 2000. *France in the Making, 843–1180.* 2nd ed. Oxford: Oxford University Press.

Economic Report of the President, January 2001. 2001. Washington, D.C.: U.S. Government Printing Office.

Ekelund, R. B. 1970. Price Discrimination and Product Differentiation in Economic Theory: An Early Analysis. *Quarterly Journal of Economics* 84:268–78.

Ellison, R. 1952. *Invisible Man.* New York: Random House.

Elvin, M. 1973. *The Pattern of the Chinese Past.* Stanford: Stanford University Press.

Evans, G. C. 1924. The Dynamics of Monopoly. *American Mathematical Monthly*, February, 77–83.

Fano, E. 1987. Technical Progress as a Destabilizing Factor and as an Agent of Recovery in the United States between the Two World Wars. *History and Technology* 3:249–74.

Federal Reserve Bank of Dallas. 1997. *Time Well Spent: The Declining Real Cost of Living in America.* 1997 Annual Report, 5–17.

Feinstein, C. H. 1978. Capital Formation in Great Britain. In *The Cambridge Economic History of Europe*, ed. P. Mathias and M. M. Posten. Vol. 8. Cambridge: Cambridge University Press.

Field, A. J. 2003. The Most Technologically Progressive Decade of the Century. *American Economic Review* 93:1399–1413.

Finley, M. I. 1965. Technical Innovation and Economic Progress in the Ancient World. *Economic History Review* 18:29–45.

———. 1985. *The Ancient Economy.* 2nd ed. London: Hogarth.

Fogel, R. W. 1986. Nutrition and the Decline of Mortality since 1700: Some Preliminary Findings. In *Long-Term Factors in American Economic Growth*, ed. S. L. Engerman and R. E. Gallman. Chicago: University of Chicago Press.

Forbes, R. J. 1955. *Studies in Ancient Technology.* Vol. 2. Leiden: E. J. Brill.

Freeman, R. B. 1978. Job Satisfaction as an Economic Variable. *American Economic Review* 68:135–41.

Frey, B. S., and W. W. Pommerehne. 1989. Art Investment: An Empirical Inquiry. *Southern Economic Journal* 56:396–409.

Gimpel, J. 1976. *The Medieval Machine: The Industrial Revolution of the Middle Ages.* New York: Holt, Reinhart and Winston.

Gomory, R. E., and W. J. Baumol. 1998. A Country's Maximal Gains from Trade and Conflicting National Interests. C. V. Starr Center for Applied Economics Research Report no. 98-22, June, New York University.

Grilliches, Z. 1979. Issues in Assessing the Contribution of Research and Development to Productivity Growth. *Bell Journal of Economics* 10:92–116.

Hamilton, A. 1913. *Report on Manufactures*. Washington, D.C.: U.S. Government Printing Office.

Hamilton, B. H. 2000. Does Entrepreneurship Pay? An Empirical Analysis of the Returns of Self-Employment. *Journal of Political Economy* 108:604–31.

Harberger, A. 1954. Monopoly and Resource Misallocation. *American Economic Review* 44, no. 2: 77–87.

Harding, A. 1993. *England in the Thirteenth Century*. Cambridge: Cambridge University Press.

Hausman, J. A., and J. K. Mackie-Mason. 1988. Price Discrimination and Patent Policy. *RAND Journal of Economics* 19:253–56.

Henrekson, M. 2005. Entrepreneurship: A Weak Link in the Welfare State. *Industrial and Corporate Change* 14:437–67.

———. 2007. Entrepreneurship and Institutions. *Comparative Labor Law & Policy Journal* 28:717–42.

Henrekson, M., and D. Johansson. 2009. Competencies and Institutions Fostering High-Growth Firms. *Foundations and Trends in Entrepreneurship* 5, no. 1: 1–80.

Henrekson, M., and T. Sanandaji. 2008. Taxing Entrepreneurial Income. IFN Working Paper no. 732. http://ssrn.com/abstract=1089367.

Ho, P. T. 1962. *The Ladder of Success in Imperial China, 1368–1911*. New York: Columbia University Press.

Hobsbawm, E. J. 1969. *Industry and Empire from 1750 to the Present Day*. Harmondsworth: Penguin.

Hobson, J. M. 2004. *The Eastern Origins of Western Civilization*. Cambridge: Cambridge University Press.

Holcombe, R. 2007. *Entrepreneurship and Economic Progress*. New York: Routledge.

Holland, T. 2005. *Rubicon: The Last Years of the Roman Republic*. New York: Anchor.

Holmes, T. J., and J. A. Schmitz. 2001. A Gain from Trade: From Unproductive to Productive Entrepreneurship. *Journal of Monetary Economics* 47:417–46.

Howard, M. 1976. *War in European History*. Oxford: Oxford University Press.

Huijser, A. 2003. Efact Conference presentation, September. Tilburg, the Netherlands.

Jaffee, A. B., and J. Lerner. 2004. *Invention and Its Discontents: How Our Broken Patent System Is Endangering Innovation and Progress, and What to Do About It*. Princeton, N.J.: Princeton University Press.

Jardine, L., and A. Stewart. 1998. *Hostage to Fortune: The Troubled Life of Francis Bacon*. New York: Hill and Wang.

Jaruzelski, B., and K. Dehoff. 2007. The Customer Connection: The Global Innovation 1000, *Strategy+Business*, Issue 49, Winter. http://www.strategy-business.com/media/file/sb49_07407.pdf.

Jarulzelski, B., K. Dehoff, and R. Bordia. 2005. The Booz Allen Hamilton Global Innovation 1000: Money Isn't Everything. *Strategy+Business*, Issue 41, Winter, 1–14.

Jones, C. 1994. *France*. Cambridge: Cambridge University Press.

Jones, E. L. 1987. *The European Miracle: Environments, Economies, and Geopolitics in the History of Europe and Asia*. Cambridge: Cambridge University Press.

Khalil, E. L. 1997. The Red Queen Paradox: A Proper Name for a Popular Game. *Journal of Institutional and Theoretical Economics* 153:411–15.

Khan, B. Z. 2005. *The Democratization of Invention: Patents and Copyrights in American Economic Development, 1790–1920*. Cambridge: Cambridge University Press.

Kihlstrom, R. E., and J. J. Laffont. 1979. A General Equilibrium Entrepreneurial Theory of Firm Formation Based on Risk Aversion. *Journal of Political Economy* 87:719–48.

Kirzner, I. 1973. *Competition and Entrepreneurship*. Chicago: University of Chicago Press.

Kirzner, I. 1979. *Perception, Opportunity and Profit*. Chicago: University of Chicago Press.

Knight, F. H. 1921. *Risk, Uncertainty, and Profit*. Boston: Houghton Mifflin.

Lamoreaux, N. R., and K. L. Sokoloff. 1996. Long-Term Change in the Organization of Inventive Activity, *Proceedings of the National Academy of Sciences* 93:12686–92.

———. 2005. The Decline of the Independent Inventor: A Schumpeterian Story. National Bureau of Economic Research Working Paper no. 11654, October.

———. 2007. The Market for Technology and the Organization of Inventors in U.S. History. In *Entrepreneurship, Innovation, and the Growth Mechanism of the Free-Enterprise Economies*, ed. Eytan Sheshinski, Robert J. Strom, and William J. Baumol. Princeton, N.J.: Princeton University Press.

———. Forthcoming. *Beyond Monopoly: Patents, Inventors, and the Market for Technology in the United States during the Second Industrial Revolution*.

Landes, D. 1969. *The Unbound Prometheus: Technological Change and Industrial Development in Western Europe from 1750 to the Present*. New York: Cambridge University Press.

———. 1998. *The Wealth and Poverty of Nations: Why Some Are So Rich and Some So Poor*. New York: Norton.

Lebergott, S. 1984. *The Americans: An Economic Record*. New York: Norton.

Lee, T.H.C. 1985. *Government Education and Examinations in Sung China*. New York: St. Martin's Press.

Lefebvre, G. 1947. *The Coming of the French Revolution, 1789*. Princeton, N.J.: Princeton University Press.

Lerner J., and J. Tirole. 2004. Efficient Patent Pools. *American Economic Review* 94:691–711.

Levin, R. C. 1988. Appropriability, R&D Spending, and Technological Performance. *American Economic Review* 78:424–28.

Levine, M. E. Winter 2002. Price Discrimination without Market Power. *Yale Journal on Regulation* 19, no. 1: 1–36.

Li, D. D., J. Feng, and H. Jiang. 2006. Institutional Entrepreneurs. *American Economic Review* 96:358–62.

Lincoln, A. 1953. First Lecture on Discoveries and Inventions. In *The Collected Works of Abraham Lincoln: 1809–1865*. Vol. 2. New Brunswick, N.J.: Rutgers University Press.

Lindbeck, A. 1988. Consequences of the Advanced Welfare State. *World Economy* 2:19–38.

Liu, J.T.C., and P. J. Goias, eds. 1969. *Change in Sung China: Innovation or Renovation?* Lexington, Mass.: Heath.

Lohr, S. 2009. Who Says Innovation Belongs to the Small? *New York Times*, 24 May, 4.

Lopez, R. S. 1969. Hard Times and Investment in Culture. In Metropolitan Museum of Art, *The Renaissance: A Symposium*. New York: Oxford University Press.

Lucas, R. E. 1988. On the Mechanics of Economic Development. *Journal of Monetary Economics* 22, no. 1: 3–42.

Maddison, A. 2001. *The World Economy: A Millennial Perspective*. Paris: Organization for Economic Cooperation and Development (OECD) Publications.

———. 2003. *The World Economy: Historical Statistics*. Paris: OECD Publications.

Mansfield, E. 1990. Comment. In *Productivity Growth in Japan and the United States,* ed. C. R. Hulten, 341–46. Chicago: University of Chicago Press.

Markoff, J. 2003. Is There Life after Silicon Valley's Fast Lane? *New York Times*, 9 April, C1.

Marsh, R. M. 1961. *The Mandarins: The Circulation of Elites in China, 1600–1900*. Glencoe, Ill.: Free Press.

Marshall, A. 1898. *Principles of Economics*. 4th ed. London: Macmillan.

———. 1923. *Industry and Trade*. London: Macmillan.

Marx, K., and F. Engels. 1976. Manifesto of the Communist Party. In *Collected Works*. Vol. 6. London: Lawrence & Wishart.

McClelland, D. C. 1961. The Achieving Society. Princeton, N.J.: Princeton University Press.

McNeill, W. H. 1969. *History of Western Civilization*. Rev. ed. Chicago: University of Chicago Press.

Menzies, G. 2002. *1421: The Year China Discovered America*. New York: Harper Collins.

Milward, A. S. 1970. *The Economic Effects of the Two World Wars on Britain*. London: Macmillan.

Mohnen, P. 1992. *The Relationship between R&D and Productivity Growth in Canada and Other Industrial Countries*. Ottawa: Canada Communications Group.

Murphy, K. M., A. Shleifer, and R. W. Vishny. 1991. The Allocation of Talent: Implications for Growth. *Quarterly Journal of Economics* 106:503–30.

———. 1993. Why Is Rent-Seeking So Costly to Growth? *American Economic Review* 83:409–14.

Nadiri, M. I. 1993. Innovations and Technological Spillovers. NBER Working Paper no. 4423. Cambridge: National Bureau of Economic Research.

National Science Board. 1996. *Science and Engineering Indicators, 1996.* Washington, DC: U.S. Government Printing Office.

———. 2000. *Science and Engineering Indicators, 2000.* Arlington, Va.: National Science Foundation.

Needham, J. 1954–2004. *Science and Civilization in China.* 7 vols. Cambridge: Cambridge University Press.

———1956. Mathematics and Science in China and the West. *Science and Society* 20:230–343.

———. 1987. Introduction. In *The Genius of China: 3,000 Years of Science, Discovery and Invention,* by R.K.G. Temple. New York: Simon and Schuster.

Nef, J. U. 1934. The Progress of Technology and the Growth of Large-Scale Industry in Great Britain, 1540–1640. *Economic History Review* 1:3–24.

Nelson, R. R. 1996. *The Sources of Economic Growth.* Cambridge: Harvard University Press.

Nelson, R. R., and S. G. Winter. 1982. *An Evolutionary Theory of Economic Change.* Cambridge: Belknap Press.

Norbäck, P., and L. Persson. Forthcoming. The Organization of the Innovation Industry: Entrepreneurs, Venture Capitalists and Oligopolists. *Journal of the European Economic Association.*

Nordhaus, W. D. 1969. *Invention, Growth, and Welfare.* Cambridge: MIT Press.

———. 2004. Schumpeterian Profits in the American Economy: Theory and Measurement. National Bureau of Economic Research Working Paper no. 10433.

North, D. C., and R. P. Thomas. 1973. *The Rise of the Western World: A New Economic History.* Cambridge: Cambridge University Press.

Okun, A. 1975. *Equality and Efficiency: The Big Tradeoff.* Washington, D.C.: Brookings Institution Press.

Olson, M. 1982. *The Rise and Decline of Nations: Economic Growth, Stagflation, and Social Rigidities.* New Haven: Yale University Press.

Ordover, J. A. Winter 1991. A Patent System for Both Diffusion and Exclusion. *Journal of Economic Perspectives* 5:43–60.

Organization for Economic Cooperation and Development (OECD). 2009. *OECD Factbook 2009: Economic, Environmental and Social Statistics.* Paris: OECD.

P&G. 2009. R&D's Formula for Success. Accessed 15 April 2009 at http://www.pg.com/science/rd_formula_success.shtml.

Painter, S. 1933. *William Marshal: Knight-Errant, Baron, and Regent of England.* Baltimore: Johns Hopkins Press.

Palmer, R. 1964. *The Age of Democratic Revolution.* Vol. 2. Princeton, N.J.: Princeton University Press.

Parker, S. C. 2004. *The Economics of Self-Employment and Entrepreneurship.* Cambridge: Cambridge University Press.

———. 2006. New Agendas in the Economics of Entrepreneurship: Optimism, Education, Wealth and Entrepreneurship. Presented at American Economic Association Special Session on Entrepreneurship.

———. 2007. Law and the Economics of Entrepreneurship. *Comparative Labor Law & Policy Journal* 28:695–716.

———. Forthcoming. *The Economics of Entrepreneurship: What We Know and What We Don't.*

Parker, S. C., and A. Basu. 2001. Family Finance and New Business Start-ups. *Oxford Bulletin of Economics and Statistics* 63:333–58.

The [United Kingdom] Patent Office. 2001. *The Patent Office Annual Facts and Figures 2000–2001.*

Phelps Brown, E. H., and S. V. Hopkins. 1956. Seven Centuries of the Prices of Consumables, Compared with Builders' Wage Rates. *Economica* 23:296–314.

Pinfold, J. F. 2001. The Expectations of New Business Founders: The New Zealand Case. *Journal of Small Business Management* 39:279–85.

Pomeranz, K. 2000. *The Great Divergence: Europe, China, and the Making of the Modern World Economy.* Princeton, N.J.: Princeton University Press.

Puri, M., and D. T. Robinson. 2005. Optimism, Entrepreneurship and Economic Choice. Duke University Working Paper.

Rey, P., and J. Tirole. 1997. A Primer on Foreclosure. http://www.ftc.gov/opp/intellect/020522reydoc.pdf.

Reynolds, P. D., S. M. Camp, W. D. Bygrave, E. Autio, and M. Hay. 2001. *Global Entrepreneurship Monitor: 2001 Executive Report.* Accessed 6 October 2009 at http://unpan1.un.org/intradoc/groups/public/documents/UN/UNPAN002481.pdf.

Robinson, J. 1969. *The Economics of Imperfect Competition.* 2nd ed. London: Macmillan.

Romer, P. 1994. New Goods, Old Theory and the Welfare Costs of Trade Restrictions. *Journal of Development Economics* 43:5–38.

———. 1990. Endogenous Technological Change. *Journal of Political Economy* 98, no. 5, part 2: The Problem of Development: A Conference of the Institute for the Study of Free Enterprise Systems, S71–S102.

Rosenberg, N. 1976. *Perspectives on Technology.* Cambridge: Cambridge University Press.

Rosenberg, N., and L. E Birdzell Jr. 1986. *How the West Grew Rich: The Economic Transformation of the Industrial World.* New York: Basic Books.

Ross, C. 1974. *Edward IV.* Berkeley: University of California Press.

Say, J. B. 1827. *A Treatise on Political Economy.* Trans. C. R. Prinsep and C. C. Biddle. 3rd American ed. Philadelphia: John Grigg.

Schama, S. 1989. *Citizens: A Chronicle of the French Revolution.* New York: Knopf.

Scherer, F. M. 1965. Firm Size, Market Structure, Opportunity and the Output of Patented Inventions. *American Economic Review* 59:1097–1125.

Schilling, M. A. Forthcoming. *The Collaboration Network of U.S. Technology-Intensive Firms and Their Partners.*

Schumpeter, J. A. 1936. *The Theory of Economic Development.* 1911. Trans. Redvers Opie. Cambridge: Harvard University Press.

———. 1947. *Capitalism, Socialism, and Democracy.* 2nd ed. New York: Harper and Brothers.

Shakespeare, W. 2004. *Julius Caesar*. New York: Simon and Schuster.

———. 2005. *Richard II*. New York: Simon and Schuster.

Shapiro, C. 2001. Navigating the Patent Thicket: Cross Licenses, Patent Pools, and Standard-Setting. In *Innovation Policy and the Economy*, ed. A. Jaffe, J. Lerner, and S. Stern. Cambridge: MIT Press.

Shell, K. 1967. A Model of Inventive Activity and Capital Accumulation. In *Essays on the Theory of Optimal Economic Growth*, ed. K. Shell. Cambridge: MIT Press.

Smith, A. 1937. *An Inquiry Into the Nature and Causes of the Wealth of Nations*. 1776. New York: Random House.

Solow, R. M. 1956. A Contribution to the Theory of Economic Growth. *Quarterly Journal of Economics* 70:65–94.

Spulber, D. F. 2009. *The Theory of the Firm: Microeconomics with Endogenous Entrepreneurs, Firms, Markets, and Organizations*. Cambridge: Cambridge University Press.

Summers, L. and D. Cutler. 1988. Texaco and Penzoil Both Lost Big. *New York Times*, 14 February, 3.3.

Swanson, D. G., and W. J. Baumol. 2005. Reasonable and Nondiscriminatory (RAND) Royalties, Standards Selection, and Control of Market Power. *Antitrust Law Journal* 73:1–58.

Tang, A. M. 1979. China's Agricultural Legacy. *Economic Development and Cultural Change* 28, no. 1: 1–22.

Tse, C. Y. 1996. Productivity and Research Portfolio. Ph.D. diss., New York University.

U.S. Bureau of the Census. 1975. *Historical Statistics of the United States, Colonial Times to 1970*. Part 1. Washington, D.C.: U.S. Government Printing Office.

———. 2007. *Statistical Abstract of the United States, 2007*. 126th ed. Washington, D.C.: U.S. Government Printing Office.

U.S. Federal Trade Commission. 2003. *To Promote Innovation: The Proper Balance of Competition and Patent Law and Policy*. October. http://xml .coverpages.org/FTC-InnovationReport2003.pdf.

U.S. Small Business Administration. 1995. *The State of Small Business: A Report of the President, 1994*. Washington, D.C.: U.S. Government Printing Office.

———. 2003. *Small Serial Innovators: The Small Firm Contribution to Technical Change*. CHI Research Inc. for SBA Office of Advocacy, 27 February. Contract no. SBAHQ-01-C-0149.

———. 2004. *Small Firms and Technology Acquisitions, Inventor Movement, and Technology Transfer*. CHI Research Inc. for SBA Office of Advocacy, January. Contract no. SBAHQ-02-M-0491.

van der Sluis, J., M. van Praag. and A. van Witteloostuijn. 2006. Why Are the Returns to Education Higher for Entrepreneurs Than Employees? University of Amsterdam Working Paper.

van Praag, M. 1999. Some Classic Views on Entrepreneurship. *De Economist* 147:311–35.

van Praag, M., and P. H. Versloot. 2007. What Is the Value of Entrepreneurship? A Review of Recent Research. IZA Discussion Paper no. 3014, August.

Veblen, T. 1904. *The Theory of Business Enterprise*. New York: Scribner.

———. 1919. *The Place of Science in Modern Civilization and Other Essays*. New York: B. W. Heubsch.

Veyne, P. 1961. Vie de trimalcion. *Annales: Economies, Societes, Civilisations* 16:213–47.

Von Mises, L. 1940. *Human Action*. Rev. ed. Irvington-on-Hudson, N.Y.: Foundation for Economic Education.

White, L. 1962. *Medieval Technology and Social Change*. Oxford: Clarendon Press.

Williams, M., and K. Kreitzman. 2008. Estimating Market Power with Economic Profits. Working paper, 18 September. http://ssrn.com/abstract=1167823.

Williamson, J. G. 1984. Why Was British Growth So Slow during the Industrial Revolution. *Journal of Economic History* 44:687–712.

Willig, R. D. 1979. Consumer Equity and Local Measured Service. In *Perspectives on Local Measured Service*, ed. J. A. Baude et. al. Kansas City: Telecommunications Workshop.

Winchester, S. 2008. *The Man Who Loved China*. New York: Harper Perennial.

Wolff, E. N. 1997. Spillovers, Linkages and Technical Change. *Economic Systems Research* 9:9–23.

Wright, C. 1965. *A Royal Affinity*. London: Frederick Muller.

Wright, R. E. 2008. *One Nation under Debt: Hamilton, Jefferson, and the History of What We Owe*. New York: McGraw-Hill.

Xu, H., and M. Ruef. 2004. The Myth of the Risk-Tolerant Entrepreneur. *Strategic Organization* 2:331–55.

INDEX

Ackerloff's lemons analysis, 179–80
Acs, Zoltan, 30, 183
Adolphus, Gustavus, 146
adventurers, 11–12
Aghion, Philippe, 2, 130, 188
airplanes, 30, 107
Alexander the Great, 146
American Civil War, 107, 146
American League of Lobbyists, 181–82
American Philosophical Society, 34
American Revolution, 215n9
anesthesia, 35
arms race: kinked-revenue-curve spending model and, 60–63; market mechanisms for, 57–60; oligopolists and, 40, 57–63, 67, 145–47, 150
Arora, A., 107
Arthur, W. Brian, 201n10
Astebro, T., 51
AT&T, 107, 178–79
Audretsch, D. B., 30

Baby Bells, 179
Bacon, Francis, 216n14
Bacon, Roger, 162, 169
Balazs, E., 160, 167
Bank of Amsterdam, 176
Bank of England, 176
Bank of the United States, 176
banks, 53, 84, 142, 152, 168–69, 173, 176–77

Basu, A., 177
Battle of Hastings, 146, 219n15
Battle of Lewes, 149
Baumol, William J., 55, 57, 183
Baumol's Third Tautology, 14–15
Bell, Alexander Graham, 132
Bell South, 107
Berman, C. H., 168
Berthollet, Claude, 101
Birdzell, L. E., Jr., 82–83
blackmail, 170
Bloch, M., 162
Boeing, 107
Braudel, Fernand, 82–84, 166
Brooke, C.N.L., 162, 167

Cantillon, Richard, 10, 12, 26, 198n3
Capitalism, Socialism and Democracy (Schumpeter), 128
Carnegie Mellon University, 183
Carroll, Lewis, 57–58, 145
Catholic Church, 139, 148, 169, 175–76, 215n5, 221n8
Center for Responsive Politics, 181
Charlemagne, 168
China, 6, 152, 154; banks and, 176; gunpowder and, 217n3; imperial institutions and, 175; intact historical record of, 218n11; labor and, 158–60, 167, 175; mathematics and, 221n4; near revolutions and, 217n3; printing and, 218n11

Cistercians, 162
Civilization and Capitalism, 15th to 18th Century (Braudel), 83–84
Coleman, D. C., 166
competition: as arms race, 40, 57–63, 67, 145–47, 150; creative destruction and, 128–36; economic warfare and, 139–51; heterogeneous product races and, 131–34; Level Playing Field Theorem and, 117–18; licensing and, 103–23; Red Queen games and, 145–51
computers, 16, 51, 189; advances in, 33; breakthrough of, 30; comparative earnings in industry of, 205n1; government and, 34–35; oligopolistic firms and, 206n4; optimal transfer pricing and, 106–7, 110; surgery and, 35; universities and, 34–35
Confucius, 175
Cooper, Peter, 106
corporate takeovers, 170
Cournot, A., 112, 123, 193, 212
creative destruction: benefits of, 135–36; competition and, 131–34; efficiency and, 130–31; Engels and, 128–29; heterogeneous product races and, 131–34; Marx and, 128–29; negative externalities of, 135–36; overcorrection and, 135; Pareto optimality and, 134; Ricardian rent model and, 132–34; Schumpeter and, 128–29, 131, 136; spillovers and, 130–35

Daimler-Benz, 107
Dana, James D., Jr., 36
Dark Ages, 161, 168
De Camp, L. S., 106
DeLong, J. B., 3
de Mees, A., 84
de Montfort, Simon, 149
discrimination: demand function and, 37–48, 53–54; entry effects and, 40–45; innovative oligopolists and, 67–68; interlocational, 39; intertemporal, 39; monopoly power and, 37, 40, 42, 46–47; Ramsey optimality and, 48–49; stability and, 42–45; submarkets and, 37–45, 49, 68, 202n8
distribution, 36–38; as arms race, 40, 57–63, 67, 145–47, 150; efficiency and, 104–8 (*see also* efficiency); lump-sum/

non lump sum, 78, 85–88, 92, 94, 98–100, 134–35, 208n2, 210nn22,24; modeling of, 16–17; optimal transfer pricing and, 101–27; Pareto optimality and, 78–81, 85–88, 92–94, 97–99, 134–35; poverty and, 8, 12, 23, 78–85, 96–98, 140, 203n13; real wages and, 80–82; redistributive vs. productive wealth accumulation and, 140–41; spillovers and, 77–101; as standard theory, 189–90
diving suits, 162
Douglas, D. C., 160
Dow Chemical, 107
Duke University, 183
Dupuit, Jules, 36, 88

Eastman Kodak, 107
economic warfare: democracy and, 141; efficiency and, 143–44; Industrial Revolution and, 141, 145; Middle Ages and, 145–51; productive wealth-seeking and, 141–42; redistributive wealth-seeking and, 141–45; Red Queen game and, 140, 145–61, 216n13
Edison, Thomas, 51, 183, 203n12
Edward, Prince of England, 149
efficiency, 2–5, 8, 190, 193; allocation issues and, 170, 208n2, 220n2; creative destruction and, 130–31, 214n5; defined, 208n3; economic warfare and, 143–44; efficient component-pricing rule (ECPR) and, 114–23, 126; historical perspective on, 158, 162–63; licensing and, 103–27, 223n3; Pareto optimality and, 48, 70, 78–80, 85–88, 92–94, 97–99, 134–35, 194, 209n10, 214n5; pricing and, 17, 19, 47, 51, 69, 101–27, 201n11, 203n13, 213n28; spillovers and, 77–80, 85–87, 90, 93, 97–100, 209n8, 210n24, 211n25; technology transfer and, 102
efficient component-pricing rule (ECPR): effectiveness of, 213n28; formula for, 115–18; imperfect substitution and, 121–22; as indifference principle, 118–21; Level Playing Field Theorem and, 117–18; licensing and, 114–23, 126; monopolies and, 120–21; relevant welfare theory and, 193; unregulated competitive markets and, 119–20
Eli Lilly, 107

technology: alliances and, 107–8; creative
destruction and, 128–36; elimination of
obsolete, 103; encouraging dissemination of, 105, 108–10, 114, 119, 122–23,
129–30, 134, 154, 165, 194; kinked-
revenue-curve spending model and, 60–
64; licensing and, 103–27; market pressures and, 27–30; mere imitation and,
105–7; near revolutions and, 166–67,
217n3; optimal transfer pricing and,
101–27; prevalent markets of, 107–8;
spillovers and, 7, 12, 70, 77–101, 130–
35, 194, 208nn5,6,7, 209n13, 210n15;
standard of living and, 82; sufferings
from lack of, 82; warfare and, 146–51,
162. *See also* innovation
Thomas, R. P., 111
Through the Looking Glass (Carroll), 145
Tirole, J., 108, 213n28
Tom Thumb locomotive, 106
Toshiba, 107
toys, 166
transplants, 35
Treatise on Political Economy, A (Say),
165

underpayment, 49–51
undertakers, 11–12
Union Carbide Corporation, 107
United Kingdom, 6, 106, 146–49, 163
United States, 141; American Revolution
and, 215n9; Civil War of, 107, 146;
commodity brokers and, 68–69; Constitution of, 176; GDP changes in, 81;
growth rates in, 3–7; Hamilton and,
176–77; as leader in innovation, 102;
lobbyists and, 177–78, 183; locomotives
and, 106; oligopolistic firms and, 28–30;
philanthropy and, 183–84; research
and development (R&D) growth and,
28–30; rule of law and, 173; spillovers
and, 77–78
universities, 33–35
University of Chicago, 183
U.S. Bureau of the Census, 95

U.S. Congress, 179–80
U.S. National Science Board, 107
U.S. Small Business Administration, 30, 32
U.S. Supreme Court, 179

value theory, 1, 11, 13, 38, 188–89
van Praag, J. M., 30
Veblen, Thorstein, 198n7
Versloot, P. H., 30
Veyne, P., 157–58
Von Mises, Ludwig, 9

Wales, 149
warfare, 146–51, 162, 169
Wars of the Roses, 147, 149–50, 173
Washington Post, 180
water mills, 162, 166, 168–69, 220n2
Watt, James, 51
Wealth of Nations, The (Smith), 192
Weber, 19, 173
welfare, 193–94; creative destruction and,
128–36; externalities and, 7–8, 128–36;
greed and, 182–83; growth and, 3–7;
historical perspective on earnings and,
84; intertemporal analysis and, 7–8;
licensing and, 103–27; lobbyists and,
182–84; major role of, 9–11; market-
driven innovation effects and, 69–70;
market failures and, 2–3; monopolies
and, 2–3 (*see also* monopoly power);
optimal transfer pricing and, 101–27;
pre-Industrial Revolution conditions
and, 82–84; spillovers and, 77–100;
static efficiency and, 2–5, 199n8; technology sharing and, 103–23
Whitney, Eli, 51
Wilhelmina, 82
Williams, M., 59
Wilson, Charles, 186
Wolff, E. N., 183
World War II era, 28, 178, 183
Wright, C., 82
Wright brothers, 27, 51, 65, 183

Yuan Dynasty, 167